Making Tracks

A Writer's Guide to Audiobooks

(And How To Produce Them)

AWP Nonfiction
A division of AWP Productions

ISBN: 978-1946429001
First Edition Copyright © 2012 J. Daniel Sawyer
Second Edition Copyright © 2012 J. Daniel Sawyer

All Rights Reserved

Book and Cover Design by Kitty NicIaian
Cover art © 2012 Arthur Wright

Making Tracks
A Writer's Guide to Audiobooks
(And How To Produce Them)

J. Daniel Sawyer

iv   Making Tracks

Dedication

For Tee, Nathan, Chris, and Steve
My graduating classmates from the school of hard cuts

Making Tracks

Table of Contents

Foreword to the Second Edition

Five years ago, the world was turning inside out. Publishing was in the middle of its great disruption, and that disruption was finally reaching the world of audio. Demand was growing faster than in any other segment of the publishing industry, with lots of room for expansion.

For reasons you'll learn about later in this book, audio is my art form. Yes, I'm a novelist first and foremost these days, but I still produce at least six audiobooks a year—this year, I'm already scheduled for fourteen. It's my first love, and one I hoped to be able to give a good boost on its way up.

Still, when I finished the book, I moved on. I'm a novelist, and like any professional writer, I look forward rather than back. In the meantime, *Making Tracks* became something of a phenomenon in its own little pond, and as the years went by I started getting notes asking my opinion on matters technological and business where my book had fallen out of date.

Then, late in 2016, I attended an industry conference where I had a series of conversations with novelist JF Penn as well as several representatives of some major retailers and distributors that convinced me that it was time for a new edition. Deciding to produce an audiobook of your work (or hiring someone to produce it for you) involves a number of factors, and some of the information you need to make that decision has changed enough in the last five years that it would be irresponsible of me to leave *Making Tracks* as it was.

So, here you are. This is the second edition. Inside you'll find significant changes to the sections on the business and on the technology. There are more minor changes elsewhere else, including new tips and techniques in the sections on performance, production, and post-production.

The audiobook market hasn't stagnated or stalled in the last five years. It's still heading up. New players have entered the market, and several more are poised too. Audio is now the fastest growing segment of the publishing industry.

And it's not too late to make it a thriving part of your business and career.

Introduction

The Voices In Your Head

The human race began with words muttered around a campfire, and a deep part of us still strains to hear those firelight whispers through the din of the every-day. For me, the campfire voice was that of my grandmother, who lulled me to sleep with tales of adventure and danger in the Amazon rain forest. She delivered these stories to me on cassette tapes, which arrived in the mail with Por Avion scratched on them in vanishingly thin ball-point, straight from the headwaters of the Amazon river in Peru, where she lived.

Hers wasn't the only voice around my campfire. Her daughter and son-in-law weren't above quieting a difficult and impossible-to-put-to-sleep boy with highly theatrical readings from Tolkien, Mother Goose, and Dr. Seuss. I loved those stories, but I never counted them as special. People just seemed to tell each other stories, and that's all there was to it.

In 1981, at the age of 4, I fell in love with radio. I was hiding behind the living room couch, building a Lego fortress, and NPR was playing on the living room stereo set. At the top of the hour, the program changed, and the radio drama version of Star Wars burst in upon me. I found myself awash in a version of my favorite movie that was bigger and more spectacular than anything I'd ever seen on a movie screen.

Until then, I hadn't known that words and sounds could do that.

This love affair with the spoken word never slackened. I was the kid who stayed up late to record Classic Radio Theater at midnight on ABC, who played my read-along records till they wore out, who borrowed every audiobook in the library, who studied Foley and accents from the time I was old enough to know what those words meant.

I recorded my first audiobook when I was 12: The Adventures of Sherlock Holmes. I read it for my brother who was battling a protracted sinus infection. Once I learned the knack, I couldn't stop. For the next several years, using Dad's old boom box, I produced comedy shows, sound effects, and readings from my favorite books.

I lost interest when my abilities finally outgrew my recording equipment, but the interest re-awoke with a mighty roar when I discovered that I could do multitrack mixing on my PC. In 1998, I produced my first multitrack, stereo-mixed audio drama: the (thankfully) short-lived Internet sensation Bevis and Butthead vs. Darth Vader.

A couple years and a few productions later, at 23 years old, I was marshaling forces for my first attempt at a feature film. I was fortunate enough, while standing in line for Jay and Silent Bob Strike Back, to meet one of the early pioneers of electronic musical instruments and his business partner, a sound mixer who'd earned her stripes mixing for the Benny Goodman Band and hadn't stopped since. The two of them agreed to produce the audio for my film, and teach me their craft in the process.

For the next seven years, I ran my one-time hobby as a full-time production services business, producing films, stage plays, soundscapes, corporate video, and audio theater. In 2007, Scott Sigler convinced me to start producing my own content as well as content for clients. Since then I've produced a number of my own full-cast audiobooks, and performed in dozens more for other DIY producers and authors. Now, the kid who listened to stories every night gets to spend his life writing and performing stories for other people, and, as a bonus, I've been privileged to get a front-row seat to the biggest revolution in spoken-word audio since the invention of the wax cylinder phonograph.

How We Got Here

Once upon a time, audiobooks were called "Books On Tape." They were something that appealed primarily to truck drivers, long-haul commuters, and—the most reliable consumers of audio literature—the blind. They came in white plastic clamshell cases and pretty cardboard boxes, they were abridged recordings, and they were usually read (rather than performed) by people with clear—but often dull or harsh—voices.

Starting in the 1930s, the audiobook was one of two forms of spoken-word narrative. The other, the radio drama, was a kind of theater performed live for audiences across the nation. From the 1920s to the 1950s, the so-called "Golden Age of Radio," American airwaves were crammed with soap operas, science fiction plays, Shakespeare adaptations, mysteries, horror stories, romances, children's bedtime stories, broad comedies, and improv shows featuring the greatest voices, performers, musicians, and Foley artists working in show business. The result was a rich medium, painted in sound, bursting with the ability to tickle the imagination in ways that film and television still can't match. In America, the most famous single broadcast was the 1938 Mercury Theater production of The War of the Worlds by H.G. Wells, directed by Orson Welles in the style of a real-time news broadcast. Its vivid production convinced some listeners (who missed the opening credits) that they were hearing coverage of a genuine alien invasion.

American radio drama died a long slow death between the 1950s and 1980s, but the art form survived in Britain and in the British Commonwealth—leading, incidentally, to the second most famous radio drama of all time: The Hitchhiker's Guide To The Galaxy (which came before the books, the TV show, or the film).

During the 1980s, the cross-pond popularity of The Hitchhiker's

Guide and other BBC productions, coupled with the continual late-night rebroadcast of Golden Age radio dramas, helped revive interest in the medium. But it wasn't until the early 21st century that things really started to pick up steam again in the United States.

> Note: the difference between a "radio drama" and an "audio drama" is how it's published. From this point forward, I will exclusively use "audio drama," except when discussing a production in relation to radio broadcast.

Throughout most of their history, the audiobook and the audio drama have been distinct beasts. Until the late 1990s, the audiobook was technically inferior (in every respect) to other contemporary spoken-word entertainment.

Older audiobooks were lackluster for three reasons—one political, one technical, and one economic.

First, the early audiobook industry was essentially a government program, established by an act of Congress, to give blind people access to more literature than that which was available in braille. Until the ubiquitous adoption of the audio cassette player in the 1970s, libraries for the blind comprised the bulk of the market. A negligible market supported by subsidies resulted in an audiobook landscape that was the artistic equivalent of standing in line at the DMV.

Second, the low quality of older speakers and the lower fidelity of older tape and record players dictated that, for maximum intelligibility, a clear, cutting voice with sharp consonants was a must. Voices like this are often not pleasant to listen to, but you can't fail to follow a story read by one. This technical demand dovetailed nicely with the third reason for mediocre quality:

Audiobooks are expensive.

The expenses start with the voice actor, the studio time, the recording engineer, the director, the editor, the mixer, and the mastering—but they only start there. Until the 21st century, all audiobooks were distributed on vinyl, cassette, and CD. That means package design, printing and duplication costs, shipping costs, warehousing costs, and a retail distribution infrastructure.

To ship audiobooks to market at a price that wouldn't drive the customers into bankruptcy, the recordings were often heavily abridged (which also incurred the cost of an abridging editor, though at far lower expense than the increase in distribution cost incurred for every additional tape or CD in a title). As the market grew through the late 1980s and in the 1990s, production quality at most audiobook companies went from mediocre to stunning. Celebrities and professional voice actors became regular readers, new performance standards moved in, and new recording formats (multi-voice, full-cast, and full-production) brought audible variety to the market.

As consumer demand grew, so did demand for unabridged recordings. The costs, however, meant that only bestsellers were ever released in unabridged format—the label "unabridged" on an audiobook box became a premium mark, deserving of a premium price. As prices crept upward and CD ripping became common, audiobooks joined pornography and Top 40 pop music as the most common targets of pirates in the age of dial-up and low-end broadband Internet service.

But what the Internet took away with one hand, it gave back with another. From 1999 through 2003, the Sci-Fi Channel sponsored Seeing Ear Theater, a streaming showcase of dramatizations of classic and new science fiction, fantasy, and horror stories starring the luminaries of the genres and written by such giants of the field as Jack Vance, James Patrick Kelley, Dean Wesley Smith, J. Michael Straczynski, Neil Gaiman, and Octavia Butler.

Meanwhile, on the other side of the world, audio equipment companies sensed a market opportunity brought about by the fragmentation of the music industry. They brought advances in chip fabrication to bear on their products, driving down the cost of recording studio gear on a Moore's Law schedule.

Moore's Law

Moore's Law states that every eighteen months, the number of transistors on a processor doubles, while the price halves. Thus, the power and quality available at any given price point increases exponentially. Businesses that become subject to Moore's Law tend to experience radical destabilization and democratization, resulting in tremendous opportunities for small business and content creators.

By 2005, a high end sixteen-channel recording studio (which cost $40,000 in 1995) could be had for as little as $3000. If you wanted to record a single reader instead of a rock'n'roll band, you could set yourself up in business as a voiceover artist for as little as $300 (assuming you already owned a computer).

Then, these two technology curves (home recording and Internet) collided head-on with a third one: the iPod. In 2005, Apple included the Podcast—serialized spoken-word audio content—in the iTunes store. Not long after, three people—Scott Sigler, Tee Morris, and Mark Jeffrey—got the idea, independently, to start podcasting their own audiobooks for free. Releasing a chapter a week, Morris and Jeffrey used their podcasts to drive customers to their print books. Scott Sigler, on the other hand, released new content unavailable in other media as part of a long (and ultimately quite successful) campaign to build himself a devoted bestseller's audience. Their success had a few consequences:

1. Along with the authors they mentored (including myself and bestselling authors Nathan Lowell, Philippa Ballantine, Mur Lafferty, Seth Harwood, and others), they contributed heavily to a growing demand for author-read audiobooks.
2. The formation of Podiobooks.com (co-founded by Morris with social media pioneer Evo Terra), a donation-funded distribution hub for podcast audiobooks and the second major entrant into the online audiobook distribution market (after Audible.com,

founded in 1999). Podiobooks has, at the time of this writing, just merged with Scribl.com to create a new platform for commercial and semi-commercial audiobook distribution.

3. Together with a handful of theater companies that helped revived audio dramas on the Internet, the birth of The Parsec Awards, one of the major industry awards in audio fiction.

All these factors, coupled with ever-increasing customer demand, have created something even better than the Golden Age of Radio. We're now in the Platinum Age of Audio Fiction—never before in history have audiobooks been so easy to produce, so profitable to distribute, or so frequently enjoyed, and never before has the author's voice been heavily in demand.

Once upon a time, audio rights were nearly worthless. Publishers bought them for a song and sold them on to production companies to help offset the cost of the author's advance. Now, they're gold—and when they're read by the author (assuming the author does a good job), they are the third biggest potential income stream you have at your disposal, which you can control for the rest of your life, and beyond (assuming you hang on to your rights).

And you know what? It's fun, too.

Part I
The Business

2 Making Tracks

Chapter 1

· · · · · · · · · ·

Time is Money

When someone seeks me out for advice on producing their first audiobook, they always ask me the same question: What kind of microphone should I buy? The trouble is, it's always the wrong question.

The right question is: What does it take to put an audiobook together?

The answer is not one that most first-timers will find encouraging. It goes something like this:

In the beginning is the book—or the story—that you wish to record. Once you make the decision to bring those words off the page and to your audience's ears, you buy yourself a whole heap of decisions and a potentially massive to-do list.

Under ideal circumstances, to produce a professional-quality salable product using the simplest possible production methods, your audiobook will cost you four to eight hours of effort for every hour of finished audio—two to four hours recording, two to four hours editing and mixing, giving you a production ratio range of 4:1 to 8:1. That's what happens with an experienced reader and an experienced sound engineer doing the editing and mixing. It's going to take you longer. Maybe a lot longer. This does not include the time you'll spend striking distribution agreements, wrangling your cover art, and doing whatever marketing you deem appropriate.

Now, the second bit of bad news: At the proper reading speed, an hour of audio only eats up 8,000 to 9,500 words. That means that an 80,000 word novel is going to come out at between 8.4 and 10 hours, and that translates to between 33.6 and 80 hours of work that you'll have to put in. That's up to two full working weeks for a moderate length novel, and, because you'll have to rest your voice, it's going to take you longer than two weeks to actually produce it (assuming you're not writing or working a day job while you produce your masterpiece).

I mention this now, at the outset, because the majority of people that have asked me for advice over the years never wound up finishing even their first project. Even in today's era of ultra-cheap equipment, ultra-cheap distribution, and ultra-accessible marketplaces, the investment in audiobook production is non-trivial. If you're a professional author who's expanding your business into the audiobook realm, you need to consider the costs before going in. If you're a hobbyist (i.e. no matter how passionately you love writing and recording, you do not now and do not intend to make your living from it), you need to make sure that the time required isn't going to drain the joy out of your hobby.

That's the time investment.

As far as money is concerned, producing your own audiobook could cost you as little as $250 (if you have a bare-bones studio and do all the work yourself) or as much as $10,000 (if you have a lavish production with hired performers, licensed music, and record in a rented studio or buy top-end equipment for your own). However, keep in mind that (unless you're renting the studio time) the price will drop with subsequent books, as you only have to buy the equipment once, and some of your other potential expenses are one-time deals.

Now that that's out of the way, it's time to talk turkey about the business end of this business. Before you turn your mic on, you need to make a few decisions about your audiobook. Foremost among them: What kind of audiobook is this going to be?

Formats

Your format determines everything else. When audiobooks were first invented, the formula was simple: one reader, one microphone,

one recording. Now, there are options.

Spoken-word audio productions exist along a continuum, with single reads at the simple end and audio drama on the complicated end. Here's how it breaks out:

Single Read

A single read is as simple as it gets. One person reads the text of the book from end-to-end, without sound effects or incidental music. Musical interludes or transitional sounds appropriate to your story may be used for scene breaks or chapter breaks, and introductory music may be played over the title sequence, but these are strictly optional—just make sure your style is consistent throughout.

Performance style in single reads can vary from the very, very simple to the highly theatrical. A simple read uses inflection and timing to pace dialogue and create mood, but doesn't perform different voices for different characters beyond subtle changes in vocal hardness and enunciation. Some excellent author-readers who work in this category are Douglas Adams, Neil Gaiman, and Nathan Lowell (who is an accomplished voice actor, but nevertheless chooses a very simple style for his own productions). In a very real sense, these books are read rather than performed.

A more stylized performance can be seen in authors like Scott Sigler and Harlan Ellison and in books read by voice actors Peter Lawlor and Elizabeth Ann Scarborough, each of whom give their characters unique voices and accents—Latino characters get Latino accents, male readers pitch female characters up while female readers pitch male characters down, and the narrator uses pacing to evoke the story's distinctive "voice" (speeding up in urgent passages, slowing down in romantic passages, leaving moments of silence for moments of tension or reflection, etc.).

While single-read is the simplest option, don't make the mistake of thinking it's easy—it isn't. Even a very simple production requires good vocal technique, solid engineering, and emotional investment in the material. A good reader, whether performing or simply reading, brings her subtext to the fore, and that takes practice.

It is, however, the most straightforward of the available options.

Multi-Voice Read

Sometimes, your story will benefit from more than one voice. A multi-voice read is often employed for tales with two dominant point-of-view characters of opposite sexes. A male and a female reader will trade narration duties depending on point of view, with each actor also reading the dialog spoken by characters of their respective genders. An excellent example of this technique can be found in the Star Trek audiobook Q-In-Law, written by Peter David read by John de Lancie and Majel Barret.

Multi-Voice is also frequently employed with nonfiction audiobooks, where one reader will take the main narration duties and another will read the footnotes, sidebars, insets, and anecdotes. Richard Dawkins and his partner Lala Ward have teamed up to do just this with a number of his titles, but the best job they've done so far, in my opinion, was in The Ancestor's Tale.

While no rule exists limiting the number of voices in a multi-voice book to two, using more than two is unusual for the simple reason that, the more voices you add, the more production time and cost you add.

Cost? Well, yes. From this point forward you must also bear in mind the sticky problem of paying your talent. Once you step out of a one-horse DIY operation from end-to-end, you're incurring labor costs. Voice actors deserve to be paid for their work. If you're doing this as a hobby, you may be able to pay them in kind (I'll read for your book, you read for mine). If you're doing this as part of your business, or you intend to sell your book at any point in the future, you'll need to pay your talent. In either case, for many reasons, you'll need to get signed vocal release contracts from your talent—I'll cover those in Chapter 2.

So, if you're considering adding that third or fourth voice, think about it long and hard. If they won't be adding something special, it might be best to leave them to one side. If they'll make the difference between a production that walks and a production that soars, and you can afford the extra time and cost, then by all means, bring them in.

Multi-voice productions generally don't contain sound effects, soundscaping, or incidental music, though there have been exceptions. Be aware that these elements also add cost.

Full-Cast

A full-cast audiobook is, quite simply, a production that uses a large cast to give each and every character in the book a unique, immediately identifiable voice. This doesn't mean that individual actors might not play a number of roles—in my experience, a good voice actor can often handle half-a-dozen roles or more in a single production—but it does mean that each character must sound unique. My book *Predestination and Other Games of Chance*, for example, had 68 speaking roles, which were covered by a cast of 33 actors. Many actors performed a single role, while others covered up to seven. In such productions, the author (if the author is involved) usually reads the narrator's lines (including the POV character if the book is told in first person) and may also take on additional roles if it suits the production.

Full-cast books are not audio dramas, because they are not dramatized. Rather, they include the full text of the original book, with one exception: dialog tags. Phrases like "she said" may, at the discretion of the director, be cut from the book so long as they do not contain any information beyond identifying the speaker. The use of multiple voices render such tags redundant, and many directors choose to omit them. However, if the dialog tag provides pacing or contains action, author voice elements, characterization, or other additional information, it should be left intact.

When you cross the line into full-cast, you open up the opportunity to create a true feast for the ears. Your actors, if well-chosen and well-directed, will give your story life in ways that may surprise you, bringing out nuances in your text that you might not be able to manage on your own.

And, if you're already going to this much effort, you have

another decision to make: Exactly how far are you going to take it?

You could take the direct route, and just ramp up a multi-voice production to a massively multi-voiced production. With good actors, you can blow the ears off your audience with the performances alone.

Or, if you're truly insane (like your humble narrator), you can opt for full-production sound and produce your book almost as if it were an audio drama, with environmental sound effects, incidental music, Foley, room-specific vocal treatments, active stereo imaging, digital FX, and other little touches that turn your book into a movie for your mind.

I love full-cast. It's my medium of choice when I have the resources available. I can't tell you the satisfaction of QC'ing a properly mixed book and getting sucked so far in that I forget that I ever had anything to do with creating it. But it's not for the timid—some author-producers (such as Scott Sigler) have described the whole full-cast enterprise (and me in particular) as "batshit insane."

And he's right. Full-cast brings extra challenges, to put it mildly. It is, hands down, the most time-intensive of all the non-dramatized formats. If you opt for an opulent production, you're going to need a script supervisor, a casting director, a source of music (either original compositions, specially licensed music, or stock), a source of sound effects, a deep grasp of audio engineering, and you'll have to be more picky with your quality control checks. All of these, naturally, also add expense and/or time.

Even if you keep your production simple, you're going to need a director. You may be able to handle the directing chores yourself, or you may need to bring someone in, but either way, your actors will need (and often expect) direction.

In my experience, a seasoned voice actor will do a superb job with written directions. However, not all actors are capable of self-direction from context or written notes (indeed, many superb ones aren't), and not all seasoned voice-over artists are actors—an artist accustomed to reading commercial copy, for example, will require a more hands-on approach: You will need to live-direct them. I will cover techniques on how to do this both in person and remotely, as well as techniques for directing yourself, in Chapter 3.

Since it doesn't have as long a tradition behind it as single reads, some segments of the audiobook audience don't like full-cast, so if you embark on it you should be aware that you're going to have to hit a very high standard in terms of production values. Where a single-read audience will often forgive merely-adequate audio quality for the sake of an excellent story, by putting the time and effort into full-cast you're signaling to the audience that you're a cut above. If your production matches the hype, you have a chance to really distinguish yourself. The audience for full-cast is an active and fast-growing market segment, and they are very vocal. Treat them right, and they will repay you with tremendous loyalty.

Highbridge Audio and Full-Cast Audio, both of whom follow the traditional audiobook studio business model (i.e. they are not author-run operations), are production companies that produce largely or exclusively full-cast audiobooks. Their work—both in their triumphs and their failures—is worth checking out if you intend to tackle this challenging form. As the longstanding professional companies who created this market, they're your gold standard.

Some author-run full-cast productions that you should also check out:

Imagine That! Studios' *Billibub Baddings and the Case of the Singing Sword* by Tee Morris

Christof Laputka's *The Leviathan Chronicles*

Chris Lester's *Metamor City*

Abigail Hilton's *Cowry Catchers*

My own company, ArtisticWhispers Productions, also produces full-cast audiobooks with full-production audio.

Audio Drama

Like a full-production full-cast audiobook, audio dramas are immersive audio universes. Unlike full-cast, though, an audio drama is, well, a drama. If the drama started life as a book, it must first be dramatized.

To turn your book into an audio drama, you must adapt your text so that you eliminate most or all of the narration, shifting the narrative load into dialog. However, there are two important exceptions to this rule:

- In a first person story, where your POV character is your narrator.
- In a third person story, your narrator can sometimes be a distinct character with its own highly eccentric point of view. The classic example of this is *The Hitchhiker's Guide To The Galaxy*.

However, even in these cases, you will still strip much of the narration. Exposition will stay with the narrator, but description and sensory details will be the responsibility of the characters, while sounds will be carried by your Foley artist.

Dramatizing books is an art form in and of itself, and requires a lot of practice. A good basic primer on scriptwriting that covers the peculiarities of the audio drama format is J. Michael Straczynski's Scriptwriting, and I highly recommend you pick it up if you intend to pursue audio dramas.

Aside from the script, audio dramas also frequently record actors in groups. Drama truly is a piece of theater, and actors tend to do better when playing off each other (it also saves you a lot of time in post production, as it's easier to record repartee live with natural timing than to create it artificially in the edit bay).

For models of production and script quality, check out the BBC. They have long been—and still remain—the gold standard in the audio/radio drama world. Additionally, if you wish to work in this format, you'd do well to familiarize yourself with some Golden Age radio series, particularly *Lights Out*, *X Minus One*, and *The Black Museum*. While the acting is often stylistically dated, they feature masterful Foley work from which you can learn a lot. Some other contemporary radio/audio theater companies that have grown into truly gorgeous production houses are Decoder Ring Theatre, The

Atlanta Radio Theater Company, and Prometheus Radio Theater.

However, the single most sophisticated producer working in the format today is Dirk Maggs of Above The Title Productions. If you want to hear what can be done with audio drama using contemporary, off-the-shelf equipment and software that is within reach of a modest budget, pick up anything he's produced in the last fifteen years. His work has, hands down, the best production quality in the world.

A Matrix of Rights

As an author, you own the copyright to your work, and you can slice and dice that copyright any way you see fit. The above list covers the most common forms of audio productions—it's not exhaustive. There are currently thirty-six different possible permutations of the audiobook format, and someone will probably invent a new one tomorrow. Keep that in mind as you consider licensing proposals for your audiobook rights, and draw up your contracts accordingly.

As a producer, do bear in mind that, so long as you have secured the rights from the author (if you're producing your own books the rights shouldn't be too difficult), you can do whatever the hell you want, the categories I've just outlined are not divine mandate. There are no firm rules, only industry norms, so you can mix and match these categories to your heart's content. I've seen people bring full-fledged audio drama production values to single-reads. However, such instances are unusual enough that this sidebar is the only places you'll see them mentioned.

Roles in an Audiobook Production

As with a movie, an audiobook is a big job and requires the DIY producer to wear a lot of hats (or hire other heads to wear them for him). I'm assuming you already have a writer with a finished book (i.e. you). In addition to your writer, you're going to need:

• *Voice Talent*

No matter what format you pick, you're gonna need a voice. If it's a single-read, you may pick yourself or you may hire it out. If it's any other format, you'll need more talent, and to do that, you'll need to be (or hire) a...

• *Casting Director*

When casting, you're entering a world of subtlety. Not only are you looking for the actors that can embody your characters, you're looking for actors who sound different enough from one another that they won't create confusion in the ears of the audience. If you're casting one actor in multiple roles, be careful that those roles don't appear opposite each other in the same scene—or if they do, be careful that your actor can create voices distinct enough from one another that the audience won't be able to tell they're played by the same person. A good voice actor can do this: in one production I directed, I wound up with one actor playing three characters who all appeared in the same room talking to each other, and he pulled it off marvelously. If you do put an actor in this position, make sure you test them on the problem scenes first, don't just listen to their different voices in isolation.

•*Foley Artist*

Foley is the discipline of creating, editing, and timing sound effects. Named after Jack Foley, who invented the discipline, Foley artists create texture for movies and audio dramas to fill in the audible world left bare by recording in a studio. A wonderful visual demonstration of this art form can be seen in the film Radioland Murders.

Once done in real-time as a live performance, the advance of portable recorders and digital editing means that pre-recorded Foley is de rigeur, while live Foley is a rarefied art. I'll cover a bit of both in Chapter 12.

• *Music Director*

The music director is the person who picks, arranges, and edits your music. Many—though not all—modern audiobooks have music. In the opening credits/front matter, as in the opening credits for a film or a TV show, your music sets the tone for your listeners. This does not need to be the tone of the entire book, but it should lead your audience into the emotional space appropriate for the start of your story.

We'll get into the ins and outs of procuring music in Chapter 16.

• *Script Supervisor*

This is basically a fancy name for the person who formats your reading copy, adds direction notes to the margins, keeps track of what's been recorded and what's still to come, and prepares scripts for retakes (and trust me, there will always be some re-takes).

• *Director*

The Director is responsible for the performance(s) of your reader(s). She sets the timing requirements, makes sure the proper emphasis and nuance comes through in the performance, sets the emotional tone, pays attention to flubs and mistakes that the actor can't hear, and requests alternate takes of problematic passages.

For tips on directing techniques, including self-direction, direction through notes, and remote-direction, see Chapter 3.

• *Production Engineer*

Of course, all this performing and casting and sound and music work doesn't mean much if you can't record good clean audio. A Production Engineer is responsible for the audio signal, from the selection and customization of the room to picking the cables and equipment to creating the signal chain. During recording, he keeps one eye on the V/U meter (which measures signal level) and the waveform to make sure that the signal is good and strong, but doesn't clip, and then he saves and backs up the files once recorded.

No matter how good the performance(s), no matter how masterful the text or music or Foley, if the production engineer doesn't do his job properly you won't have a salable product. This is the make-or-break job in the production—so important that all of Parts 3 and 4 of this book are devoted to this job.

Every other job in the production has a greater margin for error.

• *Post-Production Engineer*

This is where it all comes together. Post-production is everything that happens between asset acquisition (recording, sound effects, music) and your final product. Editing, special FX, noise cleanup, sweetening, mixing, balancing, panning, mastering to delivery formats, and tagging. For a detailed treatment of all these topics, see Chapters 13 through 18 inclusive.

• *Art Director*

Once you've got a finished product, you need to package it for distribution. At the very least, this means cover art properly formatted for the online marketplaces where you distribute.

For physical distribution—which you should consider, for reasons we'll discuss later—you'll need CD silkscreen art, box design, jewel case inserts, and other little touches to make your product stand proudly next to offerings from Simon & Schuster Audio and Blackstone Audio in bookstores, at truck stops, and in big box stores. If you're not a competent graphic designer and are intent on pursuing physical distribution, this is the one job that you really should consider subbing out.

That's a big production team—nevertheless, with the exception of extra voices, all of the jobs above can (and often are) performed by an individual or a two-person team. As with anything else, practice in each area creates expertise. If you have Full-Cast or Audio Drama ambitions, but no background in some of the above areas, start simple and build complexity with each succeeding production. Doing it this way, you'll see (and hear) your skills improve and your costs drop with each project as you get better and faster at what you do. If you work very hard and get very good, you might even do what Nathan Lowell has done:

Reduce your production ratio to 3:1.

Chapter 2

Bringing it to Market

The big three book market segments are, in this order, paper and electronic (primacy varies by market segment), and audio. The fastest growing market segment is audio (21%, market growth in 2015, according to the Audiobook Publisher's Association).

In the last few years, the markets opened up for audio like they did for ebooks in 2009. Like ebooks, worldwide Internet distribution means that anyone, anywhere, can buy and consume an audiobook so long as they have a smartphone or a data connection. And, like with ebooks, after a few initial years of out-and-out market monopoly by Amazon, other markets are beginning to appear, open up, and become viable venues for authors and small publishers alike.

Ebooks, however, have two fundamental limitations that audiobooks don't: Literacy and language.

Who Listens? And Where?

To consume a book, you must not only fluently speak the language in which it's written, you must read it fluently as well. With an audiobook, you do not need to read the language in which it's performed—and you don't necessarily need to speak it either. Audiobooks are a popular way for non-native speakers to acquaint themselves with colloquial English—as an author and producer it's not unusual for me to receive emails from fans using my audiobooks to up their colloquial facility (i.e. idiom and profanity. In the words of one fan, "I can finally fucking swear, goddammit!"). Around the world, the ability to speak English translates to economic power. As Africa and India come online with mobile broadband in the next few years, the international market for English audiobooks will explode.

But we don't have to wait for Ragnarok to make audiobooks worthwhile—we've got plenty of adoption growth in the English speaking world. After all, anyone who owns a smartphone or an iPod or a car stereo or a computer can listen to audiobooks, and audiobooks offer a non-destructive escape from desk-work drudgery and long-haul commutes (in other words, you can enjoy them while doing other things). Audiobooks have long been a staple of truck drivers and road trippers, a major component of literacy programs for learning-disabled adults, and a go-to solution for the blind.

People listen in the bath, on the commuter train, in the car, on airplanes, at work, at the gym, while gardening, while jogging, in the field on an archaeological dig, and in bed at night. Anytime the eyes are too busy, or too tired, it's an occasion where someone, somewhere is listening to an audiobook.

Is it any wonder it's the fastest growing form of fiction today?

Commercial Markets

The current audiobook market consists of a number of major online retailers and a number of major and minor offline retailers. Although I can't hope to provide an all inclusive list, here's a quickie rundown on the current state-of-play.

The major online retailers are:
• *Audible*
In the world of audiobooks, there's nobody bigger. Audible is currently the single biggest audiobook dealer on the planet, both as a

direct retailer and as the exclusive downloadable audiobook distributor for iTunes and Amazon (its parent company). Industry estimates I've seen (which are notoriously difficult to verify) are that Audible currently owns 70-90% of the domestic audiobook download market.

• *Amazon*

In addition to selling downloadable books provided by its subsidiary Audible, Amazon sells physical CDs (both CDs filled with MP3s and traditional audio CDs) from third party vendors and publishers.

• *Audiobooks.com*

The first also-ran in downloadable audio.

• *Barnes & Noble*

Sells downloadable and physical audiobooks through their online storefront.

• *Emusic.com*

One of the larger music stores on the Internet, they also carry a wide variety of spoken-word titles, including audiobooks.

• *SimplyAudiobooks.com*

The Netflix of online audio, they rent physical audiobooks through the mail. They also sell downloads and physical audiobooks through their website.

• *Scribd*

An ebook retailer that also carries audiobooks.

• *iTunes*

The deal that makes Audible the exclusive source of paid audiobook content on iTunes is scheduled to expire in the next year or two. Due to the deep and bitter rivalry between Amazon and Apple, the former strategic partners may decide to go their separate ways rather than renew the deal. If this happens, expect iTunes to open up to premium content from small audiobook creators in the same way that the iPhone app store is now open to small software developers. Keep your eyes peeled.

• *Gumroad*

A digital fulfillment service that allows you to sell downloadable and hard goods (i.e. distributed on physical media), including ebooks and audiobooks, on very favorable terms.

• *LearnOutLoud.com*

Another one of the big outlets specializing in spoken-word audio of all kinds. It's a site with some interesting windows into the broader market, worth browsing around on.

That's a sampling of the online marketplace. It has grown enough since the first edition of this book that I can't include all the players here, so I've gone for the major and/or interesting ones. The offline marketplace, though it isn't as big as it once was, is still huge and should not be neglected. Major retailers include Barnes & Noble, Target, and Wal-Mart, but they are dwarfed in by the far-reaching minor retail culture. These include:

• Indie Bookstores
• Truck Stops
• Hotel and Casino Gift Shops

Bear in mind that this is the shape of things in the US, but the audiobook market is truly international. Canada, the UK, New Zealand, and Australia all have different market landscapes. If you're in these countries, or looking to push into these countries, you will need to research their markets and find your way in.

Commercial Distribution

As a small publisher (which is what you become the minute you start producing and marketing your own audiobooks), you're going to have a tough time getting good distribution terms. The audiobook market was never as closed as the book market used to be, but like the traditional book market it's a retail business model. As a publisher working through offline channels (and sometimes with the online channels), the majority of your sales will be to retailers rather than to customers. The terms you can get out of a retailer depend entirely on how much value you bring to the table, and in this market that value is based on two things:

the number of titles in your catalog and the sales profile of the authors in that catalog. Because of this, in the early days you may be well served to access these markets through a distributor that aggregates the catalogs of a number of companies. As your company (and your catalog) grows, you may reach a point where it's worth your time to make deals directly with retailers or major distributors on an a la carte basis, rather than going through channels set up for the small frys.

In the online world, you may distribute both audiobooks on physical media and audiobooks that can be downloaded directly from the web. Your distribution options in the online world are as follows:

• *Android and iPhone App stores*

The market for smartphones depends on small-scale software developers building applications that let people do more with their phones. A lot of those developers are available for hire, and fairly inexpensively. Putting together an app that delivers a single audiobook—or a subscription to your audiobooks, ebooks, podcasts, blog, and anything else you can package as bits—is trivially easy from a developer's point of view. You can price these apps at any point you like, including recurring payments for subscriptions to serialized content. Just decide on your business model and set aside the money to pay the developer.

Of course, if you're a developer yourself, you can do this without a cash outlay.

• *Music Distributors like Tunecore and CD Baby*

These services, and ones like them, will distribute both physical and downloadable audiobooks as "Spoken Word" titles. In their catalogs, they do not differentiate between lectures, stand-up comedy, audiobooks (let alone genre), or other kinds of spoken-word material. Needless to say, since the online world is search-engine driven, this is not an optimal placement strategy—however, both of these services have storefronts that you can get into without opting into their extended distribution channels, and these may be worth pursuing depending on your business strategy.

• ACX

Amazon's Audible Audiobook Creator's Exchange Service (ACX) is a marketplace designed to match actors and producers to audio rights holders with an eye toward getting the resulting productions into the Audible store. If you want to get your audiobooks produced, but are not interested in producing them yourself, this is the place to go. The talent there can either be hired on an hourly basis or can be had for a 50/50 split between the rights holder (that's you) and the producer.

These choices do have consequences.

If you opt to pay for hired talent, you're going to pay between $200 and $500 per finished hour for professional-level voice talent. If you hire the talent this way (or you read your own book) you will retain all rights to the production, and you can sell it or distribute it anywhere you see fit. With ACX, this will allow you to choose either an exclusive or a non-exclusive distribution contract.

On the other hand, if you opt for the royalty split, ACX automatically gains exclusive worldwide distribution rights over the production, and they handle the bookkeeping. Because ACX acts as the fiduciary for this contract, the production can not be taken out of their ecosystem unless and until you make a separate deal with the producer (who retains the copyright to his or her work).

ACX offers royalties of 20% for non-exclusive distribution rights, and 40% for exclusive distribution rights. Both ACX's exclusive and their non-exclusive contracts have seven year terms, and they auto-renew unless canceled in-writing before the renewal date. ACX's exclusivity claim covers the story, not the production, so by signing an exclusive deal with them (including a royalty-split deal) you forfeit your option to make other licensing deals with your copyright, or to make enhanced audiobooks or full-cast productions, or to make deals for broadcast rights, etc.

Unlike the ebook market, which currently works on the agency pricing model (where the publisher sets the price), the audiobook market works on the traditional retail model (where the vendor sets the price). Although there has been some movement on this front in recent months, none of it has come from ACX or Audible. Audible prices by length of production, and they control the pricing.

Because of Audible's relationship with Amazon and their current relationship with iTunes, going through Audible is the only way to get downloads into both stores. Since Audible will not deal directly with small publishers through normal channels, ACX is your only direct route into the Audible ecosystem. However, you should be aware that, in addition to the restrictions listed above, ACX claims that it will not accept any production that has ever been made available for free, in any form, anywhere on the Internet, and they require most-favored-nation pricing status.

This claim is not quite true, as some of their star featured authors (such as Scott Sigler) sell versions of their books on ACX that are identical to versions available for free via podcast or through freemium sites like Scribl.com. Transgress this rule at your own peril—it works for some authors, and not for others.

I said that ACX is the only direct route into the Audible ecosystem—it is not the only one, and some of the other routes in can sometimes bypass some of ACX's more draconian conditions and demands, though they are frequently more labor-intensive. Also, If you're not living in the US or doing business through a corporation based here, ACX has no obvious avenue into the store for you, so these other methods provide a path for you to get into Audible's distribution channel.

• *Overdrive*

Overdrive supplies audiobooks and ebooks to the lion's share of libraries in Australia and the United States. Now a part of the Rakuten empire, which also owns Kobo. Currently there are two ways into the store: Through the front door (if you have a few dozen titles) or through Author's Republic (below). Due to Overdrive's recent acquisition by Rakuten, and their Kobo division's history of aggressively courting independent authors, I believe it likely that this is a market which may open up radically to smaller players in the coming years.

• *Author's Republic*

A distributor for audiobooks that hits thirty or so of the major players in the market, it is attempting to do for the audiobook market what Smashwords and Draft2Digital do for the ebook market. At the time of this writing their contract is pretty decent, and extends to a seven-year term. They do demand exclusivity of a limited sort—they claim exclusivity over the *production*, not the *story*, and there are exceptions to their exclusivity for author-controlled channels such as direct website sales, hard goods (i.e. CDs, DVDs, tapes, MP3s on memory sticks), and digital fulfillment sites like Gumroad and Patreon. They encourage authors and production companies with larger catalogs to contact them directly to negotiate *a la carte* deals.

• *Other Small Press Aggregators*

There are a few other companies that attempt to distribute to a number of major platforms. Big Happy Family Audio is currently the most well-established. They do hard goods and Internet distribution, and have been around for a number of years now. They negotiate contracts on an *a la carte* basis.

Other companies are coming and going all the time—Author's Republic came out of nowhere last year, and in the next year I expect at least two more major players to enter the market. Whether they are successful or not, time will tell, but the marketplace has never been more ripe for disruption.

I offer no warranties or recommendations about any of these companies. Engage their services at your own risk, and always have a lawyer look at any contract you negotiate with any distributor.

Thus far, I've been able to find no monolithic distribution provider that hits the sweet spot of market reach, money, speed of payments, and freedom. In the current climate, the best option is probably to cobble together a patchwork of distributors with access to different markets. The bigger your catalog, the better rates you'll be able to command. Once you have a healthy catalog (several dozen titles or more), you will be in the position to deal directly with storefronts and cut distributors out of the mix, assuming you have the time and resources to build your own distribution channel. It will net you more money at the expense of more time and paperwork.

Physical Distribution

The hard goods audiobook market, just like the hard goods music market, is declining, and for the same reasons. Fewer people have CD and DVD players, and fewer people want to tote around physical media. It is possible that the market will disappear entirely in the next few years, or that it will be replaced by memory sticks, or that, like the market for paper books, it will stabilize at a lower level than it started out at, but will stick around more-or-less forever.

Whatever its future, the hard goods market is still with us for now, and it's still large enough to be worth paying attention to. Here's the trouble. Audio CDs aren't paperbacks. Almost nobody does good Print-On-Demand, and the few who do (and also ship directly to retailers) are very expensive. For a while Createspace would do it—they still do it for music—but when Amazon bought Audible in 2010, Createspace quietly stopped printing spoken-word CDs or accepting digital downloads with a running time of longer than an hour. For the moment, we're back in the old-fashioned world of physical printing, warehousing, and distribution. Unless you land a distribution deal that includes duplication (difficult to find, and hard to get good terms on, but not altogether impossible), if you want to do physical distribution you're going to have to establish a relationship with a print shop. That's the bad news.

The good news is that printing and packaging costs for moderate sized runs of CDs have come way down. There are plenty of print shops who will deliver burned and packaged discs at very good prices, and will drop-ship print runs to retailers—though the smaller your print run, the higher your per-unit price is going to be. Without particularly recommending any one of these companies, here are some printers with good reputations who are worth checking out—some I've done business with, some I've only heard of, and I'm not saying which is which:

- Accutrack
- TrepStar (also does POD fulfillment to Amazon)
- efulfillmentservice.com
- Kunaki

The first three are full-service operations. The fourth is a little bit different—it's one of the presses that large indie bands and medium-sized audiobook publishers use. It's completely automated, and everything is done over the Internet. They have a solid reputation and good prices, but all the onus for QC is on you—Kunaki provides no telephone contact or customer service whatsoever.

This list is meant to get you started. There are literally dozens more companies that do this. Do your comparison shopping not just on price (including shipping prices) and quality, but on turnaround speed and shipping options as well. When you get to the point where you're drop-shipping a few hundred units at a time, those qualities will make or break your business relationship with your retailers.

Accessing those retailers, on the other hand, can range from dead easy to pretty tricky.

Distributing Yourself Physically

• *Amazon Direct*

While Amazon is difficult to deal with when selling downloadable files, they're pretty easy to deal with when selling physical merchandise, including audiobooks. Becoming an Amazon seller costs $40/mo, and gives you access to a number of goodies, including having Amazon warehouse your stock and fulfill your orders. It's worth looking into.

• *Brilliance Audio*

Brilliance Audio is Amazon's hard goods audio division—they are to physical audiobook distribution what Audible is to downloadable audiobook distribution. They have existing deals for distribution to truck stops, book stores, and all sorts of other nifty places. Normally, they acquire their inventory by poaching Audible's catalog—if your book hits bestseller status on Audibile, you may get a call from Brilliance. However, they will talk to you directly if you call and ask to speak to an acquisitions rep. Be prepared for an active negotiation and to show that you bring significant value to the table, and to be told just to deal with ACX until your catalog is bigger.

• *Book Stores*

Since the collapse of Borders, the bookselling retail space has contracted, but indie bookstores have rebounded to fill in much (though not all) of the giant gaping hole in the market. That means that, as a publisher, you've got easier access to a greater percentage of the available shelf space than you would have had just five years ago. For a list of independent bookstores in the United States, join the American Bookseller's Association as a publisher. As with everything else, the more titles you have (in this case: audiobooks, books, and anything else that might fit in a bookstore), and the better your catalog is presented, the more likely you are to develop dependable customers. To see how a catalog should be presented, pick a few up at a book industry trade show, or call some other publishers posing as a bookstore owner and get them to send you some, or visit your local independent bookstore and ask if you can have any old catalogs they have laying around.

• *Truck Stops*

Truck stops are where one of the biggest, most dependable market segments live and breathe: truckers. They're also a cultural world all their own, with their own protocols for doing business. Much of this world (on the supply-side) still works on something like the old traveling salesman model: They prefer to do business with outside sales reps with whom they have an established, face-to-face relationship, and who carry a varied catalog of merchandise (either their own or that of a distributor) that will appeal to truckers and tourists.

If you have a large catalog (at least few dozen titles, or at least a few dozen mixed items including swag, knick-knacks, audiobooks, calendars, gadgets, and anything else that might interest a trucker), you will find them receptive to a relationship-establishing sales pitch. Keep in mind that many owners and managers will prefer that you (or your sales rep) make that pitch in person.

I said that much of that world prefers to do business that way. The balance are big business operations—chains, franchises, etc.—which obtain their stock through distributors. To get your product into these chains, you need to deal with their distributors. To find them, ask the manager at a truck stop for the name and number of their distributor's sales or customer service rep, then follow the food chain up until you find the acquisitions rep. As will all retail distribution, expect to do some heavy negotiations with a lot of give and take in order to be guaranteed good placement in the shops.

• *Gift Shops*

These live in hotels, casinos, museums, and other tourist traps. Like truck stops, they have a particular culture that varies a bit from industry to industry. There are two ways in: the first is to ask directly who their purchasing agent is, and send that agent a catalog. The second is to ask who their major suppliers are—chances are that they buy mostly from aggregate distributors—and then call those suppliers and establish a relationship.

• *Big Box Stores*

Wal-Mart, Target, and other big box stores and shopping clubs represent a large potential market. I've personally not delved into this market yet, but I'm told by those in the know that, as with gift shops and the larger truck stop chains, the best way to access them is through a sales rep or distributor who already deals with them, and the second best way is to contact their purchasing department and find out what their purchasing protocols are. Shelf space in big box stores is at a premium, notoriously difficult to access, and frequently expensive.

Marketplace Requirements

Most marketplaces will require you to have a unique ISBN for every edition of your audiobook—this means you'll need one ISBN for your digitally-distributed audiobook, one for the version you distribute on an MP3 CD, and one for the version distributed on traditional audio CDs. All of these ISBNs must be different from any ISBNs you already use for your ebooks or paperbacks. In the US, ISBNs can be purchased individually or in batches from Bowker, or from any one of a thousand resellers.

You will also need a Universal Product Code (UPC) number for every version of you package for physical distribution—not just one for the MP3 CD and one for the audio CD, but a unique UPC for each style of packaging you do (jewel case vs. display box, etc.). You can obtain UPCs directly by registering a GS1 account, or you can buy them from a reseller. Many print shops include UPCs as part of their service packages, or will sell you one for a reasonable price.

Subsidiary Markets

A number of subsidiary markets exist for spoken-word audio content, including audiobooks. The currently-active marketplaces are:

• *Broadcast*

From local public access stations to independent radio stations across the continent, if your books or stories meet broadcast content restrictions for profanity (or can be edited to meet them), you can get them on the radio. Business models (including the money you'll make and the costs you'll incur) vary by station and market—some require you to buy airtime and then sell advertising to recoup your costs, others (such as the BBC and its affiliates throughout the commonwealth) buy content directly from writers and publishers through legally-established submission channels.

• *Satellite Radio and Cable*

With thousands of hours of airspace to fill—and no content restrictions—satellite radio and cable providers have, from time to time, made licensing deals with audiobook publishers and distributors. In this kind of market, every deal is unique.

• *Streaming Internet Radio*

Over the last few years, a number of Internet Radio networks have grown up distributing indie music and spoken word content of various lengths.

Payment schemes, profit potential, and audience reach for these markets vary not just from industry to industry, but from entity to entity. Do your homework before diving in. Also, bear in mind: These entities will sometimes walk through your door looking for you specifically, which puts you in a far stronger bargaining position. Produce solid content and get it before a big enough audience, and chances are good that you will get calls from some or all of these markets asking to license your content. When deciding to pursue these on a cold-call basis, be sure to carefully weigh the value of your time.

Semi-Commercial and Non-Commercial Markets

Not all markets worth investigating are markets that pay directly. Here are a few that pay indirectly, but can pay off very well for the judicious producer.

State Libraries for the Blind

Most states maintain Libraries for the Blind—braille and audiobook archives that work as a free resource for blind people, and accessible through schools, other public institutions, and (in some cases) over the Internet. They are not profit centers, but many of them are open to donations from small press publishers (which includes any of us independents who operate as a publishing company and/or production house, rather than just operating as authors). Getting your audiobooks into these libraries can take a little work, but it's worth the trouble—it's a whole audience of people who you won't otherwise have access to as a writer, and some of those people will recommend you to their sighted friends. While you're at it, it doesn't hurt to donate braille rights to the libraries, so that they may (if they see fit) prepare braille copies for their lending collection. Even though there's no immediate payoff, it's a decent thing to do, and it can pay dividends in the long run.

Podcast

A "Podcast" (iPod+broadcast) is a method of delivering serialized audio content over the Internet by piggybacking downloadable files on RSS feeds, which all blogs (and many other content hosting platforms) generate automatically. All blogging platforms, and most Content Management Systems, have freely available podcasting plugins—install one, make a blog post, upload your mp3, hit "publish", and you've released an episode. You can list that podcast at iTunes, in the iPhone Podcast app, and in a handful of other places around the net (listing costs nothing). As with anything else on the Internet, your cover art, blurb, genre, and metadata comprise your baseline discoverability.

Many of you who have heard of podcasts are likely most familiar with podcasts of existing radio shows, and of knock offs—what one author once described to me as "blabbermouthing and loudmouthing and other ways to waste your time and alienate your audience." It's true that a lot of podcasts are essentially talk radio or NPR for the ubergeek set, or pirated music played by people who want to be disc jockeys, but that's not the kind of thing I'm talking about.

I'm talking about podcasting your audiobooks and audio dramas.

So why in the hell would anyone in their right mind release their work for free? Particularly work that's doubly time-consuming (first you had to write it, then you had to produce it) and can command a premium price in the major commercial markets?

Taking the reasons in order from the weakest to the strongest (in my opinion):

• *Ego*

People love to talk, and the idea that there's someone out there listening is a seductive one for folks who crave approbation. Artists are disproportionately approval-seeking folk, and authors are no exception.

• *Fun*

Podcasting is a tremendous amount of fun, and if you can make it make business sense, there's no harm in combining business with pleasure. If you can't make it work business-wise, though, be honest with yourself.

• *Visibility/Loss-leader*

"Obscurity is a far bigger threat to creative artists than piracy."—Cory Doctorow

Podcasting your fiction works as a kind of advertising. If you approach it strategically, it can be an extremely potent form of advertising. People who hear your book in your voice are making a personal connection with you, and they are more likely to care about you and your success than are people who read your words on a page.

Don't worry about diluting your market by releasing something for free. The podcast market is a tiny niche in the world of people who listen to spoken-word audio, and the podcast fiction market is a tiny sliver of that tiny niche. However, that fraction of a fraction is made up of people who are highly social, very likely to leave reviews, and very likely to spend their money on paper copies of books they've already listened to. In other words, these are people who are into being "true fans," or what Malcom Gladwell's The Tipping Point calls "mavens."

In any given advertising campaign, you're doing very, very well to get a 1% conversion rate—if 1 out of any 100 people who are exposed to the advertisement buy your product, the campaign is a wild success. My experience with podcasting is that, when I'm podcasting regularly, my conversion rate on new retail products, promotions, and crowdfunding campaigns that I push on the cast is around 3%.

Artists like Scott Sigler and Nathan Lowell, who were much quicker at figuring out how podcast fiction works as a business and more consistent about working it, have better conversion rates. The podcast audience is the active section of our fanbases that drives the word-of-mouth that our print fiction sales are built on—in Sigler and Lowell's cases, those sales run into the thousands of units per month (and neither they nor their publishers price their work anywhere near the discount ghetto).

• *Profit*

Back in the early days, podcasting was strictly a cost only. In the last few years, the direct content creation market has matured to the extend that it is now possible to monetize podcasts, vidcasts, and most other kinds of art on the Internet. If you build a large enough audience, you will be able to make money from them, and not just as a loss leader. A little later in this chapter I discuss the different ways you can make money from your podcast directly.

• *Direct Access to Fans*

When you podcast your audiobooks, you're creating a regular point of contact with these true fans. It's a point of contact you can use to announce new releases and drive people to the review sites, to announce new projects, to solicit fan activism, and to drive listeners to your subscription services and other products. Think of it as a sort of audible mailing list.

When Sigler, Morris, and Jeffrey started podcasting fiction, nobody really had a clue how or if it would work for anything but increasing an author's name recognition. In the years since, those of us who have hammered away at it have figured out pretty well what works and what doesn't. Here's the current best-of-what-we-know for making your fiction podcast an effective venture:

• *Write a damn good book*

Which should go without saying.

• *Produce a damn good audiobook*

See Parts 2-6 of this book for detailed instructions.

• *40 Minutes or Less*

Make sure your episodes are short enough that they can be listened to during an average commute. People HATE having to choose between finishing an episode and getting into work on time.

• *Consistent Lengths*

For the same reason people hate long episodes, episode running time that varies all over the place drives them crazy. Pick your length, and stick as close to it as you can. If the structure of the story makes this difficult, be creative with the value-added parts of the show (i.e. everything in your episode that isn't story).

• *End Every Episode on a Cliffhanger*

Just like serial television, ending on a cliffhanger leaves your audience hungry for the next episode. If you write well and are careful about where you cut your episodes, you should be able to end nearly every episode on some kind of cliffhanger or question mark. Leave your listeners dying to find out what happens next.

• *The Story So Far*

For books that release irregularly, on a loose schedule (less than weekly), or that have multiple plot threads, a 20-30 second recap of previous events to lead off the episode will not go amiss. BBC has been doing this with their radio serials since the 1940s, and serial TV shows like Lost, Fringe, 24, etc. all use this device to orient the viewer. It's an optional device, but it is very useful—as long as you keep it short. If it stretches longer than 20 or 30 seconds, your audience will get bored and start reaching for the "skip" button.

• *Engage the Community*

Involving other podcast authors in your production casts a wider net. If you're using the "story so far" device, invite other authors to read it for you in exchange for the opportunity to drop their URL and name. They'll usually mention the appearance to their audience, which gives you a nice cross-fertilization window. Also, create a 30 second promo (like a radio ad) to send to other authors to put in their podcast episodes, and put promos for other authors' books in your episodes (in places where it won't interrupt the flow of the story, such as the very beginning, the very end, and the transition between the story and the post-show talk portion). Podcast authors are very generous about trading promos and publicity, so long as there's good reciprocity involved.

• *Be Everywhere*

The entire Internet is constructed of links, and every link leading back to you is an avenue of discoverability. Listing yourself in podcast directories costs nothing but time, and not much time at that (about 5 minutes to fill in a form and submit a link). Getting your podcast into app stores will cost you a couple hundred bucks for software development, but you can also charge a nominal fee for that app and recoup those development costs.

• *Use A Stats Service*

FeedBurner, Blubrry, Libsyn, and other similar services track the number of downloads and will localize the IPs of your fans, so you can get an idea what countries, states, provinces, and regions house your best concentrations of fans. This is useful data if/when you decide to engage in other marketing and advertising activities, or in crowd-sourced funding projects.

• *Engage the Fans*

Provide your web address and a voice mail number and email contact in each podcast episode. Take a few minutes before your story starts or after it finishes to update your fans on the doings in your shop. Keep the anticipation high, and make sure your listeners know that they're appreciated.

• *Be Consistent*

"When you release regularly, you become part of people's lives. They set their watch by your stories. They start to depend on hearing your voice." —Scott Sigler

Podcasting your stories on a regular basis (weekly, bi-weekly, monthly, it doesn't matter as long as it's dependable) attracts an audience that will grow to love your voice and depend on their "fix." Stoking that desire is like feeding a crack habit—podcast fiction fans call themselves "junkies" (Sigler's fans), "addicts" (my fans), and a lot of other variations on the theme.

• *Play A Long-Term Game*

As with any entry into a new arena, it can take time to accrue a critical mass of fans to push your success. If you're podcasting regularly using these best practices, expect it to take one to three years before you see a substantial payoff.

• *Keep Your Audience Engaged*

Podcast audiences like to feel included. Special feedback episodes (see chapter 12), guerrilla marketing campaigns, and other special events you create give them an excuse to focus their energy and remind them to tell their friends about your books.

• *Don't Take Your Audience for Granted*

The flip side of the above—don't demand too much of your audience. Be clear about the bargain you're seeking to strike with them. And if you fail, for heaven's sake don't blame them, especially not in public. Public author meltdowns—in response to bad reviews, poor sales, and other disappointments—have cost some authors years off their career and thousands off their annual income. Releasing your content for free is advertising, not commerce. You want to foster an environment where your listeners feel loyal and enthusiastic about you, and where they're happy for the chance to give back to you, but never, ever make the mistake of thinking that they owe you anything. You're an entertainer; whether you podcast or blog or write novels or sing songs, your career is contingent upon your ability to make your audience happy, not vice versa.

• *Make Sure Your Loss-Leaders Lead Somewhere*

Back in the early days of podcast fiction, before monetization was really possible, a lot of us made two fundamental mistakes: we concentrated too much on promotion and not enough on writing, and we had a loss-leader that wasn't leading anywhere. We podcasted stories as fast as we could write and produce them. Some of us even took to podcasting works-in-progress to keep the channel filled. We learned the hard way what a lot of people in other businesses have known for decades:

Never use a loss-leader unless it's leading somewhere.

Even if you're monetizing your podcast—and even if, for some stretch of time, you're making more money off of it than you are ebook or audiobook sales—you should treat your podcast as a loss leader.

Why?

The audience for podcasts is tiny compared to the audience for books, and you want as broad and varied an audience as you can get. Among other things, it'll help insulate you as the different markets goes through normal fluctuations.

That's why you should *always* have more books available for sale in audio and in print than you have available in audio for free. When you start to podcast a book, make sure the production is already either available on paid sites or will be by the time episode four drops—episode four is the point at which most listeners decide whether they're hooked, or whether they're going to bail. Many listeners will happily pay to get the rest of the story early (in audio or in print), but then keep listening along for the pre-show or post-show talk portions.

Think of your catalog as a shelf. When you podcast, you take a book off the shelf and read it to someone. If your work connects with them, they're not going to want to wait until you're ready to read them the next chapter, or the next book, or a book from another series—they're going to want it now. If you can write four books a year, record all four and post them for sale, but podcast no more than one or two. If you can only write one book a year, then devise a release schedule that you can stay a nice long way ahead of.

The point of a loss-leader is to drive your audience toward your paid content. The year that we all started to figure that out (2009-2010) was the year we started to make money.

To that end...

• *Use That Point of Contact*

When you release a new short story, or sell one to a magazine, mention it on your 'cast. Drop a link to it in your show notes (the blog post that accompanies the podcast episode). When you release a new audiobook, drop the first chapter or two to your podcast feed as a sampler. When you release a new ebook or paperback, drop a PDF or epub of the first three chapters to the feed. Keep your audience fed on samples of everything that's coming, and everything that's available.

• *Avoid Exclusivity*

Podcasts work best when they're most widely distributed. Don't get locked down in exclusivity agreements.

Now, all that said, here are a few ways you can make money

directly from podcasts:

- *Tip Jar*

Always have a tip jar on your website, make sure it's highly visible and easy to use, and direct people to it at the end of every episode. SquareCash, PayPal, and other similar payment services that don't require membership are the way to go with these. If you use PayPal, you can also set up recurring monthly payments through your tip jar, though it does require the customer to set up an account with PayPal to do so. Offer the option—some people will take it.

- *Smartphone and Tablet Apps*

Though these don't work as well as they once did where audience retention and conversion is concerned, some of authors still make a nice little stream pricing a app for their podcast at one or two bucks. Apps that access your free content and contain a purchase option for premium subscription content/bonus content/other audiobooks also give you the ability to up-sell regular subscribers.

- *Patreon, Flattr, and Gumroad*

Patreon and Flattr are designed for ongoing subscription-style crowdfunding. Setting up one or more of these creates a hook for a recurring income stream (paid monthly or by episode, depending on how you set it up and which platform you're working with). Listeners join, select the rate they wish to be billed at, and from that point forward (until they quit) they pay you a token amount each month. Of the three, Gumroad's structure is set up the most like a traditional subscription: you deliver the content they're paying for, and you set the price. Flattr is more like a recurring tip jar, and is designed to encourage people to pay for free content in order to enable the open web. Patreon is strucutred like an ongoing crowdfunding campaign, with rewards levels and bonuses that you can set in order to encourage participation. Each one of them will require tending each time you release a podcast episode.

- *Value-Added Premium Content*

Blooper reels, special stories, deleted scenes, and other ancillary content have a cash value to your audience. Use this content to feed your subscription-based smartphone apps, and as bonus content for your subscribers and patrons, whether they come to you through Paypal recurring payments, Patreon, Flattr, Gumroad, or some other avenue.

• *Advertisements*

Networks like Libsyn, Blubrry, and FeedBurner don't just provide stats, they also sell advertising time. The money you make will be based on the number of downloads, but if your cast has several thousand regular listeners, this income stream can net you a few hundred bucks a year. Many companies (like Audible, GoDaddy, and many others) also offer direct commission-based advertising to podcasters, using the same paradigm as the Amazon Associates program. Using ads during the show also gives you the option to offer an ad-free podcast as one of the inducements for listeners to switch to a subscription feed from the free feed.

• *YouTube*

Like podcasting networks, YouTube also sells advertising space and shares revenue. To release on YouTube, embed your cover art as the video stream and your podcast episode as an audio stream. Chances of generating a lot of revenue this way are slim, because YouTube has its own ecosystem and community, and leveraging that community is the most reliable way to build an audience there. Nonetheless, some podcasters do pretty well this way. Most typically, podcast mirroring on youtube will generate a trickle of ten dollars here, ten dollars there. Not much, I grant you, but every little bit helps.

• *Scribl (formerly Podiobooks.com)*

This is the other big (non-public domain) audiobook site on the net. Its catalog exclusively contains free-to-listen audiobooks delivered via podcast, and also available for sale at an algorithm-determined dynamically set price (i.e. the more popular your book and those like it are, the more expensive it is). Purchased books include the ebook version along with the audiobook version, and do not contain pleas for donations or opening/closing credits for each installment. Because of their freemium-podcast model, Scribl is able to list audiobooks for sale in the iTunes store in the podcast section, and does). The storefront also feeds ebooks to the major storefronts at your option, setting itself up as a potential competitor to places like Smashwords and Draft2Digital.

Reviews and Awards

When it comes to publicity and promotion, you must strike the proper balance for your business between time spent bringing new products to market and time/money spent creating buzz for those products. I fall very far toward the "make new products and screw the marketing" end of the spectrum, except when the marketing I engage in also helps create new products, but this is very much a judgment call for what's appropriate to my business model. The right balance for my business model may not be the right one for yours.

Audience reviews aren't something you need to worry about, they will take care of themselves—the most effort you should put into them is to mention "leave a review on iTunes" in your post-show if you have a podcast.

For high-profile reviews, you'll need to do for your audiobook just like you'd do with any book, and send out review copies. Places like AudioFile Magazine, SFFAudio, Audiobook Haven, and dozens of others serve as the audiobook industry equivalent of Publisher's Weekly, Kirkus, and maven fan review blogs. If you intend to send out review copies, start building a list anytime you see a review referenced while you're out and about on the wilds of the Internet, then use that as a hit-list for your next release.

Then, of course, there are awards. As with book awards, you can either campaign for them vigorously, or you can pretty much ignore them and only send in samples when you get an email telling you you've been nominated. Some of the major awards that net you pretty badges that you can put on your audiobook packaging are: The Audie Awards, The Odyssey Awards, and The Galaxy Awards (for commercially-released audiobooks), and The Podcast Awards and The Parsec Awards (for podcasts).

Legal Considerations

Finally, we come to the elephant in the room: The law. If you're going to be producing audiobooks, there are a few things you must have in order if you wish to avoid the risk of financial ruin.

First, do you actually own the audio rights to the story you're intending to produce? If it's one you've previously published with a publishing company you do not own (even a magazine or anthology), you should check your contract and be sure. If you don't own those rights, then someone else does, and if you exercise them you'll be liable for infringement, which is expensive, unpleasant, and—since you'd be paying fines for producing your own stories—embarrassing.

Second, if you record someone's voice without their written consent, you risk running afoul of Federal and State wiretapping laws (depending on your jurisdiction). Check up on the specifics of the law in your country and locality, and make sure you stick to them. Since, in most Berne-convention jurisdictions, performers have copyright claims on their performances, you should always get a properly-worded, signed vocal release from any performer who isn't you. If your production/publishing company is a corporate entity (an C-Corp, S-Corp, a LLC/LLP, etc.), you'll need to sign a vocal release to the company in order to legally perform in its productions. It's a good idea to do these anyway, even if you're just a sole proprietorship, since if you ever do incorporate you won't have to fuss with filling in mountains of paperwork just to keep your existing revenue streams auditable. Some radio stations and distributors will insist on seeing signed vocal releases for every voice in every production before they'll carry a production.

Third, if you are hiring outside talent for a commercial recording, be sure to pay them. It's only ethical, since you'll be making a profit off their work—and if you don't pay them but have them working for you under contract, and you wind up with a big hit, they might hire a clever lawyer to sue you, claiming that since there was no consideration (i.e. payment in cash or in kind) given, then their vocal release is ipso facto invalid. Even if they lose, it's a headache you don't want.

Fourth, as with vocals, so with music and sound effects. If they're not in the public domain (see chapter 17), make sure you obtain licenses for them, and keep the records of those license agreements.

And, finally, be sure to clear your cover art as well. Just because you or your publisher has a license for the paperback, the hardback, or the ebook doesn't mean that license extends to the audiobook (it probably doesn't). Be sure you've got the right to use the artwork you're using before you drop it on the market. If you're using stock, make sure you keep up to date on your stock license payments and keep copies of your stock licenses on file. If you're using your own artwork, be sure you've got image releases that allow for commercial use for any identifiable people in the photo or painting.

I am not a lawyer, and none of the aforementioned is legal advice. Always consult an IP attorney when drawing up and evaluating contracts related to your publishing and production businesses. A little money spent now will keep things nice and uneventful on the legal front—which is exactly how you want them.

After all, this is a business.

42

Making Tracks

Part II
Managing the Production

Chapter 3
. . . .
Managing the Production
Scripts, Casting, Directing, and Asset Management

Recording an audiobook isn't as straightforward a proposition as you might think. There are enough fiddly-bits, even in a simple production, that you can lose a lot of time bootstrapping yourself the hard way. Managing your performances, scripts, and recorded tracks will make or break the time budget for your production. This chapter will walk you through what you need to know.

Choose Your Medium

In order to record your book, you need something to read it from. The option that leaps immediately to your mind, however, may not be the best one. The "best" one depends on your work environment and your ergonomics, so here's a list of the available choices, and the disadvantages of each:

• *Bound book*

Reading from a paperback or a hardback is very convenient—you don't have to worry about mixing up your pages, you know everything you need is right there in front of you. However, bound books are heavy, and they will wear on your arms during long sessions. You can fix this by using a felt-covered music stand (see part 4 of this book), but there are other problems as well. They also often have typefaces small enough that, even with good vision, you're likely to accidentally skip lines or misread the occasional word. Since they don't have generous margins or wide spacing, you're going to have a hard time annotating them (which you may need to do). Books also make noise when you turn pages, so you must be careful not to be talking when you're turning the page—otherwise you'll have to do a re-take to fix page-rustling problems that you only discover when you're editing.

• *Loose Manuscript*

A double-spaced loose manuscript with generous margins, on the other hand, has plenty of annotation space. Combine those with a bigger font size, and you've solved most of the problems you'll encounter reading from a bound book. With a loose manuscript you can also annotate as you go, so if you encounter a trouble spot and need to stop to mark it up, you can do it on-the-fly with a highlighter and a pencil (it's always better to use a pencil than a pen, since you might need to try a few alternate approaches if you hit a particularly difficult tongue-twister or a section with complex grammatical nesting and several layers of subtext).

Loose pages do suffer from a couple disadvantages. You're always at risk of dropping them and getting the pages mixed up, which will cost you time putting them back in order. They also tend to rustle, a lot, particularly if you're inclined to hold the pages yourself while you're reading them.

The first problem is easily solved by securing the pages in a three-ring binder. The second, by using a music stand (~$20-30 at any musician supply store) which you then cover in felt in order to prevent reflections (see part 4 of this book). Alternately, you can clip the pages to a mic stand or otherwise suspend them at eye-level.

The last disadvantage this approach suffers from is that it eats a LOT of paper, which gets expensive. Unfortunately, there's no workaround for that.

• *Computer screen*

If you want to eschew the paper approach altogether, there are a few ways you can pull it off. The most obvious is to use the screen on your laptop. Aside from being paperless, this has the advantage of being infinitely scalable (you can zoom in as much as you want and get the type as big as you like), and infinitely annotate-able (you can input instructions to yourself, in-line, on the fly using your keyboard). On the downside, doing it this way means you'll have to bring a computer into your whole studio, which means you'll have fan noise and/or EM interference to worry about (see next section on Cell Phones). Since "How do I get rid of this computer fan noise" and "why are there stray beeps and buzzes on my audio track" are one of the questions I get most often from newbie audiobook producers, this might not be your best option for going paperless.

• *Cell phone*

If you've got a smartphone, you can load an ebook version of your manuscript onto the phone and just read it off the phone as you would off a computer screen. Cell phones, of course, can't accept meaningful annotations without a lot of trouble, so in order to do this successfully, you'll have to pre-annotate your manuscript.

Cell phones present a further problem in that they're radio transmitters—a quality they share with tablets and computers with wifi and/or mobile data capabilities. Cell-tower sync signals can create a distinctive patterns of pops in some recording equipment. WiFi signals create sporadic harmonic spikes in the 2000-4000hz range, which are hard to eliminate. If you're using a cell phone to read from, switch it to airplane mode first, which will turn off all the radios in the phone (come to think of it, if you're using a computer or tablet, be sure to turn off bluetooth, wifi, and mobile data as well).

Cell phones are generally too small to usefully rest on a music stand or clip to another mount, and thus share the same arm-fatigue hazard as bound books.

• *Tablet or E-Reader*

These are better than cell phones if you're itching to go paperless. They're usually big enough to set on a music or clip to a mic stand if such is your preference, and they have almost all the advantages of a computer screen and a cell phone with almost none of the drawbacks, save that they're difficult to annotate as you go.

Note that most e-readers and tablets have wifi, some have

bluetooth, and some have mobile data. Be sure to turn of these antennas before you start recording.

Script Preparation

There are two complimentary ways you can prepare a script.

The first is to annotate it. Annotation is markup within (or on) the script that reminds you of intention, subtext, action, and timing.

• *Intention*

In every scene, your POV character (and often your supporting characters) have goals that they're looking to accomplish. Your narrator may also have a goal; for example, to mislead the audience, or to clue the audience into something that the characters don't know. These various goals are the intention of the characters and/or of the scene. Some readers find it helpful to explicitly write the intentions out at the beginning of a scene or chapter, to remind themselves when they're recording. For example, if Joe and Barry are hunting, and Joe is trying to impress Barry to get him into bed while Barry is obliviously heterosexual, you might put "Joe is trying to seduce Barry" in bold at the top of the page before the opening of the scene.

• *Action*

Making note of the physical actions your characters are performing makes a difference in how you perform them, but when you get into the zone of reading you may find the flow of words keeps you from being aware of what actually is going on in your scene. In such a case, making margin notes like "Joe is picking up a heavy box" or "Barry is walking away from Joe and talking over his shoulder" will help you nail the performance that your narration has told your listeners to expect.

• *Subtext*

Some stories trade as much on what's not said as what is said, and for scenes with a great deal of subtext it can be helpful to make a note, on the page, of what the subtext is. Not just the emotional curve (though this is certainly part of it), but sometimes the actual spelled-out subtext, particularly when it's at odds with the actual words.

• *Timing Beats*

The "beats" of a paragraph are the phrase-chunks it's broken into, and, depending on how you want to perform it, may bear only a tangential relationship to the way the text is punctuated. The beats are basically your breath-marks. If, / for example, / I was to read this sentence out loud / I might break it up as I'm doing here / using forward slashes to indicate pauses / or breathing.

You can also leave yourself a note to create an empty beat. When you use an ellipsis in a sentence, an empty beat is one of the possible interpretations, but your pause length between other words (or between sentences) is more open to interpretation, and sometimes, you want to leave your audience hanging, like so:

"George's eyes settled on the gun...Ginny's gun." vs. "George's eyes settled on [beat] the gun. [beat] [beat] Ginny's gun."

The amount of annotation you do is a highly individual thing. Some readers do none at all, some do it extensively, others annotate dialog but not narrative, etc. Using annotations is the most basic form of self-direction, and is also useful in directing others if you're using performers other than yourself in your production.

Breakout—the other preparation technique—basically involves reformatting a story as a script without changing any of the text. This has the advantage of making it easier for the performer (i.e. you) to keep track of which character is speaking or which block of narration is in play, and to include in-line annotations in a way that doesn't interfere with the text. If you use a screenplay program instead of a word processor to do this, it comes with a host of other production management advantages as well. They include:

• *Character profiles*, which include scene catalogs that let you see whether two characters who might have similar voices share a scene. This lets you adjust your characterization pro-actively, rather than finding yourself in the position of having to go back and re-record a character or scene. The profile screen will also have a field for characterization and/or casting notes, and it will let you keep track of actors (if you're using more than one).

• *Per-character word count*. Useful when scheduling your studio time, and essential if you're using other actors, as this is how you pay them.

• *List of Foley (sound effects) cues*. If you're using Foley, note where your major cues are as you break out the script. A good script program will then give you a list of the sounds you've specified. This means you can gather all your clips before you start editing, which will make your post-production go much faster.

• *List of music cues*. Ditto for what I said about Foley.

I speak from experience: Because it reduces reading bloopers and accomplishes so many related production management tasks as a side-effect, breaking out a script can reduce pre-production and production time on single-reads by a factor of two, and on full-cast productions by a factor of four-to-six.

Breaking a novel out into a script takes between four and eight hours, depending on how long the book is and how quickly you work. You can do your breakout in a word processor, or in a production management tool like CeltX, or in a screenwriting tool like Final Draft. Whatever you're comfortable working with will serve.

Annotation and breakout are not mutually exclusive methods—they actually compliment each other quite nicely. Use either, or both, as appropriate for your production.

Casting

Casting is one of the key artistic decisions you'll make in your production. If you've cast yourself in a single-read production, then you're done! Move on to the next bit.

If you've got a book that needs voice talent other than yourself, though, you've got a little work ahead of you.

First, you need to decide what kind of voice or voices you want. Male or female? Voice-of-God authoritative or something more approachable? Young, middle-aged, or old? Rank your criteria—but remember that the more specific you get, the more difficult it will be to find appropriate talent.

Second, you need to recruit your actor(s). There are a number of ways to do this, from asking around among your friends to putting ads on Craigslist to prowling professionals at places like ACX.com and Voices.com. Keep in mind that you'll need a signed talent release from each actor, and in that release you'll need to specify how you can use their voice and how you're going to pay them for their work. You can find a variety of sample contracts online—consult your lawyer before using any of them.

Third, you'll need to do auditions. Each actor should get a two-to-five minute sample to read—resist the temptation to require anything longer. It won't tell you anything new, it'll eat up valuable time on both ends of the process, and it will annoy your candidates. For single-reads, pick a scene or two that represent the emotional and tonal range you're looking for, give a sentence or two of direction at the beginning of each scene. For multi-voice reads, you'll need to prep a short sample script for each character, headed by notes on that character's general age, demeanor, gender, etc. On multi-voice scripts, send full scenes so that actors auditioning for a particular role can read and understand the context to which they're performing.

A note of caution: when auditioning actors, don't specify more than age and gender in your listing unless a particular accent or style is absolutely vital to your story. There are a lot of excellent actors out there who will fit your story in ways you can't anticipate, who might not opt to audition for an overly-specific listing.

Fourth: Once you've got your auditions, listen to the recordings. Throw out the ones that obviously aren't a good fit. Narrow the field as much as possible. If you wind up with a couple readers who are both just right for a given story or part, flip a coin or do a second round of sample scenes.

Another note of caution: If you're hiring talent that will be recording remotely, don't just listen to the performance. Listen to the recording. The audio you receive (always demand uncompressed file formats for your auditions and recordings) should sound at least as good as what you'd expect and demand for your home studio. Also listen for mic technique and breath and mouth noises, as these are things that you'll have to clean up/correct for in post. The goal, as with recording in your own studio, is to get the cleanest possible audio with the smallest possible time investment.

A final note of caution: When listing your audition, be sure to specify if the book includes profanity, explicit sex and potentially controversial themes such as homosexuality, adultery, kink, rape, racism, sexual abuse of children, blasphemous attitudes toward any currently-popular religion, or graphic violence (or anything else that a significant segment of the population finds potentially objectionable). Some semi-pro voice actors will flat refuse to appear in books with such content, and it's better to save everyone the time by warning them up front. You'll also get better performances out of actors who are enthusiastic about the project than actors who are grudgingly performing content that upsets or offends them.

Fifth, choose your performer(s) and send them their contract. Be sure to specify payment schedules, delivery schedules, and quality standards in the contract.

Sixth, once you get the contract back, send off the script. If the performer will be using your studio, schedule studio sessions (no more than four hours at a stretch, and preferably less).

Seventh, when the audio starts coming in (or after every in-studio recording session), listen to the tracks ASAP while reading along. Make a note of every flub or flat performance, and make sure that you get corrections in the next session/delivery. Do your rough-cut editing as you go, it'll save you a lot of time later.

Finally, once all your audio is in, you're ready to move into editing and mixing.

Directing

In order to get the performance you want, you're probably going to have to do some directing. In the best cases, the context of your narration will be all the direction you or your hired talent needs. In most cases, at least some additional direction will be necessary. While directing is an art that takes a lot of practice, the basic nature of the job is surprisingly simple:

The job of a director is to manipulate the talent into giving the desired performance. This is true whether you're self-directing or directing someone else. Perfecting your skill as a director is nothing more or less than figuring out different tricks for pulling that performance out of your talent.

Self-Directing

If you've never done interpretive reading or voice acting before, you'll likely find self-directing to be a little tricky. In order to do it in real-time, you have to cultivate the ability to perform and listen to yourself at the same time, which means engaging both your creative and critical faculties simultaneously—not an easy trick. Very experienced voice actors can do this, less experienced ones usually fail miserably. Fortunately, real-time self-directing isn't the only option.

One of the best techniques for self-directing is one we covered above: script annotation. By pre-loading your instructions into the script, and then trusting those notes, you free yourself up during performance to find the story with your voice within the channel you've already outlined.

Another effective technique is time-delayed directing. Record a scene or a chapter, then go into the edit bay and listen to what you've done. If you're not happy with your first pass, make some notes to yourself about how you want to approach the material. If you are happy with your first pass, make some notes that will remind you of your approach next time you're in the edit bay, and also make note of any flubs, malapropisms, mispronunciations, or pacing problems, and go back in to re-record just that material. Edit the fresh take into the original take to get your rough track, then move on and do the same thing with the next chapter. As time goes on using this technique, you'll get more and more used to interacting with your own voice as if it's something outside yourself, and your ability to self-direct on the fly will grow naturally.

These two techniques—directing via prophylactic script annotation, and directing via time-delayed notes—are also very useful for directing remote voice talent.

Directing Hired Talent In Your Studio

In-studio directing of hired talent is the most hands-on directing technique. You accompany your talent into the studio, or speak to them over an intercom, and guide them through the scene to the performance you're looking for. It's similar to film and stage directing in that the performance emerges from the interaction of the director and the actor, but dissimilar in that you don't generally rehearse beforehand.

There are five basic techniques to live-directing.

1) Setting the scene

Explain the subtext, the motivations of the characters, and the narrative goal of a given scene/chapter/storyline, then turn your talent loose.

2) Reading the opposing lines

If you're doing full-cast, reading the other lines in the scene and letting your actor respond to your performance can give your actor the prompting they need to pull their character off the page.

3) Technical tricks

Sometimes, like all readers, an actor will get stuck on a stilted delivery. When this happens, have them stop and take a breath. Tell them a joke. Get them a fresh drink. Suggest changes in body posture. Help them find the beats in the line that might be different from the punctuation on the page. Once they've forgotten the original reading, have them attack the lines afresh.

4) Headspace Shifting and Motivation Games

If the technical tricks don't work, you'll need to dig a level deeper. Get your talent to attack the lines or the scene from a different emotional angle. Have them envision a different context, or emphasize a different element of the scene. The trick is to get their internal emotional map to line up with how you want their performance to sound. What sounds like wry sarcasm in an actor's head might sound flat when it hits the microphone, or it might sound cutting and cruel. Work with your talent to find their right emotional groove to get you the performance you're looking for.

5) Line Readings

This is a last-ditch technique, and many actors find it insulting. If you've got a line the actor just can't hit, read it for them the way you want to hear it read. You have to be a pretty good reader yourself to pull this off and get anything useful back, but sometimes, particularly when working with inexperienced actors, it can save your bacon.

Just as the techniques for self-directing also apply to directing others, so too do these general directing techniques work when self-directing.

Directing Hired Talent Remotely

The techniques for directing talent remotely are the same as the above techniques for in-studio directing and self-directing, but you have to adapt them to account for distance. Just as with the previous two cases, you can either do time-delayed direction or live-direction.

Remote live-direction requires an extra computer or phone hookup at the talent's studio. Skype (or similar VIOP chat services) is a good choice for this, since it lets you speak to the talent through their headphones as they perform—just make sure their phone or net hookup is coming in over a wire, rather than over the air, or you'll introduce EM noise into the signal.

Remote time-delayed direction is conducted through text notes over email, and, in cases where a line reading is necessary, by attaching small audio files (typically MP3s of the line readings) for the talent to model their performance on.

Marking the Waveform

When you catch yourself making a flub as you record, or when you record a particularly good take, it's a good idea to mark your waveform with a series of spikes. By using a dog clicker or snapping your fingers, make one loud click for flubs and three loud clicks for great takes. When you go to edit the track, you'll be able to see these clicks. It sounds simplistic, but you'll be surprised about how much time it saves.

Asset Management and Backups

As you can imagine, producing an audiobook produces a god-awful amount of paperwork and computer files. Scripts, contracts, raw recordings, rough-cut vocal tracks, editing notes, sound effects, music tracks, project files, audio masters, and other miscellany can grown like The Blob and take over your life, and if you don't keep them organized they can grind your production to a stop.

Deal with these proactively. For every project, create a directory structure that sorts your data and is easily navigable. Here's a sample taxonomy from one of my own full-cast projects.

1) Down From Ten audiobook (project root directory)

1. Script Breakouts
    1. Character scripts (by character, including Narrator's script)
        1. Retake scripts (ditto the above)

2. Contracts
    1. Actor Contracts
    2. Licensing agreements (for music)

3. Audio Projects
    1. Mixdown projects (one per chapter)

4. Audio Assets
    1. Raw audio per chapter
    2. Rough cut audio per chapter (noise-cleaned)
    This includes each actor's performance for a given chapter with names like "ch01_kevin_cleaned.wav." It also includes "Story So Far" and "Post-show Chat" segments, which I insert at the beginning and end each episode if the book is being serialized via podcast, radio, streaming, or satellite service.

2) Music

    1. General score tracks

This includes the main title music, closing titles music, transition music and other bumpers, and incidental music/character-specific themes that recur throughout the book

    2. Chapter-specific tracks

This includes incidental music that only occurs in one chapter, such as music for the big reveal at the end of the book.

    3. Public Domain and Stock music

I keep these separate because they don't have licenses that restrict them to use in this particular book as my score tracks do, since my composer writes them for the particular project and retains all other rights to them.

    4. 3rd-Party Licensed music

I keep these separately from the other two sorts of music because they often have unique license restrictions, and can cost extra money if they're used outside of a very narrow context (often a single scene) that they were licensed for. This narrow licensing keeps the cost of the music low.

3) General audio bumpers

Including the production company tag, and (for serialized stories) paid advertisements and promos for other books.

4) Sound Effects

    1. Type of effect

My Foley directory has separate subdirectories for fan noises, appliances, kitchen sounds, doors, footsteps, wind, rain, snow, weapons, and just about any other kind of sound you can imagine.

5) Masters

    1. Uncompressed masters (in .wav or .aiff format).

These are the finished deliverable files, with no extras, that go out to audiobook retailers and distributors, and are pressed to CDs for physical distribution.

2. Compressed masters (in .mp3 or .ogg format)

These are downloadable files for sale off my own website.

3. Vendor-specific compressed masters, with any bumpers and extras that that vendor requires.

6) Artwork

Cover art, blurbs, and other packaging materials.

The assets for this particular audiobook totaled about 200 gigabytes. If you're doing a full-cast book, you can expect similar space requirements. But even if you're doing a bare-bones single-read book, you're still going to eat up at least 20 gigabytes for a 100,000 word book.

Needless to say, you don't want this much work sitting around where it's vulnerable to a hard drive crash or a power surge. I learned this one the hard way when I was in film production, and once lost a month's worth of work (at a replacement cost of $10,000 plus a couple hundred hours of my own sweat) to a power surge that fried every chip in the computer.

When you're actively in production, you must back up your work every night. The easiest way to do this is to get a very large external hard drive, plug it in at the end of the day, and copy your entire project directory tree across to the external drive. Once the copy is done, unplug the drive from the wall and from your computer, and store it in a safe place. If you're truly paranoid, get two drives, and keep the second one off-site. Use the off-site drive for weekly backups, as insurance in case of fire or burglary.

Chapter 4
Velvet Vocals

Reading an audiobook aloud isn't merely about getting the words out in the proper order—any Kindle's text-to-speech feature can do that—it's about getting the story into the brain of the audience as well as, or better than, they could do it themselves were they to read the paperback. The words, in a limited (but very real) sense, don't matter.

As a producer, you're the one who makes the creative decisions for the production. Your job is very simple: make the audience forget that you and your other voice artists exist at all. Become transparent. Your job is to work your ass off getting out of the way of the story.

It's true that, the better a story is, the more an audience will forgive background noise, poor mixing, bad edits, tape hiss, and other aural offenses. It's easy to annoy your audience with bad production, but—the many valiant attempts I've heard notwithstanding—it's pretty hard to utterly ruin a great story with bad production. Not that it's an excuse for shoddy work. Most marketplaces won't let clumsily-produced audiobooks into their catalogs.

The performer, though, is a different story. Your performer(s) is the key to the production. It is very easy to ruin a good story with a poor performance.

In this chapter, I'm going to ignore the different things you can do to "play" your microphone to enhance your performance (see chapter 7 for more info). This isn't about the mic, or the equipment, or the studio. This is about what happens behind your lips.

Performing The Book

In the beginning, there were records and cassette tapes. And lo, the tapes were noisy, and the records scratchy, and the customers, having no sight, were unable to read for themselves the books that were not printed in braille. And into the universe entered the boring performance: a basic technique for getting every word out unambiguously, in a neutral accent, with no editorialization whatsoever. And the gods of publishing called it good, and there was sleepiness and boredom in the 60s, 70s, and 80s.

Things have changed since then. The audience has grown exponentially, and is now dominated by folks that are accustomed to performance rather than reading. The difference between the two is the difference between Ben Stein reading a lecture and your mother reading Dr. Seuss to you at bedtime. The first is meant to convey only information, the latter is meant to convey emotion, pacing, tension, characterization, and information in one tidy package.

But none of that extra effort matters if you don't first master the basic five points of vocal performance: Posture, Diction and Breath Control, Hygiene, and Inflection.

Posture

Your breathing is controlled by your diaphragm, an organ situated right at the base of your sternum. Because this is where your wind comes from, your posture will profoundly affect your performance.

If you have the ability, it's best to record from a standing position with your shoulders relaxed but un-hunched, reading from a script or screen positioned at eye level, much as you would give a public address. Good posture opens up all the resonance cavities in your body and takes pressure off the muscles that control your voice, giving you the maximum possible dynamic range, tonal control, and breath control. Hunching forward or dipping your chin changes your vocal timbre, which is useful for doing character voices, but generally undesirable when narrating.

Standing for the hours on end that it takes to record a book is exhausting work. Be sure to take regular breaks (every hour, or every half-hour) to give your voice a rest and stretch your legs, back, shoulders, and neck. Try not to engage in conversation during those breaks—you won't get any rest if your "break" consists of arguing with vendors or gossiping with friends on the phone.

If you aren't able to record when standing, use a chair that encourages good posture, and position the reading material at eye level. It's easier to slouch when sitting down, and recording while sitting down is only slightly less taxing than recording while standing up, so keep those stretch breaks regular.

Diction and Breath Control

Unless you're fortunate enough to be born with a crisp Received Pronunciation (BBC English) or middle-class Ohio accent, or have since trained in oratory, chances are your diction is less than perfect. In real life, diction only matters in some contexts, and the rest of the time a slur, a grunt, or a hurried blur of sound will do the trick.

But when you're speaking into a microphone, your diction has to be clear. You may choose to muddy it up for certain characters, but narrators need to be crisp and all your characters must be (at the very least) intelligible.

The secret to precise diction is to speak with a nimble tongue, with the tip of your tongue doing the consonant work at the front of your mouth. Depending on where you're from, this can take some time to master—many accents (including my own native ones) feature lazy diction as a fundamental part of the way people speak. If you're from the California coast, the deep south (middle or lower class), or most of New England (or, if you're in the UK: Newcastle, Yorkshire, and Wales) you've almost certainly got mud in your mouth. If you're not from these areas, you don't have to feel left out—you've probably got a little mud, too.

Practice your diction. If you have difficulty hearing your own accent or vocal sloppiness (as many people do), try recording some audio with an unflattering EQ (equalization—see chapters 4 and 15) curve and listening back to it. Making notes of the places you stumble, slur, mispronounce, swallow your vowels, and soften your consonants. Learning to hear your own voice as if it were someone else's is one of the skills you must master in order to do this job.

Or you could take a page from Demosthenes, the famous Greek orator who, to his great shame, couldn't speak clearly. He solved this problem by keeping his mouth full of pebbles and learning to speak around them. After a bit of practice, he found that the effort of speaking around them had trained the muscles in his mouth to ultra-precision, and he could speak clearly even in the crowded agora.

Whether the story is apocryphal or historically accurate, the trick actually works. When I return to performing after an absence of more than a few weeks, I have terrible mush mouth. The muscle re-training that the marbles (easier to deal with than pebbles) offer gets me back into narrating shape in a few days.

Learning how to control the muscles at the front of your mouth will cure mushmouth. It won't fix the other three persistent diction problems common to English speakers: nasal-gag, strangle-throat, and sharp-S (note: these are colloquial terms I learned from my college voice instructor. Your colloquia may vary).

Nasal-gag happens when the back of your tongue presses hard against your soft palate, pushing all your breath up into your sinuses and making a slight gagging sound (don't worry if you can't hear it, the rest of us can). This makes your voice sound half-swallowed and overly nasal, particularly in syllables with guttural consonants like "g" and "k." If you have a weak soft palate, or sleep apnea, this problem sounds even worse and is a bit harder to correct. Nonetheless, it is correctable. Speak with an open throat—don't pitch your voice down, just use your laryngeal muscles to open up your throat—and deliberately move your tongue forward when making your gutturals. This will keep your tongue from blocking your throat and forcing all that good sound up into your sinuses.

This will, in turn, will make you sound less like Gollum.

Strangle-throat is closely related—it's where your throat spontaneously closes up in the middle of words, making you swallow your vowels and make phlegmy gurgling noises. This usually comes from throat fatigue and poor breath control. To correct it, relax. If it helps, take a half-shot of booze before recording (don't take more than a half-shot—it'll make the rest of your diction sloppy long before you're legally drunk). Learn to consciously open your throat. You can do this using the same muscle that you use to close your throat when you've accidentally inhaled your drink—just push it the opposite direction you normally would. Thirdly, do warm-up exercises before recording; actual, traditional singer warm-ups (sing scales, sing tongue twisters, etc.). Finally, use those singing exercises to refine your breath control.

Breath control is basic to all oratory (and music, too), so it deserves a little exploration here:

Make sure you've got enough air for the sentence (but not so much that your diaphragm itches and you cough uncontrollably), then let that air out in measured ways to give your diction the punch and volume you want, without running out of air before you're done with your phrase. Basically, you want to use your breath as punctuation. If you pause for a second and take no breath, it creates suspense. If you take breaths every other word like you're panting, it amps up the adrenaline. If you speak cleanly and easily, with breaths only at the commas and the periods, you convey clarity and purpose. All of these are valid techniques, and there are a number of others (see Appendix C for resources to deepen your familiarity with breath control and voice acting techniques).

What you don't want to do is take breaths that you don't intend to, or take breaths that will interfere with your ability to edit (any breath that runs under a phoneme or slurs with a phoneme will interfere with editing). And, unless you're using your breath to illustrate actual heavy-breathing, you don't want the audience to notice your breaths. Since you're literally breathing in their ears, they're going to notice a hell of a lot more than if you were just breathing at them from across the table. If you're having trouble mastering your breathing, a supporting technique can help:

Any time you have to take a breath, turn your head away from the microphone, then turn back when you're all topped up with oxygen. This will attenuate its volume without interrupting your flow too much.

The best way to learn breath control, no kidding, is to join a choir. If you're not the churchgoing type, look for ad hoc caroling choirs at local Christmas events. If no good choirs are on offer in your neighborhood, or if you're someone who can't carry a tune, singing is still your best bet—just do it in your car or shower. Sing along to the radio, and try to match the vocalist's breath rhythms as closely as possible. It may sound silly, but this kind of parrot-fashion work will make you aware of all the muscles in your tongue, throat, and diaphragm and help get you in shape for the long-haul marathon that is audiobook performance.

The final of these high sins of diction is the sharp-S and its close cousin, the lisp. Some of us, let's face it, have less than perfect teeth, and when we make an "s" it's a harsh, almost whistling sound. Usually the easiest way to take care of this is with a de-essing filter (see chapter 15), but if you want to solve it before you record, or if you have a lisp, there are some things you can do to make it better. Lisping and sharp-s problems have everything to to with tongue position. The closer to your teeth that your tongue gets, the softer your "s" will sound. If you actually touch your tongue to your teeth or your upper gum, you're going to make a "th" sound (a lisp), and if you pull it back too far, you're going to whistle. Practice your "s"es deliberately, paying conscious attention to your tongue position, to retrain yourself. This is basic speech therapy, and it can take weeks or months (or years), depending on how re-trainable your muscles and how ingrained your habits are. For some people, the neurological map is such that they can't retrain their basic phonemes without formal speech therapy. For others, it's as easy as changing clothes. Most people fall somewhere in the middle.

Hygiene

You want a clean sound, and nothing makes your sound grimier than mouth noises.

Your tongue is a wet tendril of meat flapping around in a drippy, mucousy, meat-lined chamber perched at the top of something that looks like a giant eel and works like a clarinet—except that it uses folds of meat instead of a reed to make its noises. In the middle of this appetizing package, you have thirty-or-so little white pebbles growing up out of the meat—and that's if you're lucky. If you're unlucky, you've got fewer, and maybe you've got some machinery in there to make up for the missing pebbles. Let's face it, the fact that any of us ever says anything that doesn't sound like a slimy, gurgling fart is pretty damned impressive.

This means that, at the best of times, human speech is possessed of a certain plopping moist squishy quality as the saliva swishes around, the meat slaps together, and the teeth clatter and chomp. At the worst of times—if you have crooked or missing teeth, dental appliances, a lazy tongue, or a too-dry or too-wet mouth—these sounds start to dominate.

In everyday life, we're not assaulted by these grotesque noises from anyone but ourselves, because they're quiet enough and at high enough frequencies that only the barest shadow of them reaches our ears in normal conversation.

Speak into someone's ear—which is exactly what you're doing when you're recording—and those mouth noises come through loud and clear as a Sunday morning alarm clock. I've described them in the most nauseating way possible, so as to convey the feeling it will engender in a good segment of your audience. For many people, hearing mouth noises in an audiobook is like watching someone chew with their mouth open. It's not appetizing. Even people who don't find it nauseating will find it distracting, because the clacking, slapping, splashing sounds will be fighting with your consonants and breaths for attention. I've known people to miss major plot points when listening to books because the narrator had bridge work that dried his mouth out and didn't take care to stay hydrated.

Here's how you beat mouth noises:

• *Record at a reasonable gain level* on a decent microphone (see chapters 6 and 11 for more information).

• *Brush your teeth.* Not only does it make you feel cleaner, the desiccants in toothpaste dry your mouth out, the rinsing gets rid of the gunk, and the whole process stimulates fresh saliva.

• *Stay properly hydrated.* Dry mouth makes for clacky smacky sounds. Keep a drink of water, coffee, tea, or Gatorade at the ready. If you're at all lactose intolerant, don't drink anything with milk products in it: in the lactose intolerant, it can stimulate mucous production, which will compound your problem. Hot and cold beverages are better than room temperature ones, as they stimulate your mouth and remind you of where all your speech parts are. If your mouth feels tacky, or you can hear smacking sounds when you talk, it's time to take a sip. Try not to drink so much that your back teeth are floating, as this will affect your performance in other ways. Be aware that some prescription drugs have "dry mouth" as a side effect—if you're taking one of these, be prepared to sip early and sip often.

• *Don't record when* you have a cold, have recently cried, or are in any way congested. Congestion makes your mouth, throat, and sinuses slimy, which can lead to the too-wet sound, and it'll ruin your nasals and gutterals.

• *If you smoke* (see chapter 9 for information on how to protect your equipment from smoke), try varying your smoking schedule to manage your mouth moisture.

• *Make sure your bridgework* is well seated. If you wear a retainer, take it out.

• *Practice your diction*, and pay attention to the correlation of phonemes to mouth noises. You'll find that, even if you're not normally prone to mouth noises, there are particular phoneme pairs that will make you slap your tongue down hard against the floor of your mouth and make a splashing sound, or make you twist up your tongue in a way that makes a whistle or a gurgle. Make note of these sounds, and then record these sounds with a breath in between the phonemes (which you'll cut out in post). If these pairs occur in the middle of syllables or words, practice those sounds particularly, finding ways to move your tongue to produce the same sound without the accompanying mouth noise.

And before you ask, no, there are no fancy digital signal processing tricks that can reliably eliminate mouth noises. It's best not to record them at all, and then clean up the occasional (between-words) mistake with editing.

Inflection

Someone once asked Don LaFontaine, the voice over artist who everyone knows as "the trailer guy," what his secret was for delivering stunning vocal performances. He said "You have to find the music in the words."

Although he did advertising work—and most of the rules for advertising voice overs are not the same as those for audiobook narration—finding the music is still the cardinal rule of the game. When you're talking, you naturally find the music. When you're reading, you have to extract that music from the words. You have to decide where the emphasis goes. Where will you get soft? Where will you get hard? Where will you pitch up and where will you pitch down? What will match the text you're performing?

Remember, you have to manage your inflection in a way that will translate to your audience no matter their native dialect. For those of you from the Northwest and the Midwest (or, if you're from the UK, from Newcastle and Yorkshire), you have an extra challenge, because your native dialect tends toward "up-speak." This is where you pitch up at the end of a thought or a clause, whether the source of the pause is a comma, a period, a question mark, or an exclamation point. In conversation in your native environment, this sounds completely natural, but to folks who speak other dialects, it's anxiety-inducing. Spoken in up-speak, for example, the Preamble to the United States Constitution sounds something like this:

We the people? Of the United States? In order to form a more perfect Union? Establish justice?...

You get the idea.

If you don't come from one of the named areas above, don't worry, there are a lot of microcultures throughout the English speaking world where up-speak is the default mode of conversation—usually in places with deep cultural roots in agriculture and in slavery. Up-speak is a submission cue, and egalitarian and downtrodden microcultures use it to preempt and defuse potential conflicts. In these cultures, up-speak is a way of checking if your conversation partner is with you, of drawing them along to the conclusion of your thought. A few generations on, even after the culture shifts, the speech patterns remain, often times transmogrified into a form of dominance posturing.

However, even in areas where up-speak is part of the native accent, it's usually not something you hear from newscasters, announcers, lecturers, and other public speakers. These are people who speak with authority and decisiveness, and as such they end their sentences on an assertive, authoritative down-pitch.

Another problem that new narrators run into is the "reader rhythm." You'll discover as you start reading aloud regularly that you have a particular mental tune that you repeat sentence after sentence, paragraph after paragraph. When you do this, you're fitting the words on the page to your mental template of how people should speak. It creates a hypnotic, soporific rhythm for your listeners. When you're recording your own words, which are written in your own voice, you run the risk of doubling up on this error and falling into a deep abyss of reader rhythm.

I won't lie to you—this is the hardest fundamental for most actors of any sort to get right. There are a variety of tricks you can use to jog yourself out of it:

• *Record, listen, then re-record*

When you're new, you have to learn to hear your own performance as you're performing, and often the only way to do this without tripping yourself up is to time-shift your performance, take some general notes, and then take another run at it.

- *Mark up your script*

If you're having trouble getting the right emphasis on your words, or you're struggling against up-speak, or you're treating every comma as a period, or you're EM-PHA-SIZ-ING EV-ER-Y SYL-LA-BLE, annotate your script. Use capitals or italics to tell you where to emphasize and accent, use underlines to tell you where to quiet down. Then, use those notes as your direction when you perform.

- *Rephrase the sentence in your head*

Sometimes, despite your best efforts, you'll get stuck in a rut with a sentence or a paragraph that just won't come out right. When that happens, often the only thing that will help is to mentally reset. Envision the emotional context of the problem passage. Redo the sentence or two leading up to it. Stop focusing directly on it, and let your subconscious take over. It might take a couple tries, or even a five minute break away from the mic, but you'll eventually nail it. And don't worry, it occasionally happens to even the most experienced performers.

- *Get some training*

If inflection is proving a persistent problem for you, join Toastmasters. The active feedback and coaching can help even the most timid person develop a masterful stage and mic presence.

While relying on your default reader-rhythm can sink your book, as you gain experience you will develop a style where your natural voice—enhanced with performance acumen—will emerge. Don't be afraid of it. The reader-rhythm is only a problem when it gives you an audiobook that's soporific and stilted.

Similarly, the voice of your narrator and characters should trump other performance considerations. If your book is narrated in first person by a valley girl, it should be lousy with up-speak, earlier advice notwithstanding. While it's worth bearing in mind that attenuating a narrator's strong accent or irritating qualities is desirable for the overall presentation of the product, don't attenuate it so much that you lose the flavor of your story.

There is one other classic inflection problem that new readers stumble on: overacting. Interpretive reading always runs the risk of crossing over into Captain Kirk territory. Unless you're doing a full-cast production or an audio drama with highly dramatic aesthetics, keep your performance range narrower than you might find in real life or even on TV. Even with a very dramatic production, your narrator should have a bit of distance. If you're worried that you're pushing the envelope and crossing over into cheesy acting, hand some samples to an acquaintance and ask their opinion.

Audiobooks are a product with broad appeal—audience members often have broader listening tastes than they do reading tastes. Even though audio is more expensive than print, popping an audiobook in to listen often represents a smaller commitment in the mind of the audience than does sitting down to a thick stack of pages (which presents an opportunity to expand your audience). A disinterested test listener will help you gauge whether your performance is over-the-top, flat, or just right. Listen to their opinion.

More than any of the other basic four, inflection is the do-or-die of your performance. Any of the other four might make your work sound unprofessional. Inflection will make your audience fall asleep if it's too flat, and it'll wear them out if it's too energetic.

As a narrator, you are the authority in your book. Your individual characters may use any speech patterns you choose, but the narrator is the voice that holds the book together. It should inspire confidence, wield authority, and provide the stable base for the listener to sink his teeth into.

Taking It To The Next Level

The dynamics of your performance are what bring your story's voice to life. We've talked about the basics, now it's time to tackle the sparkle.

Pacing

Think back to Junior High, when you started having to do oral project presentations a few times a year. Remember the purgatorial length of one-page and half-page reports read by pre-teens who buried their face in the paper, reading the words one after another without any regard for syntax, meaning, or emotion? That is the sound of stage fright.

Stage fright amps up adrenaline, which screws up the time sense and flattens the emotional response. That's a double-whammy that kills performance pacing dead.

Pacing is a two-pronged beast. The first prong is your overall speed, and it's governed by how quickly people can comfortably absorb information. Too fast, and your listeners will miss the story. Too slow, and they'll get impatient. Your target average word-rate is 150-155 words per minute, or just under 9300 words per hour.

The other, trickier part of pacing is the way you vary that pace on a sentence-by-sentence level to hit that average. Just as when you write you control the pace at which your audience reads by the way you construct your sentences, when you perform you control the urgency, intimacy, humor, and suspense by the rate at which you read those words into the microphone, and the cadence you use. Your goal is to bring out the pacing variations you originally wrote on the page by:

• *Variation*

Subtly speeding up and slowing down your word rate.

• *Playing the silences*

In music, the difference between a competent amateur and a virtuoso is that the virtuoso takes the page as the starting point, not the goal. The amateur plays the notes, the virtuoso plays the silences. Even more than the emotion in your voice, the pauses in your performance elicits the emotional response in your audience. Know when to give your audience breathing room. Use dramatic pauses, extra beats, quick rushes and sudden stops.

• *Playing the Words vs Playing the Story*

In your writing you use tricks like assonance, dissonance,

alliteration, and rhythm. Sometimes it's appropriate to plays these textual elements up. Sometimes, it's more appropriate to underplay them. An audiobook is a different creature than a book. In a book, you have the luxury of reveling in language for its own sake. In an audiobook, you have to let the flow of the story tell you when playing up your linguistic brilliance will enhance and when it will detract. For example, puns based on the visual appearance of the words are less likely to work than puns that you can hear, while gorgeous imagery in service of evoking feelings of beauty can be lingered over a little longer than your reader might do on their own. In such cases (and the thousands of other cases like them), the *flow* of the story must be your guide.

Characterization

Also known as character voices (for dialogue and first person narration), the basic purpose of characterization is to help keep your listener oriented. In the car or on the train or in the gym it's easy to miss a "George said," and lose track of who's speaking. Introducing some characterization to distinguish your characters helps obviate this problem, and adds depth and richness besides, since it echoes that oldest of human art forms: the campfire story.

There are more ways to do this than there are writers under the sun, from a very little character variation at all to full-on cartoon voices, but all are built using a few basic tools:

• *Pitch and Pacing*

Pitching your voice *slightly* higher or lower and your words slightly faster or slower can change the gender of your character. Quicker breathy speech gives you a character who's harried and overextended, slower speech can (depending on how it's played) indicate uncertainty or authority, harder quick speech makes your character sound like a savvy operator, etc. Your delivery style, even if you don't vary the other characteristics of your voice, can weave a wonderful character.

• *Mouth Shape*

Change your mouth shape and you change your voice. Pinched

in, small movements give you an entirely different sound than an open throat and a wide open mouth. Give different characters different mouth shapes, and you'll hear the story come alive.

• *Musicality*

Some people have a mechanical way of speaking, while others have an almost operatic musicality about how they speak—most folks fall somewhere in the middle. Choosing your characters' level of musicality, and sticking with it, is a good quick way to differentiate them.

• *Dialect*

Put pitch & pacing together with mouth shape, throw in some exotic vowel substitutions and consonant styles, and you've got a full-on accent. If you're going to go this far, make sure that you can do the accent on the page—very little sounds more jarring than a fake accent, and if your audience contains people whose accent you're doing, they can take umbrage at a poor attempt, or (worse) mistake it for a parody. If you're doing a single read and you have a character whose accent you can't do, you've got a couple choices. First, you can give the sense of dialect without diving in by concentrating your speech in the part of the mouth characteristic of that accent/language. For example, Upper-Class British English is spoken as far forward in your mouth as you can push it, with every consonant tight against the teeth and the lips parted slightly more than normal, High German generally happens toward the back of the throat for both consonants and vowels, Parisian French is spoken as if you were talking around a mouthful of porridge, etc.

The second option is a little more radical. I love doing accents, I'm better-than-average at them, and I also prefer to produce full-cast books (partly because of my love of accents). If I find I've got a character whose accent I can't nail, or I've got an actor who's perfect for a character despite the accent, I will rewrite the character's backstory for the sake of the production. I will only do this if doing it will not affect anything else about the story, and I will only swap it for another dialect with similar slang and speech patterns. It usually involves less than one or two sentences worth of work, because I write with this production step in mind. Unless you want your audiobook production considerations to impinge upon your writing, pick the former path. Do as I say, not as I do.

That's your palate. Whether you choose to paint in bright brash colors or in striking gray scale is completely up to you. Choose what you want to do based on what you can do well. Audiences will accept compromises (a male reader using a slight pitch and inflection change for female characters) more readily than they will accept clumsiness (an accent that sounds fake). And there's a reason for that...

Conviction

Fact: it's easier to lie to someone in person than it is to lie to them over the phone. The human ear is very sharply attuned to detect social falseness, but it can be more easily fooled if fed visual cues that match the words being spoken, even if the tone of the speech bears a note of falseness. On the phone, with no visual cues, this falseness radar is on full alert, with no confounding factors.

For you as a voice actor, that means that you have to utterly believe the words you speak. You have to buy into the story. You can't let self-consciousness, the critical voice in your head, or worries about your parents hearing you read that sex scene get in your way. Just as your writing can be ruined by self-consciousness derailing your creativity, so too can you ruin your audiobook by indulging in feelings of awkwardness, self-doubt, anxiety, or make-believe. Your story about the talking unicorn who saves children from a serial killer might be played for laughs or tears, but when you stand in front of that microphone you must sink down into the words and speak them as if they were the dictates of God. If God wants you to be funny, then you trust that the story is funny and you deliver it as if you're sharing that secret with your audience. If God wants you to make your readers cry, deliver the tragic news sincerely without ever letting them hear you thinking "Wow, I could write this scene so much better now"—because, trust me, they will be able to hear you thinking that.

Flubs, Bloopers, and Screw-Ups

You will inevitably find sentences in your stories that simply do not want to come out of your mouth, and you'll stumble over them time and time again in the recording booth. You'll make other mistakes. too—mistakes of timing, pronunciation, characterization, emphasis, dialect, and more. When you make those mistakes, you need to stop and fix them immediately, and you need to do it in a way that'll make your editing painless.

First, when you make a mistake, stop. Take a breath.

Second, back up at least a full phrase before the mistake, if not a full sentence, and start recording from there.

Do not just pick up from where you stumbled. It won't cut together in post. In order to splice different takes together, you have to find points where the pitch, volume, and pace match, at least for a few phonemes. It takes an exceptionally practiced voice actor to pick up at the stumble point at the same pitch, volume, and pace, and to continue on as if nothing happened. The rest of us (i.e. 99.999% of us) need to create as many possible cut points as possible, so that we can be sure that the screwed-up sentence will splice together well once we get into the edit bay. The more you overlap your takes, the more potential splice points you create in post.

Be sure not to back up too far—you're likely to stumble over the same point, because the run-up to the place where you previously flubbed can create anxiety. The Goldilocks zone for the overlap is "the beginning of the thought," which can be anywhere from as short as a single phrase to as long as a sentence. Resist the urge to go back further than that, unless you decide to approach the performance for that segment from a different angle (in which case you'll not need edit points).

Keeping it Straight

Up to this point in this chapter, I've been more or less assuming that you have a particular image of audiobook reading in your mind:

you and the book standing in front of a microphone, reading page after page in sequence, as you would read it if you were reading it for your own enjoyment. Usually, this is exactly how it works.

Usually, but not always.

Whether doing deep differentiation or subtle variation, some people find it difficult to manage switching between so many voices while reading straight through a story. Such a reader may find himself using the wrong voice, or forgetting to switch voices, or taking a few words to ease into the new voice, etc. If you discover yourself having this problem, fear not. There is a solution.

We live in the age of non-linear editing, and you're going to be doing a lot of it no matter how sparse your production is. Because you can take any bit of sound from any recording session and, as long as its sonic profile matches, mix it with any other sound from any other session, you can record your book out of order. You can even record your voices separately. Just break your script out as if you were preparing it for different actors (see chapter 3), and then record each role on its own as a module. Once you've got all the roles recorded, piece them together in your DAW (see chapter 11).

There Is No Wrong Way

The style you choose for your book depends entirely on you. All styles are marketable, and any good quality production will have broad appeal. You might be like Nathan Lowell and decide you prefer the sparest of styles, the most subtle vocal differentiation, and the most even pacing in the world, even though you're an accomplished voice actor capable of doing several dozen accents flawlessly. You might be like Neil Gaiman and just not have it in you to do voices other than the one you were born with, but you can still do an excellent job by letting your story carry the day. You might have grown up in the circus and have boundless energy, and, like Harlan Ellison, pour your heart and soul into every word you read, treating it all like a spectacular piece of theater. Or, like Scott Sigler, you might be a guy from Detroit with tons of attitude and not much finesse, but you believe in yourself and your story enough to pull out every cheesy cartoon voice in creation and perform them with such conviction that they embody your work better than a full cast of professional actors could ever hope to.

So long as you keep your conviction high, your performance good, and your voice true, there is no wrong way to do this.

Librivox

If you're new to all of this, and you're nervous about dipping your toe into producing your own work for fear that you'll just need to do the whole thing over once you get your feet wet, there is a place you can practice your performance and production chops: Librivox.

Librivox is a website that aims to be the Project Gutenberg of audio. It accepts uploads of performances of any public domain book (fiction or non-fiction) or short story. Just pick a book you like, make a recording of it, and upload it. You'll be able to work the kinks out of your setup, practice your craft, and give back to the community all at the same time. Everybody wins. Find out more at http://www.libravox.org

The Centipede's Problem

An Ant and a Centipede met on a leaf one day. The Ant stopped the Centipede and said:

"Excuse me, sorry to interrupt, but I see you out here every day and I just have to tell you how much I admire you. I wish I had it in me to do what you do."

The Centipede, bemused, said "Oh? What is it I do?"

The Ant said "You work out here everyday on your own, and you never trip or fall or make a mistake. I have six legs and I can barely keep them straight. But you never stumble, you never falter, even with dozens and dozens of legs. I've always wondered how you manage it. Do you lift the left ones all at once, then the right ones? Do you alternate each pair? How do you do it?"

"Well," said the Centipede, "I...I...I don't know. I never really thought about it."

And the next time the Centipede tried to move, he fell over.

I've just spent the last five-or-six thousand words telling you how to read aloud for a microphone. Your job now is to practice the techniques enough that you can banish them from conscious memory. Performance is an organic, creative process with technical demands, but you must never let the technical run the show. Let it tweak the show, but never let it steer. Your technical mind doesn't know an ass from a mule when it comes to virtuosity, and if you let it drive you'll be forever stuck with the Centipede's Problem, when he realized that he didn't know how to walk.

Don't fret. Just do, and through doing, improve. If you look back in five years and think "wow, that first audiobook is way below my standards. I'm a *much* better performer now," you can always re-record it...*if* you really want to. But keep in mind: that's time you won't be spending writing or recording the next book.

80

Making Tracks

Part III
Acoustics

Chapter 5

Mastering the Wild Waveform

When you venture into the world of audio, no matter how shallowly, you're going to encounter a dizzying array of technical terms. If you don't know what those terms mean, you're going to find yourself groping around in the dark, having to learn everything the hard way through blind trial and error. This chapter will give you the basic vocabulary to understand everything that follows.

The Basics of Acoustical Science

Imagine a pond in a quiet forest, in the morning, before any creatures are awake, before any winds have risen. Imagine the surface of that pond—glass smooth, so perfect that if you photographed it you wouldn't be able to tell which side of the photo was the original and which was the reflection. Now, toss a stone into the water. Use a high arc so that the stone falls in vertically. Notice how the ripples spread out in a perfect circle?

The glass-smooth surface is silence. The ripples from the stone are sound.

Sound is a pressure wave. When you record sound, the microphone transforms the pressure wave into an electrical current that preserves the shape of the pressure wave. Because of this, you can view the sound in your editing software—in fact, all modern editing software is based around the waveform display.

In the real world, sound pressure is measured in absolute decibels (dB)—the greater the pressure, the higher the number of decibels. In the electronic world, decibels are a measure of relative signal power, with 0dB being the reference maximum capacity of any given piece of equipment.

But getting back to the ripples on the pond, since sound is a pressure wave, those waves on the water aren't just *like* sound waves, they *are* sound waves, albeit propagating at such a low frequency that you can't hear them.

Frequency

The frequency—measured in oscillations (wave-peaks) per second, or Hertz (Hz)—is what defines the pitch of your sound. A waveform of 440Hz (the same pitch as the middle A on a piano), for example, looks like this:

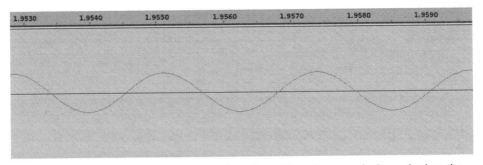

Figure 5.1: A standard 440Hz reference waveform. Time, in seconds, is marked on the horizontal axis along the top of the picture.

440Hz is the *fundamental* frequency of the middle A on a piano, but the signal above is not a piano, it's synthesized. You can tell just by looking at the waveform. A piano generates harmonics as well, and they would show up as sub-ripples in the larger ripples.

In real life, anything that vibrates has a fundamental frequency (the note you hear) and harmonics, which provide texture and depth to the sound. Harmonics progress as integer multiples of your fundamental frequency. Thus, a fundamental of 440Hz would, if played in the real world, generate harmonics of 880Hz, 1320Hz,

1760Hz, 2200Hz, and so on. Understanding harmonics is key to understanding EQ and mixing, so we'll deal with them more extensively in chapter 15. Specific harmonics are very hard to pick out in a waveform, but they're easy to spot in a Spectrum Analyzer. See chapter 11 for more information on spectral analysis.

Looking at the waveform above, you'll see that a time meter, marked in seconds, runs across the top. You can see (or calculate) the fundamental frequency, amplitude, signal density, phase, and the number of channels and the balance between them (in a vocal waveforms, you can also see the phonemes). The frequency we've already seen. Let's take the rest in order:

Amplitude

In the waveform as shown, the amplitude is the vertical distance between the peak and the trough. This tells you the volume of your signal—the bigger the amplitude, the more volume the signal has. Amplitude is one of the components of loudness.

The amplitude of your signal must remain within the recording equipment's *dynamic range*—that is, the range of allowable signal levels between complete silence and complete saturation (0dB). When you oversaturate a digital signal, you get an artifact called *clipping*. It looks like this:

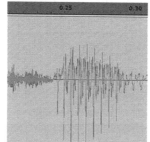

Figure 5.2: A vocal waveform, clipped.

Notice how some of the peaks are straying outside the track? These are places where the amplitude exceeds 0dB. All the information in those peaks is lost. There's no recovering from a clipped signal, and it sounds like crap to boot. When you're recording, the most important thing to watch for is clipping. Avoid it at all costs—it's one of the giveaways of an amateur production.

However, while the volume of your signal corresponds to the peak amplitude of your signal, it doesn't correspond to the loudness. Instead, the loudness corresponds to the signal density or the RMS (Root Mean Square—a description of the mathematical equation used to derive the loudness from the amplitude of various frequencies over time). The signal density shows on the waveform: here's how to see it:

Notice the difference between the sample 440Hz waveform and the vocal waveform. Notice how the sample has one set of regular peaks and valleys, while the vocal form looks like a bunch of sine waves that have been stacked on top of each other? The vocal form has more frequencies interacting on it, and the signal density is greater.

To increase the loudness on that vocal waveform, more of the quieter frequencies need to be pushed to a greater amplitude, which increases the amount of signal being pushed at any given millisecond. The reason that computer-controlled dynamic range compression has become the go-to tool for levels control is because current listening environments (like cars and iPods) often have to compete with high levels of background noise, and it's easier to throw a severe compressor on the track in order to maximize the loudness.

By pulling down the peaks and pushing up the floor, a compressor increases the signal density of your mix while preventing clipping—but, because it does this indiscriminately, it makes your signal sound like crap when you use it for loudness maximization. Instead, compression is properly used with a very light touch to protect from clipping (see chapter 15). To maximize your loudness, you'll want to use a different trick: Mixing (covered in chapter 14).

Phase

The phase of a sound is described by the position of your peaks and valleys, and it both contains some of your sound's directional information and dictates how the sound will interact with other sounds in the mix. The sounds here have a 0 degree phase relative to one another:

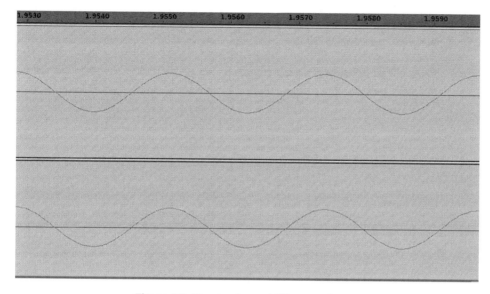

Figure 5.3: Two in-phase 440hz waveforms

When you duplicate a waveform, you get two waveforms that are in-phase with reference to each other, as we have above. When you add two in-phase waveforms together, you reinforce the peaks and valleys, doubling the amplitude, like so:

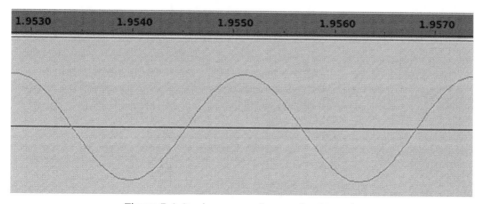

Figure 5.4: In-phase waveforms mixed together

Waveforms interact with one another on the basis of phase, using the principles of simple addition.

The opposite of this effect is when you have to phase-reversed signals, like so:

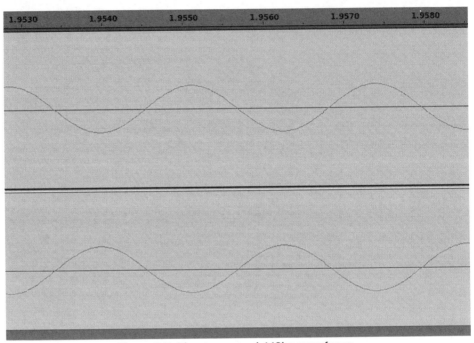

Figure 5.5: Phase-reversed 440hz waveforms

Knowing that these two will be added to each other in the mix, you might expect that the net result will be a flat waveform...

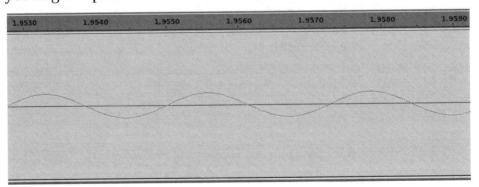

Figure 5.6: Mixing down opposite-phase signals

...and you'd be correct. This may seem elementary, but it is the one of the basic tricks to performing noise reduction. Isolate the noise, phase-reverse it, then add it back to the original signal.

The games phase plays are what give sounds their flavor. It's what makes the difference between the sound of a bare room and that same room with furniture in it. It's why using reverb and EQ judiciously can sweeten your sound and bring depth and life to music (and if this sentence doesn't make sense to you yet, don't worry—it will by the time you finish this book).

Phase games can also be used for special FX—one such, called a *phaser*, uses the interaction of offset phase duplicates, a synthesized waveform, and a feedback loop to create something that sounds like it's been fed through really crappy electronics. It's popular in industrial rock music on vocals and guitars, and also useful as part of a "spoken over a bad radio" effect.

Channels and Multiplexing

Each of your inputs constitutes a single channel of audio. Adding those channels together for a final delivery format (rather than blending them into a single channel) is called "multiplexing."

A single channel of audio is called a mono (monaural) signal. If you have two tracks (left and right) carrying exactly the same information, you have a dual mono signal packaged in a stereo file. Since all current consumer delivery formats require at least a stereo signal, dual-mono is the best choice for single-read audiobooks.

Two channels of non-identical audio (left and right) are called a stereo (stereophonic) signal. For audiobooks, you will be recording either in mono or stereo, and mixing down to either stereo or dual-mono for delivery. In between those two points, depending on how extensive your production is, you will be working with anywhere between one and thirty tracks. When viewing a stereo waveform, you will see two waveforms stacked, one atop the other, on the same track strip. The waveform on top represents your left channel, the one on bottom represents the right channel.

The difference in volume between the left and right channel is called the balance of the sound, and is important in stereo positioning, both active (called *panning*) and static, which we'll cover in chapter 16.

Four or more channels is a surround signal. Over the past 20 years, the most popular flavors of surround sound have been Prologic, 4.1, 5.1, and 7.1. Surround sound is most common in games and movies, occasionally shows up in music, and some very rare audio dramas (such as those released by *Above The Title Productions*) are available in surround as well.

The market for surround-mixed audiobooks is very, very small, the software and extra hardware you need to mix it properly tends to be quite expensive, and it takes an enormous amount of time and practice to get it right. For these reasons, I will not be covering surround sound in this book.

Real-World Waveforms

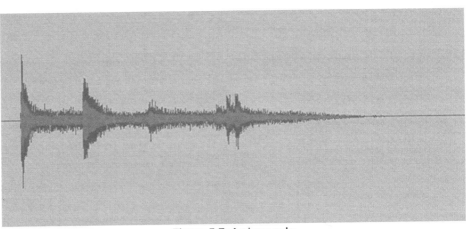

Figure 5.7: A piano solo

Here, we have a waveform from a real piano playing a series of six notes. Looking at it, you can see the components of a sound:

• *The attack*

This is the beginning of any sound. It's also a term used by plugins to describe the initiation of action upon a waveform.

• *The sustain*

As the name implies, the sustain is the resonance of the sound that carries beyond its attack. It can be the continuation of a vowel, or the sustained vibration of a guitar string, or the reverberation of a stone dropped in a warehouse.

• *The decay*

The decay is the way the sound falls off to zero.

Every sound has an attack, sustain, and decay, and by paying attention to the shapes they take for different phonemes, you will eventually learn to "read" the words in a vocal waveform. The better you get at this, the faster things will go for you in editing, so it pays to pay attention to what shapes you're seeing on the screen when you hear yourself speak.

Signals and Noise

In production engineering, there is one measurement that is more important, and more basic, than any other: the signal-to-noise ratio.

Think back to the pond illustration that I opened this chapter with. The perfect glassy surface has no vibrations on it. It's perfectly silent. When you toss the pebble in, you create a sound—a signal. The signal is the part of the sound that you intend to record.

Now, imagine instead that there's a breeze blowing across your pond, and subtle ripples race every-which-way. Now when you throw your pebbles in, you get a signal of the same size, but it doesn't rise as far above the surrounding surface as it did before, because these other ripples—the noise—are at a non-zero level. The noisier the surface is, the worse the signal-to-noise ratio gets. If it gets noisy enough, it will be impossible to tell the ripples your pebble makes from the ripples already on the pond.

Noise comes in these varieties:

• *Room Tone*

All the noise that comes from the room you're recording in, whether it's leaking in from the outside or coming from your computer fan or air conditioner. See chapter 6 for instructions on minimizing problems caused by your room.

• *EM Interference*

Radiation from dirty power and old appliances bleeds off into the atmosphere, and can get picked up by your equipment as if it were a radio signal. Cell phones and wifi and bluetooth all throw off radio signals that can get picked up by your mic. See chapter 6 and 8 for instructions on finding and minimizing electromagnetic (EM) interference.

• *Ground Loop Buzz*

A 60Hz buzzing sound that comes from poor grounding of your equipment. Essentially, this is the sound electricity makes in your walls, and when your equipment isn't properly wired up, that sound will leak through into the rest of your setup. See chapter 6 for instructions on finding and killing the Buzz.

• *Impedance Matching Noise*

For reasons we'll get into in Part 4, the signal traveling through your cables can run at different power levels, called "line level" and "mic level." Mismatching these signals can create a couple characteristic sorts of noise. If you cross-connect line level signal to a mic level input (see chapter 9), you'll get an ultra-hot signal with a lot of static hiss. If you plug a mic level signal into a line level input, you'll get a very quiet signal with a lot of static. Either way, it's not a happy sound.

• *Power Supply Switching Noise*

This is the sneakiest of all, because it doesn't come from your audio equipment. It comes from your computer's power supply. As a power supply's transformer ages, it will start to throw off static, and that static goes straight into a computer's electronics. It results in a very characteristic static punctuated with semi-irregular popping noises. It usually comes in at a low level, so you'll be able to hear that the noise exists, but you'll have to amplify the noise to be able to tell it apart from Impedance Matching Noise or Ground Loop Buzz.

The good news is that, if you're recording on a laptop, fixing this one is easy. Just unplug the power supply and record on battery power (of course, you'll want to be sure not to run your battery dry, and to plug it back in when you're not recording). If your laptop has a dead battery (as may be the case if you're using an older one), you'll need to replace either the battery or the power supply.

If you're recording on a desktop, you'll need to replace the power supply. High quality desktop power supplies are usually devoid of switching noise.

Noise also comes in "colors," which describe the frequency profile of common kinds of noise. These are useful to know if you find yourself needing to dig deeper into noise reduction techniques:

• *White Noise*

Just as white light comes from combining all the frequencies (or colors) of light at equal intensity, white noise is noise that combines all parts of the audible spectrum at roughly equal levels. The hiss you hear on old vinly LPs, or from an overdriven preamp, is typically white noise.

• *Pink Noise*

Pink noise is distributed logarithmically up the spectrum, with the loudest noise being down low. Since human hearing works on a logarithmic curve, pink noise registers as flat, loud, and maddening with the human ear. In audio engineering, it's used to "tune" a room. By playing pink noise into a room and listening to the result with a spectrum analyzer, you can isolate which frequencies the room will reinforce, and compensate for any that might sound harsh or unpleasant to the human ear. This is useful if you don't have the latitude to physically modify your recording studio to your satisfaction. If you take that frequency map and use it to notch down the hot frequencies on your outboard EQ, you can compensate for defects in your studio's acoustical treatments. This process is called "ringing out" or "pinking out" a room.

• *Brown, Blue, Violet, and Grey*

These colors describe different amplitude relationships between frequencies, and are generally used only in electronic engineering and in designing high-end music recording and live performance installations, therefore I won't explore them here. If you're curious, check out the Yamaha Sound Reinforcement HandBook (a must-have reference for the serious recording engineer).

Practically speaking, it is impossible to completely eliminate noise from a system, but it is possible to minimize it. The target level for signal silence in a studio environment is -60dB or better, assuming that your signal is nice and strong. The trick to recording clean audio is to maximize the Signal-to-Noise (SN) ratio. A SN ratio of 20dB will be marginally listenable, a SN ratio of 40dB or greater will sound nice and clean, and a SN ratio of 50+dB is the kind of measurement you should expect out of a professionally-designed and outfitted studio.

As you get used to mixing sound, your ears will become hyper-attuned to hearing noise (studio ears). Resist the urge to sink your whole life into making things ultra-quiet. Unless you're dealing with irregular noise or the Buzz, any noise below -60dB in the finished mix will be transparent to the listener. However, when recording, lower *is* better. After you edit, you'll be mixing, which will involve pushing parts of the floor up to get a consistently-listenable signal. The lower your noise floor is when you record, the more latitude you have when you mix.

If you're having trouble tracking down your noise, run a sample of the noise through a spectrum analyzer. You can find a primer on spectrum analyzers in chapter 11.

Spectrum and Equalization

When an object vibrates, it does so at a certain frequency. Each frequency corresponds with a particular pitch. The combination of those frequencies, and the phase games they play with each other, add up to the sounds that you hear. Those frequencies exist along a spectrum—an infinite number line that stretches outward from 0Hz. This spectrum is what you see when you use a spectrum analyzer. The audible part of the spectrum runs from approximately 20Hz to approximately 20kHz, with some variation depending on genetics, age, and cumulative hearing damage.

Equalization (EQ) is the process of selectively cutting and boosting specific frequencies to tweak the character of a sound. EQ is the single most powerful tool for post-production engineering, useful for everything from noise reduction to enhancing character voices to creating orchestral arrangements. You can learn all about it, and how to use it, in chapter 15.

Sampling

An analog recording—such as you get on a vinyl record or a tape—is one made by analogy (hence the term). A physical process (a sound wave) moves diaphragm in the microphone, creating an electrical signal, which moves a magnetic field (in a tape recorder) or a needle (in the case of a record).

A digital recording, on the other hand is *sampled*. Since everything on a computer is comprised of 1s and 0s (these are the "digits" in "digital"), analog sound (such as your voice in the microphone) needs to be converted to a stream of 1s and 0s. Digital recording equipment uses an Analog/Digital converter (A/D) to accomplish this through *sampling*: taking discrete slices (samples) of sounds of a given "bit depth" (the amount of information contained in each sample, expressed in bits) at a certain "rate" (number of samples per second—expressed in kilohertz). Some A/Ds come as outboard gear, some come built-in to sound cards, mixing boards, handheld recorders, and other devices.

Because sampling takes snapshots and plays them back in order, the effect is to the ears what a movie is to the eyes, and, just like a movie, it can suffer from a weirdness called the "even division" problem. When a movie or video camera films a fan or a wagon wheel or a helicopter rotor, the blades or spokes can appear to spin backward, or move slowly, or do other things that are obviously at odds with reality. This happens when the rate of spin is evenly divisible by the frame rate, resulting in the loss of location and movement information. In sound, frequencies that divide evenly into the sample rate lose their phase information. This isn't worth worrying about for vocals, but if you get seriously into Foley, you'll need to learn to compensate for it. Such compensation techniques are beyond the scope of this book.

Generally speaking, the higher the sample rate and bit depth, the higher fidelity the recording. However, practically speaking, above a certain limit most people can't hear the difference, and the result of infinite pursuit of higher sample rates is that you eat up a lot of extra disk space for no really good reason.

Music and Foley can benefit from more latitude, but that latitude is usually destroyed when mixing down to consumer delivery formats. If you were mixing music for movies or reproduction in high-end concert halls, or if you're recording particularly tricky instruments (like drums and brass), acquiring at 24 bits/96 kHz has its uses.

For our purposes, however—those being spoken-word in all its glorious forms, for delivery to iPods and CDs—the highest you ever need go when recording is 24 bit/48 kHz, but you can get away with recording at your delivery-format level: 16 bit/44.1 kHz.

For reference, at this delivery-format rate, you can expect your audio to eat up about 10mb for every minutes. If you work at a higher rate (I usually work at 24/48), you can expect that figure to grow. Make sure you have plenty of hard drive space, and plenty of backup space. See chapter 3 for tips on resource management and backups.

Note: A higher bit depth means more dynamic range. If your studio is quiet, 24bit will give you a better signal-to-noise ratio than 16 bits. This means that anything you can do to improve the s/n ratio with a 24 bit signal will yield a cleaner delivery format.

Wrap-up

Now you've got the basics of acoustics, which should make the tech-speak in the following chapters make sense. So, let's move on to the hands-on stuff.

Making Tracks

Part IV
The Equipment

100

Making Tracks

Chapter 6
· · · · · · · · · ·
It's All About The Sound

Between your voice and the raw recording sits a veritable highway of electronics, cables, connectors, and capsules. This highway is your production pipeline, and it looks like this:

Microphone → Cable → [Mixer/Preamp → EQ → A/D] → [Computer/Recorder)]

You'll notice the brackets in the diagram—that's because these components can be bought as separate components or as integrated packages, and each approach has certain advantages which we'll discuss in a bit. But first, we need to take a hard look at a concept that most people never give a second thought to: Silence.

The Sound of Silence

Picture this: You're in a cocktail party, packed shoulder-to-shoulder with hundreds of people all trying desperately to mingle. The conversational din is somewhere around 130 decibels—about as loud as the sound of a jet engine when you're standing on the wing—and you've just run into the top editor in your genre. She's just fallen in love with your writing and wants to get to know you and learn your career ambitions, because she'd consider publishing your next book a major feather in her cap. How are you going to carry on a conversation with her?

Unless you have a (fairly common) audio processing disorder called, appropriately enough, APD (for Audio Processing Disorder), you just exert a little effort to tune out the noises you don't want to hear, much the same way you'd focus your eyes on a needle and thread so that you can sew a button on. As far as your senses are concerned, you just shut out the rest of the world in favor of that needle, or that conversation.

You have this ability because, though you're rarely conscious of it, you're picking up phase, panning, time delay, frequency, amplitude, and other information through your ears that your private computational genius—your brain—can use to triage the signal coming in. So, if the editor is an alto, the brain will throw away most of the information below 250Hz, since altos generally don't have fundamental frequencies that low. If the editor is in front of you, your brain will throw away any sound coming from behind you (since the shape of your ears effects the phase of sound coming from front and back), and the microseconds between a sound hitting your right and left ear create discontinuities that tell your brain how far away the sound is, and in which direction.

At any given time, your sensory system is throwing away upwards of 80% of what you're perceiving. That chair you're sitting on? Some part of your brain is actively throwing away all the microscopic details of its texture, the way it reacts to moisture, the way the upholstery interacts with the fabric of your trousers, how much it's making the backs of your thighs sweat, and a thousand other details that you have no use for whatsoever. Your brain is actively doing the same for every square nanometer of skin, most of your visual field, the several hundred-thousand taste buds in your mouth, the olfactory glands in your nostrils, most of what you're hearing, and the sensations of movement and equilibrium that monitor what's going on with your organs. The heavy curtain the brain hangs between your conscious mind (the prefrontal cortex) and the rest of your awareness is what allows you to have a life rather than going catatonic from sensory overload.

But if you've ever tried to use your cell phone to record a lecture in a cavernous theater, you'll have noticed something: The recording is almost impossible to listen to. If you strain hard enough, you can make out the speaker's words, but it's exhausting work liable to drive you half out of your gourd. That's because recording does to sound what photography does to images: it flattens everything. When you look at a photograph, you're at the mercy of the photographer's judgment in the selection of lenses, color depth, focus, light response, and exposure time. By throwing away most of the information available, the photographer, for better or worse, creates a fixed interpretation of reality that the viewer can either engage or ignore.

Likewise, the very act of recording a sound removes from it much of the information that the brain would normally use to focus, discriminate, and customize that sound for your listening pleasure. The result is something flat and uninteresting, where irrelevant noise competes with desirable sound (signal) for your attention. If your signal-to-noise (SN) ratio isn't very, very favorable, your recording will sound amateurish at best, unlistenable at worst.

Getting the best possible SN ratio is the sum total of the job of the recording engineer. There is an entire industry of long-term professionals in film and music who do nothing other than clean up noise and maximize good signal (and get paid quite handsomely for it).

Since every step of the recording process—including every piece of equipment in your production pipeline—introduces noise into the signal, you must protect your signal at every step of the way, starting with your room.

You're going to need a quiet room—and I'm using the word "quiet" in a technical sense, not a colloquial one. Quiet enough to go to sleep, to hear a whisper, or to listen to a mouse's teeth chattering can be too loud for a good recording if you pick the wrong equipment. It you really want to create a space that's quiet enough to record in, you have to learn to listen to the sounds of silence.

So, find your room (see next section), close all the windows, and stand in it. Give yourself a good five minutes for your ears to adjust, then listen for sound leakage. Can you hear the refrigerator in the kitchen whirring? How about the air conditioner, or the furnace? Is there noise coming through the duct-work from other parts of the house? Do you hear a computer fan, or a spinning hard drive? Can you hear the white noise of traffic or wind? Did you just discover that you're under the flightpath of a major international airport, or a small commercial one? Are you suddenly aware that your son has a deep bass hum coming from his room—then when you went to check it you found that he has a dirty fan perched precariously on a window frame that's transmitting the vibrations into the bones of the house?

What you're hearing is your "room tone." Now, we've got to fix it.

Building the Room

Fixing "room tone" assumes that you have a room to start with. If you don't have any obvious candidates for your room, you're going to need to either repurpose a space in your existing domicile (or office), or you're going to need to build a room from scratch. When selecting or building your room, the first thing you need to worry about is the shape.

Like waves in a swimming pool, sound reflects off surfaces. If you've been around enough pools or lakes, you'll have noticed that with some of them, landing a leaf on the water is enough to cause ripples that carry on rippling for quite a while, but with others, the waves from a cannonball dive seem to die away pretty quickly. In small pools, like a bathtub, you may even have seen standing waves, where the whole surface seems to rise and fall in such a way that the water itself seems sluggish and distended and inclined never to stop. These different behaviors are a result of the shape of the pool itself, and particularly a result of the ratios of the different sides. Different distances require different amounts of times for the ripples to hit.

In a pool that's 10ft wide by 20ft long, for example, the waves will take twice as long to bounce off the walls at the end of the long axis as they will the walls at the end of the short axis. In the meantime, the ripples from those early reflections will cross and interfere with the ripples still radiating out from the primary splash, causing lots of little pyramidal ripples on the surface of the water. Then, when they meet their opposite numbers, they will either reinforce or cancel each other out, according to how their phases line up (which depends entirely on the relationship between the frequency of the ripples and how wide the pool is). When those waves reinforce each other perfectly, you'll get much taller waves at the same frequency. If they reinforce each other sporadically, you'll get clumps of taller waves. When they cancel each other out, you'll get a flat surface. When they reinforce and cancel each other out willy nilly, you'll get a constantly varying, glittery surface with no detectable order whatsoever.

Sound will do the same thing in your studio, and the ratios of the walls in your room will determine how sound interacts with itself in the room. Get those ratios wrong, and you'll get ringing (undesirable reinforcement at certain frequencies), ultra-live sound (near-perfect reinforcement at all frequencies), flatness (near-perfect phase cancellation), or sweetness (analogous to the glittery chaotic scattering described above). In other words, the first and most important variable you want to control for is the shape of your room.

Because of those reflections. some shapes sound better than others. The ideal shape is the so-called "Golden Room" or "Golden Cube," a rectangular room conforming to the Golden Ratio (1:1.618). The width of the room should be 1.6 times the height of the room, and the length should be 2.6 times the height. In a typical house with 8ft ceilings, this gives you room dimensions of 8ft high x 12.95ft wide x 20.95ft long.

That's a lot of square footage. Chances are, it's more square footage than you've got to spare. If it is, don't worry too much. You can use acoustical treatments to tune your room and get very close to the sweetness of a minimally treated Golden Room, once you pick your space.

If you're not going to be building a room, and you don't have anything as big as described (such as a deep, unused one-car garage) that you can readily convert, here are some other good options:

• *Walk-in Closets*

A good-sized closet has the advantage, in many floor plans, of being along an interior wall, and thus maximally acoustically isolated from the outdoor din. Because they're small, they're easy spaces to treat—as long as they're big enough for you to work in comfortably. Done right, these are not a second-best option. Quite the contrary—done right, they're ideal.

• *Basements*

Though they are vulnerable from the noise transmitted through the ceiling above, basements are naturally insulated from road noise, neighborhood noise, and aircraft noise. If you've got one, you should seriously consider putting your studio in it.

• *Libraries, Bedrooms, and Offices*

If you don't have an extra room or closet available, you'll need to turn one of your existing rooms into a dual-purpose space. Bedrooms can work very well for these, as the large areas of blankets, pillows, and wooden furniture in most bedrooms work as ready-made acoustical treatment (see "Tuning the Room" later in this chapter). If you have a dedicated library, it may be ideal for many of the same reasons. Offices, prone as they are to containing large flat metal and glass surfaces, as well as computers and other noisemakers, are often (though not always), the least attractive option.

• *Living Rooms and Bathrooms*

Generally speaking, these are bad ideas, as their acoustics are generally ill-suited for the job due to their unpleasant resonance and tendency toward untreated surfaces (i.e. they're very live).

It goes almost without saying that the location of your domicile (and whether you are allowed to mess with the walls) is at least as important as where in your house you locate your studio. Thus, unless you can get a recording studio custom-built, selecting the quietest room in the house is often the best you can do. Even the quietest room in your house is probably not quiet enough, and you'll need to put some work into making it even quieter. The quieter it is, the faster your recording goes, because you'll get interrupted less often. Assuming you're on a budget like most of us, your decisions here will be compromises that directly dictate how much it costs you (in both time and money) to produce each audiobook.

For example, I once had the misfortune of living beneath the flight paths of three major international airports, and for one of those airports I'd get overflown both on takeoff and on approach. This means that, at certain times of day, I'd have to stop recording every fifteen to twenty minutes, wait for ninety seconds, then pick up where I left off. However, it wasn't the worst that the place had to offer me: I also had road noise and commuter train noise from the nearby freeway, as well as neighbors who were endowed by nature and circumstance with prodigiously loud toddlers and dogs, neither of which could be reliably silenced.

In that situation, my control began and ended at the walls. I couldn't change the flight paths, or convince the airports to confine their flight activities to the early hours of the morning, and despite the genial nature of my neighbors and their willingness to take the kids and dogs to the park if I asked nicely, there's only so long you can make demands like that and expect your apartment to remain un-spray-painted. So I needed other options.

The first option was the most straightforward: move to another location, and this is what I eventually wound up doing as the complex attracted more and more decent but noisy folks. There was a stretch of a few years, though, where moving wasn't an option, so I used option 3.

Option two involved a two-pronged approach. First, I had to deal with the airplanes. I unfortunately couldn't soundproof the ceiling. That would have involved some structural modifications that fell well outside the coverage of my cleaning deposit, as well as being prohibitively expensive (ceiling mods are always the most difficult and expensive). I quickly decided to live with the airplanes, and spent a couple weeks charting the flyover times and noting how they varied by weather, so I could schedule my recording sessions during the least annoying times of day.

With that done, I focused on the second prong: Soundproof as best I could on my (meager) budget. The results were good enough that I produced three award-nominated audiobooks this way, as well as the soundtrack and ADR for five films of various lengths and a number of instructional materials (such as lectures, corporate reports, advertisements, etc.). Don't get me wrong—even with the soundproofing, it was no picnic recording in there, but it was good enough that a determined person could pull off some very complex and demanding productions. Unless you're living in a rat-infested building underneath freight train tracks in a war zone populated by flamingos and howler monkeys, you should be able to soundproof on the merest of budgets.

Sound, and How to Stop It

Since sound is a pressure wave, exactly the same as waves in the ocean, it works by pushing and compressing (i.e. vibrating) the medium it's traveling through. The properties of that medium—its inertia, rigidity, and resonance—and its interactions with other media, shape, filter, and stop sound. Soundproofing is a matter of outsmarting the pressure waves by sticking dispersing and reflecting materials in its way.

Inertia, as you'll remember from gradeschool physics, is an object's resistance to a change in motion. For an otherwise unencumbered object, inertia is a consequence of mass. All other things being equal, the more massive an object is, the louder your sound will have to be before it will make your object vibrate appreciably.

As for an object's rigidity and textural properties, consider this: Layered fabric (fiberglass and Kevlar) can stop bullets where steel plating can't, because instead of resisting the bullet's kinetic energy, it absorbs and disperses it over a great area. For the same reason, a flexible, mobile mass (such as Sonex foam, or stage curtains in a theater) can absorb and mute sounds that a rigid body of similar mass could not.

Finally, every object in the world has a natural resonance. Resonant frequencies are those at which the object vibrates most readily, and they're determined by the object's shape, mass, microscopic structure, and chemical makeup.

In soundproofing your room (i.e. insulating it from unwanted sounds), you want to add things to the walls that will use these three properties to attenuate (or dampen) the sounds you don't want. The standard way to do this, for those of you on generous budgets, is to build a room within a room by:

• Mounting the new drywall on rubber isolation mounts, to prevent the direct physical transmission of vibrations through the walls.• If the noise outside is particularly loud and intrusive, backing these walls with mass-loaded vinyl (MLV). This is a sticky-backed plastic fabric that's very heavy, and is used to soundproof cars. Applying this to the walls further increases their mass, which further dampens sound transmission.

• When you install the new walls, you would want to insulate the space between the old wall and the new wall using a substance—such as polyurethane foam—that won't settle or shift over time. Polyurethane foam has the further advantage that it offers the maximum possible sound dispersion per cubic inch of any commonly-available insulation.

• Repeat this process with the ceiling by installing an drop-ceiling backed by insulation and MLV.

• Install double-glazed storm windows, then plug them with removable or hinged MLV+foam insulation-backed shutters.

• Replace the door with weather-stripped solid-core oak or cedar, with a rubber drag-strip along the bottom.

• For reasons of survival, an air conditioning vent (as you can imagine, one person's body heat can make such a room quite toasty in very short order).

This will get you a room that's tight and quiet enough that you can record with some of the world's best microphones and never have to worry about unwanted noise leaks. A room done up properly in this way will have a room tone quieter than the electrical noise floor of most vocal recording equipment, even if this room is in a house on the verge strip in the middle of an interstate.

As you can imagine, doing this costs an obscene amount of money—portable sound booths that you can erect in a room that give you about 80% of the sound dampening you can get with the method described above will cost you upwards of $4000.

Fortunately, that's not the only option.

If you're living in a modern insulated house with double-glazed windows, and you live with people who are willing to give you some reliable quiet time (for example, children who go to school during the day, roommates who work day jobs, a spouse who is content to read for a couple hours or run errands while you're recording), you can get away with a LOT less. Sometimes hanging stage curtains around the inside of the room will give you what you need.

If you're less lucky–for example if you live in an older apartment with uninsulated walls (as I did for far too long), and you're on a tight budget and can't make structural changes—you can use any number of easily-obtained items. Moving blankets and upended mattresses are the obvious ones. Foam-core cubicle walls can also come in very handy, particularly for separating your microphone from the fan noise of your computer (if you must keep both in the same room).

But there's something you probably have in your house already that will do wonders for dampening sound and insulating your room: books. If you cover all the walls in your studio with wooden bookshelves (filled with books), you'll be getting some of the best sound treatment that a limited budget can buy. If you double the bookshelves with stage curtains (putting the curtains behind the shelves, for reasons we'll discuss in the next section), you're in even better shape—this, by the way, is the method I used in my first studio in that painfully noisy apartment.

Be creative. Anything with mass, flexibility, and coverage will help. If you've got rolls of old egg crate foam around, tack it to the wall. If you've got moving blankets from the last time you moved house, hang them up. Grab a circular saw and some plywood and a spray can of polyurethane foam and make yourself some el-cheapo shutters. Use the old roofing shingles in your back yard as a poor-man's MLV. Chances are, you've got quick-and-easy access to things you can use to vastly improve the quality of your soundproofing—and if you can't cut out all the external noise, don't worry, there are other tricks further down the production pipeline that we'll use to help compensate for that.

But before we get to that, we still need to tune the room.

Tuning the Room

Like light, sound reflects off surfaces, and different kinds of surfaces preferentially reflect different frequencies. In light, this biased reflection/absorption game gives us color. In sound, it gives us phase, texture, and reverb, which together create the sound's character: A steel guitar gives a sharp, bright, bell-like sound, while the same steel strings on a maple guitar produce a sound that's soft, warm, inviting, and sensual.

The same song played on both instruments by the same musician will affect you in two different ways because the materials and geometry in the guitar's body color the sound in the same way that paint colors the light bouncing off of it. The guitar's body is the "room" in which its strings resonate—the interaction of the strings and the body create the guitar's voice.

Just as with guitar strings, the human voice needs a good room to bring out its desired qualities. But when it comes to undesirable vocal reinforcement, it's hard to do worse than the environment you'll find in most houses and apartments.

Mostly Dead vs. All Dead

Making the sound in your room is more difficult than keeping sound out of the room. To get a sweet sound, you have to control the reflections—creating the correct frequency bias while treading a line between a "live" room and a "dead" room.

A "dead" room absorbs all of the sound inside it, where a "live" room absorbs very little. The goal of room-tuning is simple: you want the audience to hear you, not the room. If the room is dead, the audience will hear it in the artificiality of a sound-booth voice. If the room is live, the audience will be able to "see" the shape and makeup of the room, to the detriment of verisimilitude. A mostly-dead room, properly diffused, with appropriate resonant materials, will give you a natural sound that will make your audience feel as if you're right beside them, whispering stories in their ear. That intimacy starts here, and it's what makes a good quality audiobook shine.

Most houses and apartments—some architectural styles aside—are not designed with acoustics in mind. The rooms are squarish, and don't conform to the golden room ratio. The walls are gypsum (drywall) or plaster—materials that preferentially reflect harsh frequencies—and run parallel to each other in a way guaranteed to prevent acoustical scattering. The concrete, tile, or laminate floors create another too-bright, highly reflective surface. Add it all together, even if you throw down some carpeting, and you've got the recipe for tinny, emotionally off-putting sound that can be physically painful to the listener.

Stand in an empty room and snap your fingers. You'll hear a hard slap-back reverb. If you have trouble hearing the reverb as distinct from the primary sound, it means that your ears need training. Getting your ears in is the basic skill in becoming an effective recording engineer. Fortunately, if you've got a smart phone, you've got a set of pocket training wheels (if you don't have a smart phone, head down to the local gadget shop and drop $20 on a digital voice recorder—they come in handy in this line of work). Turn the recording app on and stand in your chosen room, and talk for a couple minutes. When you play it back (be sure to listen on a pair of good headphones), you'll hear all the awful acoustics that your brain is automatically tuning out. Learn to listen for those.

That slap-back is the sound of an indiscriminately live room.

Killing a room stone dead isn't cheap, but it's not complicated: Coating every wall in acoustical foam will do the job in a flash. For reasons mentioned above, though, a completely dead room isn't desirable for audiobook vocals. For our purposes, you want a room that's only mostly dead—"mostly dead" means "slightly live" at the right frequencies.

The reason a slightly live room is desirable is that the human voice is a complex instrument, and it depends on its environment for its finer characteristics to manifest. Ideally, this means a golden room with the speaker positioned in the center. Obviously, this isn't always possible, but even with a less-than-ideal space, you can make a beautiful-sounding room.

Our first stage of vocal treatment is to dampen those high, tinny frequencies. Hanging moving blankets or quilts or drapes around the space will do the job nicely. If you're in a closet with enough room, hang a bunch of clothes on the bars and pack the head space shelves with socks and other softs. Don't cover everything, just cover parts of it.

Our second stage is the diffusion, which you can think of as "screwing with the propagation of the sound waves." To visualize this, think back to the swimming pool example earlier. When someone dives into the pool, the splash sends ripples out in all directions. When those rippling waves hit an obstruction, some of their energy is reflected. If the waves hit a flat surface at a right angle to the wavefront, they reflect back where they came from. If they hit a tree trunk, or a rock, or a boat floating on the surface, they split and reflect at oblique angles, and those reflections then intersect with other reflections.

When wavefronts meet, one of three things happen:

• If they meet so that the peaks and troughs are in phase, the waves reinforce each other according to the rules of simple addition (a wave peak of +1cm meeting a wave peak of +.5cm gives a wavefront of 1.5cm). This kind of direct reinforcement is what you get in a squareish room with hard, parallel walls.

• When they are exactly 50% offset from one another (so that the troughs from one wave line up with the peaks from another), they are said to be 180 degrees out of phase, or "phase reversed," and they cancel each other out to zero—again, according to the rules of simple addition: -1cm + 1cm = 0. Earphones with active noise cancellation use exactly this trick—a speaker in the headphones generates a tone that's phase reversed from the environmental noise.

• When they meet without perfect alignment, they are partially out of phase, and parts of the signal are attenuated and boosted according to the laws of addition. These haphazard cancellations and reinforcements are the phase games that bring the richness out in the human voice. This is what you're aiming for when you do your diffusion.

To get this effect in your diffusion, you ideally want to do two things. First, you want your diffusion elements to be non-uniform. Set your major surfaces slightly off prime, break them up with blocks and doo-dads of various materials of various hardnesses. Ideally, you want to mix wood with acoustical foam, carpeting, and fabrics.

If you're on a generous budget, head out to a pro-audio shop and pick up wood-block baffle panels, sawtooth-shaped soft acoustical foam, and medium-stiff flat acoustical foam, then position these around the room so that 60-80% of the wall surface is covered. The permanence and quality of these materials will, in the long run, pay for themselves both in terms of reduced upkeep and reduced time spent in post.

If you're on a more limited budget, or don't have the option of affixing anything more substantial than posters to your walls, don't worry. Here are a couple ideas of how you can make your room sound beautiful, whether it's a bedroom or a closet (the ideas are applicable to other rooms of the house).

DIY Acoustical Tiles
Make your own tiles using cardboard boxes and memory foam

(old mattress toppers are great for this). Cut each into 12"x12" squares, then mate them with Elmer's glue so that the cardboard provides a rigid backing to the foam. Let them dry for a day, then pluck holes in the foam near the corners so that you can reach a finger or two all the way down to the cardboard. Hang them with push-pins inserted through the plucked holes and pushed through the cardboard. Using this method you can acoustically treat a breakfast nook or alcove for between $20 and $150, depending on the size of the space and whether you already have the foam on hand.

Library

If you've got a library, or a room that is mostly covered with bookshelves, your job is easy: move your bookshelves a few centimeters so that all are at an angle to the wall (and none of them wind up at directly opposing angles to each other). Once that's done, mess the books up—push some in a bit, pull some out a bit. You only need a few centimeters, but avoid any solid walls of books. Do this, and you'll have ideal diffusion with beautiful, voice-friendly resonant materials. Wood and books both reflect warm frequencies that enrich the sound of the human voice.

Closet

Your hanging clothes will help a lot—while they won't enrich the sound, they'll work wonderfully both for dampening and diffusion. Add to them some scrap 2x4 blocks stuck to the walls and the ceiling, affixing them with double-sided paint-safe tape (if you make the blocks small enough, they will stick to the wall safely without compromising your cleaning deposit). Cover the inside of the closet door with a removable heavy drape—moving blankets, quilts, doubled-over towels, and stage curtains work well.

Other Rooms

If you're in a studio apartment or have a living room that's quiet enough, and you have the ability to treat it acoustically, the principles in the above will serve you well, but there's one other option that might come in handy:

Freestanding cubicle walls cost about $40-50 each when new, and you can frequently get them for less at office supply surplus depots. By elevating them to a height equal to where your mic will be, you can construct a portable sound booth on a very affordable basis. They won't soundproof the room, but they will save you from nasty reflections without completely killing the resonance. Used alone, they'll give you a very adequate (though not ideal) sound treatment. Used in conjunction with some of the other techniques above, they can give the final polish to make your voice shine—and they have the added advantage of folding easily away.

> ### A note on materials:
> Many of the materials you'll use to treat your room, from books to memory foam to Sonex, are combustible and emit toxic gases when smoldering. Sound booths, night clubs, and other places with lots of acoustical treatments and electricity are notorious death traps in the event of fire. Be very careful when dealing with electricity or incandescent bulbs or other heat sources in your booth—and always have a clear exit path in case something catches light.

Super-low Cost

Most of the above assumes that you have the square footage available to spend making either a dedicated studio, or a studio that shares space with another room that you can tune without ruining your living space.

However, if you're living in a studio apartment, or have a large family, roommates, loud pets, or are otherwise seriously pressed for space, the above may not work for you. If it doesn't though, fear not! There are still a couple options open to you.

First, you can do as Nathan Lowell did for his first several books: record in your car. This works best if you have a well-insulated car and/or you keep your car in a garage, but even a low-end sedan or hatchback can serve you well if you don't have any better options. There's not much in a car that will sweeten your voice, but there's also not much that will make it go tinny, and a little EQ work in post production will sweeten it right up. This works best if you have a portable recording setup, so bear this in mind in the next section when we discuss equipment selection. Needless to say, if you've got a rag-top, this is not a viable option.

For the other ultra-low-cost option, you'll need to build either a recording shroud or a desk studio.

A recording shroud is basically a box lined with acoustical foam

Figure 6.1 Picture of a recording shroud

that you mount your mic inside. It isolates your microphone from side and back reflections (good and bad) and picks up a narrow cone of sound directly in front of the microphone. If you're using one in a live room, you'll need to do so with your back to a wall against which you've hung a heavy blanket or curtain to dampen the bad resonance as much as possible.

You can build a recording shroud for about $30-40, or buy a prefabricated one for $50-60. Some of the prefabs have the advantage of being collapsible for easy stowage.

On the other hand, if you have a corner you can set aside, a desk studio may be the way to go for you. You'll need acoustical foam tiles to plaster the walls in the corner with, as well as one to sit on the desktop underneath your microphone. If you're setting up in an inhospitable room, you'll also want to hang a heavy curtain or stand a cubicle wall behind you while you're recording to cut out back-splash from the walls behind you. A desk studio setup is often the setup of choice for home voice over artists on a budget, and it will often give you markedly better results than a shroud, as it gives you access to more room resonance. Though it won't sound quite as sweet as a well-tuned room, it will get the job done with professional latitude to spare.

Clean Power

There's one more thing you need in your room: clean power. If you're using a battery-powered signal chain (anchored by a laptop or a portable digital recorder), you've got clean power already. If, on the other hand, you're using something plugged into the walls, you might be in for a nasty surprise the first time you fire up your rig (if you overlook the plug itself).

Depending on the wiring in your home, the quality of your local substation and infrastructure, and the age of the transformers hanging from power poles in your neighborhood, you might have anything from squeaky clean to ultra-dirty power flowing through your walls.

Unfortunately, while I have wired the occasional house and done many an electrical survey, I'm not an electrician, nor am I qualified to dispense advice on how to debug the electrical in your building of choice. Fortunately, however, this isn't necessary, because rock'n'roll bands often have to deal with dirty and inconsistent power, and they have an inexpensive trick up their sleeves you can steal:

A power conditioner.

These are basically glorified power strips, designed to fit into an equipment rack, that restore the power flow to an even sine wave. They don't just protect against surges, they also soften power dips and provide a common ground so that you can avoid the dreaded ground loop buzz (which we'll cover in chapter 8). They run between $40 and $100 for a good Furhman or similar, and any of these models should be more than adequate for a home voice studio.

Or, you could use a newer model UPS (Uninterruptible Power Supply) which you can obtain from your preferred retailer for computing supplies. Most models manufactured after 2014 resynthesize the power modulation to match a sine wave generated by an on-board computer, and produce exceptionally clean power. If you already have one of these, or need one for another reason, this could be your solution.

Wrap-up

The decisions you make at this step will affect every later step. The quality and location of your room determines what equipment is best suited for it, how much post-production work you're going to have to do, how much cabling you need to buy. In any of the above scenarios, you will be able to build a room that will give you professional quality sound on a budget. Make your decisions based on what's best for your budget, your production needs, and your living situation, and make notes of your decisions.

Now that you know how to build your room, you need something to put in it.

120

Making Tracks

Chapter 7
The First Question Everybody Asks

When you're building a studio from the ground up, there's an optimal order in which to select your equipment. The quality of your room affects the range of mics you can pick from. The type of mic dictates the range of recording and mixing equipment you can select from, and so on down the line.

As I mentioned back at the beginning of the book, *"What microphone should I buy?"* is the first question everyone asks. Now that we've talked about the business end of things and built you a room for your microphones to live in, it's time to actually chose the mic and the mounting equipment.

Mounting Equipment
Microphone Stand

You've got three basic choices about how to mount your microphone: The desk stand, stick stand, and the boom stand.

The great advantage that the boom has over the stick is that it gives you room to maneuver without hitting the stand. If you're a gesticulater, if you prefer to read from a seated position, or if you might have problems with electromagnetic interference due to aging power lines outside your house, get a boom stand (I'll explain that last one at the end of the chapter).

Boom stands come in a variety of sizes, from ones designed to sit desk-side to stands big enough to fly overhead microphones above a drum set, and range in price from about $30 to about $300. To get a feel for what size is best for you, head to a local

Figure 7.1 From left to right: A desktop stand, approx 5 in. tall;, a stick stand, extends to 6 ft.; a boom stand, 4ft. tall with 3ft. adjustable arm

pro-audio shop or musician's store (like Guitar Center) and try a few out, pretending to read while moving in front of the mic as you would naturally do while reading.

If you've opted to build a corner desk studio, you'll probably opt for a desk stand. If you do, be sure to float it on top of a mouse pad, acoustical foam, or use a shock mount. If you don't, then every time you bump your desk you're going to get deep thumping noises on your tracks.

Shock Mount

A shock mount is a device that allows you to suspend your microphone from a spiderweb of rubber bands of various strengths and sizes, with the aim of reducing or eliminating handling noise when you bump the stand or reposition the mic. Some microphones come with shock mounts, some have internal shock-

Figure 7.2: An AT4040 XLR Condenser mic in a shock mount

absorption (to reduce handling noise—this kind will not save you from doing re-takes when you bump the stand), and you can buy shock-mounts separately if, after you start recording, you find you're knocking your stand a lot.

Pop Screens

B, T, K, G, and D, are five of the six plosive sounds in the English language. P is the sixth and the worst. As you might gather from the name "plosive," each is accompanied (to a greater or lesser extent) by explosive exhalation. When you ram a hard front of air into the capsule (see Dynamic vs. Condenser, below), it creates a very loud pop on your recording—much louder than the rest of your vocal track. Take it from someone who has had to remove pops from poorly

Figure 7.3: A side-address mic with pop screen

recorded audio: you have never experienced tedium so profound, and you don't want to. Don't "fix it in post," get it right the first time, for the sake of your sanity as well as your time budget.

There are two ways to prevent pop artifacts. The first is to speak off-axis to your microphone. Get close, then turn your face about fifty degrees, so that all your pops fly right past the microphone. This works very well, but some find it a difficult habit to train into (especially when you don't have previous vocal experience), and it can add a layer of complication to working the presence curve on some mics (see Presence Curves later in this chapter). If you find you can work the axis angles on your microphone, you can save yourself a few bucks on a pop screen.

The second is to use a pop screen. There are basically three kinds: steel, cloth, and DIY. The price of the steel and cloth screens are about the same, but they work differently. The steel has angled vents that breaks up and redirects the hard pops, while the cloth flexes to filter and dampen the pops. They each do the same job, though cloth tends to dampen all sound at the high end, which can be a problem if you have weak consonants, as it can make you sound muddy. They come mounted on the end of goosenecks, so they can be clamped to your mic stand and easily positioned between you and your microphone. Commercial pop screens cost between $15 and $60, depending on the size of the screen and the length of the gooseneck.

The DIY screen ain't elegant, but it is lot cheaper. Simply take an embroidery hoop and stretch a single layer of pantyhose over it, then trim the pantyhose to fit. Now, find a way to mount it in front of your microphone (coat hangers and duct tape are a popular combination).

Microphones

A "transducer" is a device which transforms one kind of energy (such as mechanical) into another (such as electrical). The heart of a microphone is the capsule, which is an assembly containing a transducer and its supporting equipment. Around the capsule, you'll find the shielding, the mounting hardware, the wiring, the body, and the screen.

Microphone Selection: Considerations

The first thing to consider when picking a microphone is: "What kind of recording are you going to do?"

Given that you're reading this book, I'm assuming "I want to make audiobooks" is the answer.

However, if you catch the bug you're likely to want to expand, even if ever-so-slightly. You might, for example, want to record original Foley, or do periodic call-in or group discussion podcasts or live-stream shows where you respond to reader emails or talk about writerly things, and these might benefit from a different microphone than you'd pick for solo voice recording applications—see the "Recording Techniques" section for a quickie discussion of these.

Polar Pattern

This is a polar pattern diagram—imagine it as the "Google Earth" of microphone sensitivity. The diagram views the microphone from the top, with the capsule facing toward the twelve-o'clock (zero degrees) position on the diagram. The microphone is understood to be at the center, the dark (outermost) circle is the shape of the microphone's sensitivity to sound. The concentric circles radiating out list sensitivity in reference dB (i.e. the measurements are relative to each other, rather than relative to

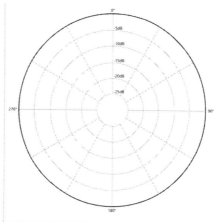

Figure 7.4: An omni-directional polar pattern

any absolute measurement), from 0dB at the outer edge, to -25dB at the innermost circle—this means that the mic is most sensitive closest in, and least sensitive furthest out, as you might expect. Since this polar pattern is for an omnidirectional microphone, it picks up sound evenly from from all angles. This won't be the case with the rest of the patterns we'll see.

Shotgun mics are so constructed that they preferentially catch sound in a very narrow cone. They're used to pick sound out from a crowd, to mic from overhead on a film set, and sometimes to

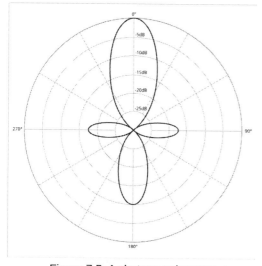

Figure 7.5: A shotgun polar pattern

mic individual instruments or voices in a recording studio.

The shotgun and the omnidirectional are the two extremes of the polar pattern range. For your home studio, you're looking for something in the middle.

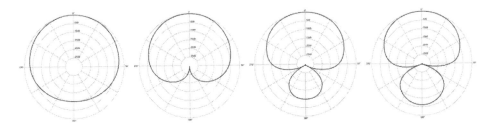

Figure 7.6: The Cardioid Family, from left to right: subcardioid, cardioid, supercardioid, hypercardioid

The cardioid pattern (second from left, above) looks like a heart, hence the name. It rejects signal coming from the back of the capsule, partially rejects signals from the side, and is most sensitive to sounds coming through a semicircular area in front of the capsule. The subcardioid (far left), supercardioid (in the second from right), and the hypercardiod (on the right) are subspecies of the cardiod, and together this family represents the Goldilocks zone for pickup patterns in a home studio. Using mics with these pickup patterns will help offset any imperfections in your soundproofing or sound treatment, while giving you the freedom to move around a little bit as you speak.

Some side-address (see *Form Factor*) condenser mics have more than one capsule, and a switch that allows you to toggle the polar pattern between omni-directional, cardioid, and dual-cardioid (which is the figure-eight pattern you see in Figure 7.7). This pattern allows two

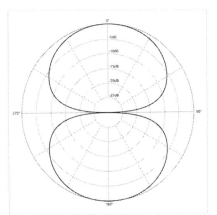

Figure 7.7: The dual-capsule figure-eight polar pattern

vocalists to share a single microphone—useful for duets, or for recording closely-acted repartee in a radio drama or multivoice audiobook.

Response Curve

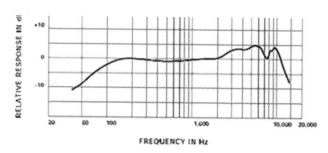

Figure 7.8: Response curve diagram for a Shure SM58

Every microphone has a response curve, such as the one above. The graph is laid out with the frequencies along the X axis and the sensitivity along the Y axis. To understand what this means for you as a vocalist, compare this sensitivity with the profile of the human voice as laid out in chapter 15.

Your mic's response curve shapes your voice before the signal even gets to the preamp. Once you get some experience under your belt, you'll be able to match a voice to a microphone with only a cursory glance at a spec sheet—well, you'll start in the right neighborhood, at any rate. Experience is the key part of the equation; the printed graph on its own never tells the whole story. For tips on getting that experience and on matching your voice to a microphone, see How to Find the Right Mic at the end of this chapter.

Form Factor

Excluding lavalieres and headsets (which you don't want to use for audiobook recording), vocal mics generally come in two form-factors: Front Address and Side Address.

A front-address microphone usually looks like a stick or an ice cream cone (occasionally it looks like a capital "P"), and the polar

Figure 7.9: A Front-Address microphone

pattern extends along the microphone's axis. They mount directly onto a mic stand without need for a shock mount, with a standard mic clip (though shock mounts are available for them). Most (though not all) dynamic microphones are front-address.

Figure 7.10: A side-address microphone with pop screen

A side-address microphone's polar pattern extends perpendicular to the mic's axis. Side-address mics often hang from above, or are mounted on shock mounts on a traditional stand. They are usually (though not always) condensers, though not all condensers are side-address.

Dynamic vs. Condenser

Since anything that vibrates can create an audio signal, people have used everything from lasers to silk ribbons to wooden tables to glass windows as the pickup element of a microphone. Some of these methods are utterly sublime (and very expensive), and others are quite hackerish and suitable mostly for surveillance and espionage.

The two microphone technologies whose price and performance

make them a best-fit for spoken word are: The dynamic and the condenser. Each of them have a nearly infinite variety of subspecies at a wide variety of price points, and the price curves on both follow a simple rule: the more accurate and sensitive they are, the more expensive they are. The most expensive can run into the thousands of dollars, and the least expensive (that are still professional quality) can cost as little as $40.

Condensers

Condensers are powered microphones that use a charged piece of foil to pick up sound. As electrons are displaced from the foil, the displacement pattern causes changes in the current, which gives you your sound. Generally speaking, they are more accurate than dynamics at any given price point. Because condensers are powered, they have two disadvantages: First, you'll need to choose a preamp that supplies phantom power (they won't work without phantom power)—this limits your options when we get to the next bit of electronics. Second, they can be more sensitive to some types of electromagnetic interference (think cell phone sync signals) than dynamics at the same price point.

If you ask the Internet what kind of microphone you'll need, you're going to hear one piece of advice among hobbyists: "Get a good condenser."

Good condensers aren't just good, they're incredible. They're also probably *not* what you want to use in your home studio.

Generally speaking, with spoken word in a home studio, you'll be micing close to the face in order to maximize your s/n ratio and to make up for any imperfections in the sound treatment in your booth. The closer you get to the mic, the less people are going to hear the room you're in, even if the room isn't a great room.

But because of their accuracy, condensers are remarkably unforgiving if you have bridge work or other dental appliances, or wet speech, or if your room is less than perfectly treated or soundproofed, or if you don't have good breath control. All the things that make condensers excellent scientific instruments and wonderful for micing Foley and film sets and choirs and jazz ensembles make them tricky customers where spoken-word home studio work is concerned. The more expensive the condenser is, the less suitable it's likely to be.

There's one further drawback, too, which you might be able to infer from the fact that condensers are sold in shock-absorbing foam. Because their elements are metal (often gold) foil, condensers tend to be very sensitive to shock—if you drop one wrong, your expensive microphone is going either into the repair shop, or into the garbage can. They're most at home in a dedicated studio where you can hang mics and leave them. If you've got a studio where you'll need to be putting things away or moving them around between sessions, think twice about a condenser.

That doesn't mean that you shouldn't use a good condenser if you can afford it and if you have one that's well-matched to your voice. Most of the mics I use for my work these days are condensers, even when I'm in ramshackle studios I've thrown together on a couple hours notice. They can serve you very well if you know what you're doing or are willing to learn. Currently, there are some beautiful cheap side-address condensers on the market in the $100-300 range that treat the human voice like gold. Now that you know the difficulties they can present, if you think the upsides of a condenser might be serve you well in your situation, it's worth starting out with testing mics in this price range.

Dynamics

Where condensers are electrostatic, dynamics are electromechanical: when you speak into one, a small magnet vibrates back and forth inside a coil in much the same way as happens inside a speaker. This generates oscillating electrical current that passes down the cable as signal. Dynamics do not require phantom power—they are thus universally compatible with anything that has an XLR port.

Dynamic microphones are the gold standard for vocal microphones in stage performance and radio studios around the world because they are, on average, kinder to the human voice than are condensers, and much more tolerant of close-up micing (i.e. they're less responsive to mouth noises). Because their mechanisms more closely mimic what happens in the human ear, they tend to yield a tone that feels more personal. Like photographing a lover in soft focus, a dynamic vocal mic projects the emotional reaction to a sound onto the sound itself, thus heightening the emotional response in the listener because of this doubling-up.

Because dynamics editorialize the voice, they tend to be less sensitive at the frequencies where unwanted noise generally occurs (these frequencies are much more obvious to the listener than background noise in the prime vocal spectrum). Because they're generally less sensitive, they're less prone to picking up sound leakage from outside the room. This means that preferring a dynamic mic to a condenser in a home studio can seriously save your bacon.

Most dynamic mics are more durable than most condenser mics. Vocal mics designed for rock'n'roll, like the AKG D 5 or the Shure SM-58, are internally shock-mounted to dampen handling noise. This means that if you brush your mic stand while recording, less of the sound will transfer to the track (although you'll still want to do a re-take). More importantly, it means that if you drop the microphone, you're probably not going to damage it.

Some of you are thinking "Ha! I'd never drop a microphone." Don't bet on it. I've seen intelligent, competent, completely sober, healthy 30 year veterans knock over mic stands, trip over cables, and drop equipment (from mics to amps to violins) worth thousands of dollars, and some of that equipment got ruined. Unless your stands are bolted to the floor, you never change your mics, and you never allow children or cats in your studio, then, sooner or later, you'll drop a mic. Everyone does.

Although most dynamic mics are durable, there are exceptions. For a long time I had a couple vintage dynamics that were extremely delicate and had to be packed in foam and treated like eggs. Why did I keep them around if they were old and fragile? Because they had unusual characteristics—one wasvery good for micing people with rich, quiet voices. The other was specially designed to pinch-hit for high-end condenser mics when phantom power wasn't available.

Most dynamics, though, are of the robust variety and designed for vocals. All other things being equal, they are an excellent fit for any home recording studio.

Presence Curves

Dynamic vocal mics also often have something called a *presence curve*. When you use them from more than a few inches away, their response curve is relatively flat. But the microphone itself has a powerful low-end resonance, so the closer you get to the microphone, the more it accentuates your low frequencies. Get within two inches, and speak quietly, and it'll give you an amazingly sexy bedroom voice. Get a little closer and speak powerfully, and you've got the Voice of God. The closer you get, the more pronounced this effect is.

The practical upshot is that you can play a dynamic vocal mic like an instrument, giving you much greater performance latitude. Come in close to whisper and to narrate, back off a few inches to play a character. With no further audio processing, you'll create an acoustically rich and varied performance. You'll have heard this (probably without knowing it) in rock'n'roll vocals. But if you watch stand-up comedy concerts, you've probably seen it: Bill Cosby, George Carlin, Richard Pryor, Dave Chapelle, and Louis CK all rely heavily on their ability to manipulate the presence curve of a dynamic microphone.

Roll-Off

Some microphones have a special feature called roll-off that solves problems that can arise in some recording situations. Such microphones can throw away all sounds below a certain threshold, without creating any of the annoying artifacts that noise gates and other digital do-dads can introduce. They won't protect you from an unquiet room, but they can attenuate a just-barely-audible rumble from the street outside. This feature is generally only available on very expensive instrument mics, but sometimes manufacturers sneak it onto lower-end vocal mics. It's worth keeping your eyes peeled.

How To Find The Right Mic

If you don't have a lot of experience with microphones yet, I highly recommend you go to a pro-audio store with a friend and test several of them before making your final decision.

Why bring a friend? Price bias. It's human nature to fool ourselves into preferring more expensive items over less expensive ones, and with microphones, that can kill you. The right microphone for your studio is the right one for your voice for that specific application. Price does not count. In fact, some of the best vocal mics in the world—like the Shure SM58, SM57, and the Audio Technica AT2020—are under $100. The Beyerdynamic M201, the BBC's preferred studio microphone, is only $300. Once you're in the pro-audio range, all that matters is "What's the best match for my voice in my budget?"

In the pro-audio shop, tell your friend your budget, and have him fetch you a selection of mics. Listen to yourself on the headphones, and have your friend do the same. Pick the one that suits you best, and don't look at the price till afterward.

I use a different mic for narration (AKG C460b—a $400 condenser) than I do for voice-over work (Shure SM58—a $99 dynamic), and a third mic for character acting (Shure SM57—the 58's kissing cousin) because of the different subtleties they bring to my voice, and I keep a collection of others around for actors and gang recording situations. For my daily podcast, I use the built-in mics on my DR-40 portable recorder (which I'll discuss later in this chapter).

For some budgets (such as mine when I was starting out), even $100 is a painful amount to spend. Here are a couple facts to take the edge off:

• Good microphones hold their value very well. If, after working with your mic, you discover that it's not a good fit, don't fret. You'll likely be able to recoup about 70-80% of the value on Ebay or Craigslist, whether you sell it off now or in five years. I have a 50 year old mic in my collection that still sells used for just under $1000.

• If you find a microphone you love, and the sticker price is too steep, there are two good ways (beyond ordinary comparison shopping) to get a better deal. First, check the competing models from other manufacturers—you might find a comparable model on special. Second, check the pro-audio rental houses in your area for used mics. You can often find excellent deals on scratch-and-dent items that have seen heavy use. Don't worry about the "heavy use" part; microphones made for the stage are designed to stand up to just about anything. If it works when you test it out, it'll likely keep working for years despite any cosmetic damage. It may even live longer than you do.

USB Mics

The age of podcasting and inexpensive studio gear has brought with it a plethora of cheap equipment with varying degrees of suitability for audiobook work.

The first of these are the USB microphones such as those put out by Blue, Rode, and MXL (and a number of other good manufacturers). These mics plug into the USB port on your laptop or desktop over a standard USB printer cable, and appear on your computer as a second sound card. If you're looking for an entry-level turnkey solution for your home studio, this could be the way to go.

However, there are some things to bear in mind. A good microphone can last fifty years or more with proper care (occasional tightening of screws, re-soldering of connectors, etc.), and it holds its value exceptionally well. The basic technological innovations that make for good microphones all happened eighty years ago—the only advances since then have been small tweaks enabled by new materials and computer-assisted acoustical modeling. Progress is incremental, not exponential, and each mic has a unique sound that remains desirable for some applications more-or-less forever. And, because they use the same connectors and cables as all other studio equipment (usually XLRs, less frequently 1/4"), if you decide to change your microphone (or add more microphones) you can do so without changing your other equipment.

USB mics are not components. Unfortunately, they are the endpoint of a studio. You can't buy more mics and cables and add them to your board to record more than one track at a time. You can't upgrade your studio without replacing your entire acquisition pipeline—since it's integrated into the mic body—and the microphone itself isn't going to last more than a decade or so.

Why not? Electronics contain caustic chemicals that eventually corrode themselves to death. And electronics also introduce the nasty specter of obsolescence: USB mics have their A/D converters and their preamps integrated into their bodies. Since the digital side of audio technology moves at the speed of Moore's Law, that means that the digital innards of your USB mic won't hold their value like normal studio equipment does. When you decide to upgrade (and you will, since the preamps in these devices are just noisy enough that they'll begin to bug you after a while), you won't recoup as much of your outlay as you would selling off used pro gear.

One further consideration with USB gear:

USB has a maximum cable run of 5 meters (just under 16 ½ feet), and USB mics pipe audio to a computer so you can record the signal. Unfortunately, almost all computers have fans, and fan noise is one of the banes of indie audio producers. Unless you're willing to punch a hole in the wall, or stick your computer on the other side of a double-glazed window in your sound booth, you may have difficulty minimizing the fan noise in your studio with that kind of limitation.

Good quality USB equipment isn't to be sneered at—the best of it is studio gear with extra bits soldered on inside. If you're on a tight budget, it's a worthy first step for your recording studio. But if you can afford to get component gear and are willing to spend a little time learning to set it up well, you'll be better served in the long run.

For reference, the price difference between a decent USB microphone setup and a pro-level (but feature-limited) component setup is approximately $70-80 at today's prices.

Portable Recorders

If you're looking to do more than just record audiobooks—for example, if you're also wanting to do an interview podcast—or if you're on the road a lot and need to record in hotel rooms in between business meetings, a portable recorder might be a better first-fit for you than a component studio.

Portable recorders are hand-held devices with professional microphones and electronics built in. They can be mounted on a mic stand when in the studio, and set up pretty much anywhere you like when you're on the road. They range in price from about $200 to about $700, with many models sporting several external XLR jacks, giving you the option to upgrade to a more suitable microphone when your budget permits, and to record larger groups on-the-fly as needed.

In the previous edition of this book, I judged these appliances unsuitable for audiobook work due to their noisy preamps. Technology has moved on since then. The preamps, while still a little noisier than I generally like when paired with a dynamic microphone, are stunningly quiet when paired with a good condenser. The built-in mics have also come into their own, to the point where I now recommend them as the best way to start a home studio.

At the time of this writing, TASCAM and Zoom make the best portable digital recorders in the business. I highly recommend giving them a serious look.

Wrap-up

More than any other single piece of equipment, your microphone determines the character of your sound, it shapes your physical and verbal performance dynamics, and it dictates the range of support equipment you need and can use. Take the time to pick the right microphone for your voice. With a little care, you can put together a studio that will serve for producing a good audiobook on even the meanest of budgets.

138

Making Tracks

Chapter 8

Connections

Cables are the nervous system of any studio, and without knowing your cables and connectors you're going to have trouble reading spec sheets to make sure all your equipment matches up.

Types of Connectors

Audio equipment connectors and their applications sort out along the following lines:

XLR

This is the XLR. In the audio world, this is the gold standard—the highest fidelity, the lowest noise, and the most expensive of the analog cables. They're the standard for microphones, and can also be used to do patch work at the mixing board and between components (though they're less common there).

Figure 8.1: XLR connectors

XLRs used in audio work are technically XLR3s, since they have three pins (positive, negative, and ground). The male end contains a spring lock (with a release button), the female contains the notch for the lock. This lock makes XLR connections very secure, enough that they can stand up to the yanking that happens when you trip over a cable—if you're running cables across walkways, it is therefore vital that you strain-relieve your cables (see "Strain Relief" later in this chapter). XLR connectors, when free from corrosion, are high fidelity enough that XLR cables can be strung together end-to-end without much signal loss.

When buying XLR cables for your home studio, make sure you get XLR3—cables with more pins won't fit any of your gear. If buying XLR cables for equipment you purchased on the gray market, make sure that the pin-outs match. Some British gear, for example, has a different ground/signal configuration than the US standard, and using a cable that doesn't compensate for this can give you a phase-reversed, muted, or otherwise screwy signal. If you're using a mix of gear with mismatched pin-outs, you may find it more expedient to make your own cables; check out this eHow article for instructions http://www.ehow.com/how_7778725_solder-xlr-jacks.html (or, if the URL has expired, do a google search for "how to solder xlr"—you'll find a number of helpful articles and videos).

XLRs are typically balanced cables, meaning that they are constructed so as to protect themselves from EM interference (when plugged into devices of equal impedance). This is important, since cables are essentially antennae, and the longer a cable is the more exposure you've got to picking up noise. Whenever possible, no matter what kind of cable you're buying, buy balanced cables.

TS and TRS

The next most common type of audio cable in a home studio is 1/4" patch cable (the TRS, or tip-ring-sleeve connector). Most commonly used to patch between equipment (from the board to the EQ or the A/D, for example), it's also the style of connector you'll find on your headphones and on instrument cables.

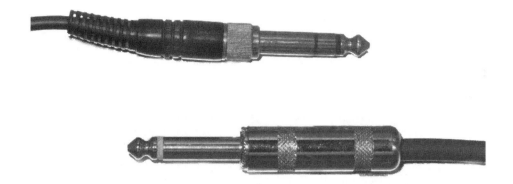

Figure 8.2: 1/4" Connectors: TRS (top) and TS (bottom)

Above to the left you see the three segments of the Tip-Ring-Sleeve connector. On the right you see the two segment Tip-Sleeve (TS) connector. Generally speaking, TRS cables are balanced, and can carry a stereo signal (though when carrying stereo they are unbalanced). TS cables carry unbalanced mono.

TS and TRS cables come in a variety of sizes, from 1/4" (sometimes called "quarter-inch" or "patch cables" rather than "TS" or "TRS") down to 1/16". The middling size, the 3.5mm "mini-jack," is what you'll find on most ear buds for portable media players.

RCA

RCA cables are ones you're probably familiar with from hooking up your home stereo or DVD player. Each cable carries a single unbalanced channel. In pro-audio applications, you'll find RCA connectors in two places:

Figure 8.3: RCA cables

• As inserts on mixing boards, for bringing CD and other consumer audio players into the mix.

• As SPDIF ports, carrying 2-channel digital signals between components and (sometimes) to monitor speakers.

Lightpipe (TOSLink)

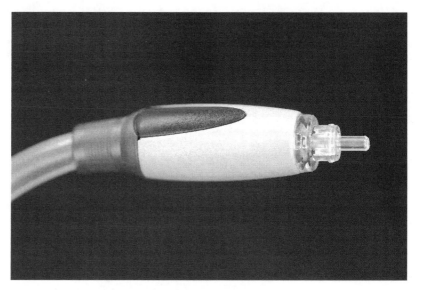

Figure 8.4: Lightpipe/TOSLink cable end

These are fiber optic cables that carry multichannel digital audio (anywhere from 2 to 16 channels). They're common on portable hard disk recorders, multiplexing A/D converters, some multichannel mixers, and on some home theater equipment—usually they will be offered instead of SPDIF, less frequently they will be offered alongside. Due to the high fidelity transmission (and their invulnerability to EM interference), I prefer them over SPDIF wherever the equipment gives me the option.

Unless/until you get into simultaneous multichannel recording, you're unlikely to run across one of these, except on the back of a BluRay player. However, if you do, there are four things to be aware of:

• These things are expensive, and you need to treat them like gold, because...

• Due to the fact that they're spun glass fiber carrying an optical signal, any kink, fray, or cut is going to render them unusable (other cables can sustain a terrific amount of abuse before they become too noisy/flakey to use)

• Not all optical cables have the same shaped connector. Your equipment will usually come with a sample cable—even if it breaks, hold on to it so you can match it to a replacement cable at the store.

• In a pinch, you can use mismatched connectors with the proper application of duct tape or silicone sealant (this is not recommended, but it has saved my bacon on a couple of occasions).

Firewire, USB, and MIDI

Figure 8.5: Connectors from left to right: Firewire (6-pin), USB mini and USB standard, standard MIDI (top) and MIDI-Joystick (bottom)

Here are the three computer cables that most often show up in home studios. Firewire and USB connect A/D converters to your computer, and MIDI (and sometimes USB) connects your computer to MIDI-controllable devices.

USB (above, middle) is the most common interface you'll find on consumer audio gear. It's quick, it's easy, the cables are the same ones that hook up your printer and your external hard disks, and almost every computer in the world comes with a USB port. USB's bandwidth is limited, so USB interfaces typically only carry two channels of audio at a time—the upshot is that, if you've got six mics feeding into your board and you're pulling it out via USB, the signal you'll get in your computer will be the mixed stereo signal you'd get from your mains. If you're building an inexpensive multitrack studio, chances are you'll start with a board that has a built-in USB A/D. See the chapter 9 for tips on picking a mixer with a built-in A/D that you won't have to throw away if/when you want to expand to a multitrack recording setup.

Firewire (above, leftmost) is the interface of choice for higher-end gear. Compared to USB, its higher bandwidth and sturdier construction mean it's capable of delivering 8-to-16 channels of audio to your hard disk simultaneously (which is a great advantage when doing gang recordings for podcasts or audio dramas, or for producing music, but isn't usually called for in audiobook production). Firewire cables tend to be more expensive per foot than USB cables.

MIDI (above, rightmost) is a cable that carries control signals rather than audio signals. It's used to control synthesizers, but unless you're using a keyboard for music or Foley you're likely only to have call to use one with external surfaces to control your mixing software (discussed in chapter 14).

Industry Standard Power Cable

Power cables that look like this are now the standard for most electronics. Since almost every piece of equipment you'll buy comes with a power cable included, it may seem silly for me to mention it here, but sometimes you get caught short—literally, when the cable that came

Figure 8.6: An industry standard power cable (with US wall connector)

with your gear is too short to make it to the plug. You also might find yourself shy a cable if you buy used gear, as people frequently hoard these things (and thus "accidentally" don't box them up with used equipment), and there's very little more irritating than having your whole operation held up by the least expensive piece of equipment in the whole chain.

My advice: Keep a couple extras on hand. Eventually, you'll need one, whether it be for your audio gear or your computer or your tea kettle or your treadmill.

What To Buy

When selecting your audio cables, be prepared for a lot of marketing bullshit. There are only four things you really need to pay attention to with your XLR and TS/TRS cables:

• *Is it balanced?*

Except on older equipment that might not play nice with balanced TRS cables in TS ports, balanced is always preferable to unbalanced.

• *Gold connectors*

Gold connectors are one of the few blingy upgrades that make a marginal difference—they resist corrosion, extending the life of your connectors. When they won't cost you more than an extra few pennies, grab them. If the price difference is more than that, don't worry about it.

• *Shielding*

When faced with a choice, the cable with better shielding is the one to prefer. Our world is only going to get noisier, electromagnetically speaking, and shielding is another line of defense against the EM noise that can seep into your signal.

• *Gauge and durability*

Unrelated to the shielding, the thickness of your mic cables and patch cables helps protect you from bending them too sharply, which makes them less prone to internal breakage during normal use. Larger girth also spreads out impact force when something heavy (like a foot or a desk) gets set on top of the cable. Don't go crazy with girth, as you still need to be able to roll your cables up and snake them through your studio, but a little extra girth can extend their lives, and is worth a few extra pennies per foot.

• *Length*

Because cables are essentially antennas, keep your cable runs as short as possible while leaving slack for strain relief, vertical runs, and ergonomic tweaking—for example, if your mic stand is six feet away from your board, you'll probably want a fifteen foot cable to connect it up.

However, if you stick with audiobook production past the first book or two, chances are you're going to want to do some gang recording (whether for podcast, for radio, or for personal memories) that will necessitate reconfiguring your studio. It's therefore a good idea to keep a couple extra long XLR cables (~50ft) and perhaps one extra long TRS cable in reserve, for special occasions.

Pretty much anything else you hear advertised about cables—platinum shielding that supposedly creates a "cleaner" signal vs. copper, or special solder or other do-dads that allege "richer, more vibrant" sound, etc.—is marketing bullshit, and falling for it can cost you a premium when you don't need to pay it.

How many cables will you need? That depends on the equipment you select. Make a list of everything you need, then buy two of each. Cables do fail, break, and sustain internal damage that can render them useless. Since they're not exactly sold at 7-11, it's best to keep backups on hand.

Adapters

Adapters let you to use one kind of cable (for example, an RCA pair) with another kind of port (such as a mini-jack). With the exception of optical, adapters exist for literally every jury-rig job you can imagine. In addition to cables, it's wise to keep some adapters around. Here's what you'll need in a basic adapter kit:

• A Y-adapter for each kind of cable you have.

• Male-to-female converters, at least one for every kind of connection you have.

• Format converters to and from (i.e. with the cable sexes pointing in both directions) each kind of non-digital cable you have. Example: XLR to 1/4", 1/4" to minijack, etc.

• A section-separated plastic box (such as you might use for fishing lures or Christmas ornaments) to keep them in.

Adapters can come either as little do-dads that you stick on the end of a cable, or as cables with mismatched ends. Each have their uses. Adapters can also be quite expensive, so the trick to building a kit without a large initial outlay is to just pick up one or two anytime you're at a pro-audio shop, or add one to your Amazon order every time you buy something there. The more activity your studio sees, the more you'll need your adapters, and having them on hand makes all the difference.

Care and Feeding

Inside their vinyl sleeves, your cables are complex assemblages of braided metal wires and insulation. The braiding gives the signal extra bandwidth over a single thick strand, and allows the cables to bend more easily, but it also introduces fragility. Repeated flexing and twisting causes metal fatigue and will eventually make the little strands of the braid break. As the strands break, your cable gets noisy, transmits signal less readily, and eventually becomes unusable.

That said, a well-maintained cable can last for years, sometimes decades. Here's how to treat your cables to get the best value for your dollar:

• Do not crush, kink, crease, fold, or step on your cables. This can break them internally.

• Coil your cables properly, and not too tightly. Coiling a cable for storage or just to get it out of the way is exactly like coiling a lasso: you want to reverse the direction of twist once per turn. The easiest way to do this is to give the cord an overhand twist on the first loop, and an underhand twist on the second loop. Varying your grip like this will give you a cable that pays out cleanly when you hang on to one end and throw the coil across the room (which is how you check if you're doing it right)—it'll also keep torsional stress from building up on those fiber-thin copper wires that you want to protect. Too much torsional stress can make some of those little wires shear.

• Always strain-relieve your cables. To do this, leave six inches to a foot of slack at each end, dangling in a loose loop secured either with velcro or just set on the desk or hanging loose from the mic stand. When someone trips over the cable (and eventually someone will), this will save your cable from sharp shock, and it'll keep your gear from being yanked onto the floor with loud and expensive consequences. And, of course, never stretch a cable taut, even if the ends are strain-relieved.

• Periodically unplug all your cables and clean the connectors. Electricity flowing over metal encourages oxidation, which impedes signal flow. From time to time, give your connectors a good polish with terry cloth or microfiber polishing cloth (don't use sandpaper, polishing compound, or a wire brush unless you can actually see corrosion—we're cleaning off the corrosion that hasn't advanced that far yet).

• While you've got your cables out, lay them out on your driveway or in a parking lot on a hot afternoon. The heat will soften the metal and help undo the cable's "memory" of how it's been run (that memory is a manifestation of metal fatigue), and once cooled and coiled it should behave just like new again (assuming there are no internal breaks).

• Eventually, your cables will start to get noisy. Assuming they haven't suffered any impact damage (see #1 on this list), this is probably either because the solder joints in the connectors have started to weaken, or the final foot of the cable (which typically sustains the most bending stress) has accumulated enough internal breaks to cause a problem. Solder joints can be inspected visually—if they need re-soldering, and you're not good with an iron, it's not hard to find someone who can do it for you for a fraction of the price of replacing the cable. If the solder is still in good condition, it's time to give your cable a haircut. Cut the last foot off each end, then re-solder the connector onto the new cable ends, and pat yourself on the back: you've just extended that cable's life by another five or ten years, at zero cost.

Best Practices

Labeling

When running cables in your studio, spare a moment to grab a sharpie and some sticky tags or colored gaff tape and label your cables. When you're setting it up, you know which cable is going where—but since even a one-channel studio usually has more than one of a given kind of cable, the chances are that in six months, you'll forget something and wind up tracing cable runs by hand (which is time consuming and can involve moving furniture). Getting color-coded cables at the outset helps a lot with this as well.

Grouping (Velcro ties)

Behind any sound board, little cable gnomes spend their time tangling things up. The easiest way to foil their evil plans is to use Velcro cable ties to group cables that are running along similar routes—but be sure not to interfere with strain-relief when you do this.

Figure 8.7: A Velcro tie used to secure a strain relief loop on an XLR cable

Keep Power and Signal Separate

Mains power, which runs from the walls to your equipment, alternates polarity 60 times per second (50 in the UK and Europe). When you run power cables next to audio cables, you're gonna get bleed-off, and that's one of the major causes of the dreaded "Ground Loop Buzz" or "60 Cycle Hum" that you'll hear sound engineers complain about loudly. No kidding: 60 cycle hum is THE worst problem in audio engineering. It is hard to track down, a pain in the ass to fix, and it ruins recordings. Where the audience will accept white noise if it's at a consistent (and low) level, they will not tolerate noise that sounds like a tone or a buzz.

Here's how to prevent The Buzz:

• *Do Not Run Power Parallel to Signal*

Parallel cable runs create the worst kind of sympathetic resonance between the cables. Keep any unavoidable parallel cable runs separated by at least a foot. If you can't avoid crossing your power cables over your audio cables, cross at 90 degrees to minimize the exposure surface, giving your audio cable's shielding the best chance of keeping out the interference.

• *Boom Stand*

Sometimes your buzz is coming from "out there." Old infrastructure—like the transformer atop the power pole in front of your neighbor's house—can bleed off a god-awful amount of noise, and none of the tricks above will help you. If you find yourself in this situation, there are two things you can do. This is the cheap one:

While your cables are balanced, your microphone isn't. Dynamic or condenser, if nothing else has worked, then chances are this is what's picking up the noise. But, like an antenna, you can orient it for better or worse reception. Plug your headphones into your board, then, listening to the noise, move your microphone around in all its axes (tilt, swing, elevation) until you find the quietest spot—typically this is where the capsule is at a right angle to the source of the radiation.

• *Faraday Cage*

This is the expensive solution to infrastructure bleed-off. Install electrically grounded chicken wire over the ceiling and all the walls. Cover them with plaster to keep the aesthetics of the room together, and install your acoustical treatments on top of it. This will create a Faraday cage for a range of the radio spectrum, and will severely attenuate the bleed-off noise—be prepared, it may also screw with your WiFi and cell reception. This is, obviously, the most expensive option.

Chapter 9
Preamps and Boards

Levels Games

In your living room, your television is connected to a number of devices: DVD or Blu-Ray or VHS machines, home theater systems, DVRs, gaming consoles, etc. If you've ever tried to tap the audio wires directly with headphones, you'll have noticed that it's so quiet you can barely hear it. This is because the signal shuttling through those cables is all at *line level,* which needs amplification before it's passed along to speakers. In a home theater, that amplification is done by the receiver.

In your studio, too, signal is passed around between your components at line level and then amplified for output to your speakers or headphones. The outboard EQ, the patch signals from the CD player or the MP3 player, and any other pre-computer gear you use will all feed signal to your mixing board at line level.

If you've only got a single-step recording setup (like a portable recorder or a USB mic), then line level is what's getting passed to the recording software.

The problem is, microphones don't produce a line level signal. They produce a far weaker signal, a *mic leve*l signal. For a mic level signal to participate in the audio production process, it needs to be amplified. Since this amplification happens before the main overall output amplification, the circuit that gives this bump is called the preamplifier, or "preamp."

A "good" preamp, whether it's a standalone unit or it's integrated into an A/D or into a mixing board, is quiet at base load and does not generate distortion when hit with a spike (like a hard P spoken into the microphone). Generally speaking, the quieter the preamp, the more expensive the appliance—generally, but not always. The last decade has seen the advent of extremely quiet inexpensive preamps in some manufacturers' mixing boards.

In an audiobook studio, the preamp is the second most important piece of equipment (the microphone is the first).

Noise Floor

The "noise floor" is the noise you hear when nothing is going into the microphone. Some of it comes from your room, some of it comes from electromagnetic interference—we've already talked about how to minimize those. The rest of your noise comes from your equipment, and you minimize it by picking good equipment. In technical terms, for a professional-sounding recording, you want your cumulative noise floor at or below -50dB—this is the loudest you'll find on any professionally-produced audiobooks, and if your noise floor is this high, you'll need to be careful in editing to keep that floor consistent while mixing (since the human ear is more sensitive to changes than it is to absolute levels).

A professional noise floor for recording purposes is -60dB or below. We'll get into how to measure the noise floor in chapter 11 where I talk about signal analysis.

Types Of Preamps

Though there are other sorts on the market, for a home studio you're usually going to want one of five basic types of preamps:

Integrated Into the Microphone

If you're going the ultra-budget route, you're going to want to take a look at the better-quality USB microphones. When you do, don't just look at the quality of the mic, test out the quality of the electronics. USB mics include their own preamps which (depending on the model of the mic) are controlled through gain knobs on the microphone body itself or through a software control panel that you'll install on your computer.

USB interface

M-Audio is one of a number of manufacturers who produce little one track or two track USB audio interfaces for under a hundred bucks. Typically they're a couple inches across, and accept one or two mic level inputs and sometimes one line level input. They're designed for musicians who are on the road and wanting to record rough-tracks, but many of them have spectacularly good preamps and are an excellent choice for a home audiobook studio.

Figure 7.1: Blue Yeti, a popular high-quality USB microphone

External Solid State Preamp

By "external" I specifically mean "does not have a USB interface." These have been around forever. Musicians will often carry them to use in clubs with substandard mixing boards, and studio owners will buy them to use on boards whose preamps have gone on the fritz, but are too expensive to fix and too otherwise desirable to replace. External preamps are available with and without phantom power supplies.

To use these in a home studio, you'll have to plug their line-out to the line-in port on your soundcard. Since consumer soundcards tend to be vulnerable to EM interference generated within the computer, this is not your best option unless you already have an upgraded prosumer-or-better sound card.

Outboard/Rack Mount

This takes the external preamp one step further. Old hands at sound recording sometimes complain that digital technology has robbed the warmth and richness from recordings. They claim that the old analog equipment made everything sound sweeter just as a side-effect of the way it was built.

They're actually right about this. Some parts of the post-production step called "sweetening" has to do with bringing warmth back into the voice that hyper-accurate digital equipment can sap away. Producers with truly extravagant tastes and budgets sometimes opt for a rack-mount tube amp.

These gadgets often sound gorgeous, and because they use vacuum tubes instead of solid-state electronics for their amplification they respond to sound in a non-linear way that is greatly coveted among audiophiles. They're best for music (vocals and instruments) but can add a subtle depth to spoken word as well. Check your wallet before you even think about it though: a good one will run between $800 and $3000, and they're very, very fragile.

Mixing Board

Mixers are devices that take two or more audio channels and allow you to control the way they interact (relative volume and pan) before you send them out into the world. A mixing board is a mixer that's laid out in such a way as to facilitate the real-time adjustment of the sound, and often include knobs to control the signal from outboard gear, three-to-five band on-board EQ, low-end roll-off, and sometimes other shinies like reverb,

Figure 9.2: A mixing board, annotated with board geography

compression, etc. Mixing boards generally have preamps built into some, though not all, of their tracks. To tell where the preamps are, look for the XLR inputs.

Preamps in mixing boards vary widely in quality depending on manufacturer and price point. Currently, Behringer has very quiet preamps, even in their $50 two-track boards—and many of them come with a perfectly adequate USB-based A/D converter.

A/D Converter

While overkill for most home studios, multitrack rack-mounted A/D converters are available for between $200 and $2000. These will often have optical, SPDIF, Firewire, and USB outputs and, on the more expensive models, allow for simultaneous multitrack recording. Many will accept both mic level and line level input, so they can be used as direct preamps or as a module in the signal chain in conjunction with your board and other outboard gear. My personal preference is to use modular equipment so that, in case of failure, I can swap out a single piece of the pipeline.

Although this is my preference, and I recommend it for large or long-term installations, I do not recommend this approach for a new producer. Every piece of gear in the pipeline is another potential source of noise, as well as another expense.

All About Boards

Although ergonomic differences exist between manufacturers, mixing boards are generally laid out so that the signal flows from top to bottom, and then from left to right. Here's how it works:

Channels

Each of your inputs is a channel (or a track). The channels are laid out next to one another in strips down the length of the board, with track one on the left, track two next-to-left, and so on. Usually, preamps are on the first few tracks, while later tracks are reserved for instruments, CD players, and such-like.

Down the channel strip, you will find, in this order:

1) Inputs, Sends, and Inserts

Some boards keep this along the top of the face, others keep them on the back, and a very few use a combination. These are the ports where your signal comes into the board. Inputs accept sound from a source (such as a microphone or a CD player) into the system. Sends take that input sound, and divert it to an outboard processor (such as an outboard EQ or Ring Modulator), while Inserts accept that sound back into the board on the same track. On channels with a pre-amp, the Insert point is post-pre-amp, so this is where you bypass the pre-amp with a line-level input.

2) Phantom Power Toggle

For boards equipped with phantom power, this is where you turn it on and off. On for condenser mics, off for dynamics. If you switch it on when you don't need it, you'll introduce extra noise into the system.

3) Pad Toggle

Only available on some boards, this attenuates the input signal by about 20dB.

4) Gain

This is the amount of amplification you're applying to your signal. So-called because it controls the amount of volume that your signal *gains* while passing through the channel.

5) Roll-off Toggle

Some boards have low-end roll-off that perform a function similar to the feature on certain microphones, though it works differently. This kind of roll-off is actually a hard-wall *high-pass filter* (meaning that all frequencies *higher* than the cutoff *pass* through), where all signal below a certain frequency threshold (typically 80Hz) is rejected outright (see chapter 15 for more info on frequency-based filtering and other types of EQ treatment). For music, this can sometimes create problems, but for vocals this is a wonderful feature to have.

6) Compressor Toggle and Knee Control

Some boards have built-in dynamic range compression,

controlled by a toggle switch and a pot (i.e. a potentiometer, or knob) that controls the threshold/knee of the compression curve (see chapter 15). While useful for live-recording roundtable discussions, resist the urge to use this when recording audiobooks. For reasons we'll explore later, this is the wrong point in the signal chain to use a compressor, and the compressors available on most boards are not well-suited to what you'll need in an audiobook when compared to those you'll have available to you in post.

7) Channel EQ

Three pots controlling the tone of the channel, corresponding to low, medium, and high frequencies. Some boards also include a sweep knob here, which allows you to control the shape of the EQ curve in the mid-range, which can be useful for attenuating undesirable frequencies while preferring desirable ones.

The channel EQ is your first opportunity for sweetening, it's also your last opportunity to clean up any noise before the signal leaves your board.

8) Pan Control

This is the first of your routing controls. It positions your signal on the left-right stereo axis. Turned all the way left, the signal will pass only to the left channel. Turned all the way to the right, it will pass only to the right channel. Position it somewhere in the middle, and it will split the difference proportionally.

9) Mute and Solo buttons

"Mute" mutes the track. "Solo" mutes all tracks except those where "Solo" is depressed. Unless you're recording live music, you won't use these much, but if you accidentally hit them and don't know it, you might panic when suddenly the sound on the board goes all wonky.

10) Routing Buttons

This is where you decide where you want the signal to go after it leaves the channel. Options typically include Mains (which sends the signal to the main output ports), Subs (which sends the channel to a second set of outputs available on most boards), and Pre-Fader Listening or PFL, which sends the signal to the headphone port. The

Mains and Subs are the *buses* on your board—they are signal control blocks that do not directly accept input from outside the system. Buses are also important in post-production, where they serve an analogous function in software to how they work in hardware.

11) Faders

On smaller boards these are just knob-style pots. On bigger boards, they're sliding potentiometers. Either way, they allow you one final volume adjustment before the signal goes to the mixdown.

Put it all together, and it looks like what you see in *Figure 9.3*.

Mixdown

Once your signal leaves the channel, it moves to the mixdown block at the far right of the board. Here you'll find, from bottom to top:

1) Faders

For both mains and subs. This is your last opportunity to control your output volume level. Typically each output channel has independent volume control (subs-right, subs-left, mains-right, mains-left, etc.).

2) Headphone Port and Headphone Volume Control

This is where you plug your headphones in to monitor the per-channel signal quality, or to listen if you prefer to monitor your performance as you read.

3) V/U Meters

These give you a visual readout of your volume. On most modern boards, this is a pair of LED strips, with green covering the lower levels, yellow indicating that you're nearing saturation, and red meaning that your signal level is too hot. Ideally, you want your mix to regularly peg theyellow range as you speak, without peaking into the red.

Figure 9.3:
A board channel

4) Output Ports

This is where your outgoing cables plug in. If the board has a built-in A/D, this is also where you'll find your USB, Firewire, SPDIF, or optical ports.

Purchase Considerations

When you buy your board, you want to consider:

- The number of preamps it comes with—even if you're only doing single-channel recording, it's always nice to have a backup or four.
- Quality of the preamps. For obvious reasons.
- Sweep EQ. If it's available, it's very nice to have.
- Built-in A/D. If this is your first board and you're working on a budget, this is very handy.
- Compressor. If the board has one, can you bypass it? If not, don't buy it.
- Roll-off. Always nice to have.
- Price. More expensive is not always better. Get the best deal that fits your other requirements.
- Sound quality. Last, but definitely not least.

Other Considerations

Because this book is concerned chiefly with a home studio, I'm only worried about noise level and value-for-money in your home studio equipment. But if you're on the road a lot and need a mobile rig, or you're shopping with an eye toward expanding into live sound work, here are some other things to keep in mind:

1) Ergonomics

If you're mixing sound live, the ergonomics of your mixing board make a huge difference. A lot of boards (like some of those put out by Mackie) which are perfectly fine for home use have poorly-thought-out button placement and other design issues that make them difficult to work with in live-sound situations.

2) Portability

Similarly, if you're shopping for a mobile rig, bear in mind the weight of the equipment, whether it comes with its own carrying cases, and how much bulk it's going to add to your luggage.

3) Durability

Anything that sees use in a club needs to be pretty bullet-proof. For such applications, prefer metal construction over plastic, and make sure the pots (potentiometers, or knobs) and faders are robust and good quality.

4) Sealing

Gear that goes on the road often has to contend with spilled drinks, rain, smoke, bird poop, and other hazards. Well-sealed gear stands up better than un-sealed gear. However, every board has open 1/4" jacks, and most of them have faders, and dust will build up even inside a well-sealed board, so eventually you're going to need to break it open and clean it, which brings us to...

5) End-user serviceability

Your board (and other equipment) has screws. Make sure you can get your hands on the screwdrivers to open it up for cleaning. Check the schematics to see how many of the parts can be replaced without re-soldering—and, if you're handy with a soldering iron, check the availability of the solder-only parts.

Things to Ignore

A lot of boards now come with built-in digital FX. In audiobook production, you'll almost never use these. Their presence should only figure into your purchase, as a negative, if they can't be bypassed.

Care and Feeding

Boards can wear out, and they can get dirty. There's

When You Need a Board

Depending on the other decisions you make about your studio, you may not need a mixing board. You'll be able to do without a board if you decide to use a portable digital recorder and won't ever need more tracks than the recorder is capable of recording, or if you have a USB mic.

On the other hand, if you're opting for a more modular setup for multitrack group recording, you'll need a board.

This need not be an either/or decision. If you want to build your setup out slowly, I'd recommend starting with a good four-track digital recorder, then adding good external mics as you can afford them, then adding a mixing board when you need to expand and/or decide you want more control over your signal before it gets laid down on the memory card.

five basic things you can do to ensure the longevity of your board—and all your other component equipment.

1) Keep Away From Pollutants

Smoke and dust are your equipment's natural enemies. Don't smoke in your studio—or, if you do, cover your equipment before you do. I once fished a $2000 sound board with a -80dB noise floor out of a dumpster because its former owner had smoked so much weed in the studio that the insides were completely encrusted with hash tar and gunk. It took two days of clean-up work with pot cleaner (that's "pot" as in "potentiometer" not "cannabis") and Q-Tips, but I wound up with a gorgeous 16x4 channel board in nearly-new condition for about twenty bucks.

Smoke isn't your only enemy. Dust that settles on the surface and infiltrates through the vents often contains metallic particles, and when those rest on unshielded traces or work their way into pots, you get noise in the system. For this reason, cover your board (and other equipment) with a cloth when not in use. A clean board is a quiet board.

If your board is dirty, or getting noisy, disconnect it from your rig (and unplug it from the wall) and disassemble it. Spray down each internal surface with pot cleaner (about $10/can at your local electronics shop) and wipe it clean with a lint-free cloth. Use Q-tips to get into the hard-to-reach crevices. Make sure all your traces and all exposed solder joints are nice and clean. After you reassemble, remove every knob and fader pad and spray pot cleaner in the seams of moving surfaces, then work the range of motion for a few minutes on each—this will dissolve the contaminants and work them up out of the connections. When done, wipe it clean and put all the knobs and pads back on.

2) Keep Away from Liquids

As someone who has, far too frequently, baptized his gear in iced tea, take my word on this: fixing a drenched electrical appliance is about as fun as wrestling a Vaseline-coated badger while naked. If your studio is laid out so that you must have a drink near to your gear, keep it sugar-free. Limit it to water, unsweetened/unflavored tea, or plain black coffee.

Under no circumstances should you allow salt, fruit juice, booze, electrolyte water, milk, horchada, Gatorade or any similar liquid near your equipment. Those electrolytes that keep you hydrated make your electronics short out far more aggressively than do other liquids.

If you do suffer a spill, here's how you fix it:

First, immediately unplug the device from the wall (and/or remove the battery).

Second, disassemble it.

Third, thoroughly rinse it in *deionized* water. You can get this at most grocery stores. Do *not* use any other kind of water, as all other water is electrically conductive.

Fourth, after rinsing the equipment thoroughly, seal the parts in a bag with either dry white rice or (preferably) silica gel and let it sit for two or three days. When it's thoroughly dessicated, reassemble it, plug it in, and continue to use as normal.

This trick works with any electronic device, but it is a big pain in the ass—better that you never have to learn how well it works.

3) Strain Relieve Your Cables

I mentioned this in the care and feeding section for cables, but it bears mention here as well. Taut cables, even when no tripping hazard is present, puts stress on the solder joints inside your gear, and will eventually work them loose, at which point the only two options are re-soldering or buying new gear. For the same reason, handle your connectors gently when seating and unseating.

4) Walk Your Board

If you have the space for a static setup, you'll be inclined to set up your studio and then just leave everything in place forever. This actually will shorten the life of your equipment, as it concentrates the oxidization in your connectors. Better to spread the wear out by moving your mic cables down the line of tracks from time to time (i.e. every three or four months).

It's good to do this with your pots and faders too. By all means, use a marker and/or board tape to label your preferred settings, but when the board isn't in use, turn the pots and faders all the way down. Even without electricity flowing through them, these pots and faders control are electrically reactive, and they will slowly corrode. Since corrosion introduces noise, it's best to make sure that corrosion happens at setting levels you don't use. If corrosion-created noise becomes a problem anyway, cleaning your board with pot cleaner (as described above) will make things better and extend the life of the gear.

5) Don't Drop Your Equipment

This one's kind of obvious, but if you live in earthquake country or have small children in the house, you want to make sure that the gear won't get dropped (or get things dropped on it). Secure it to a rack, place it on a shelf that won't topple over, or otherwise install the system so that it's not in danger in the event of natural or toddler-induced disaster.

The close corollary to this rule is "Don't stack heavy things on top of your gear."

You are the heart and soul of your studio. Your gear is the vehicle that brings that heart to your readers. Pick the best gear you can for your budget, maintain it well, and treat it gently, and it will help you reach out to your listeners for as long as you care to use it.

164

Making Tracks

Chapter 10

Capturing, Monitoring, Accessories, and Studio Assembly

After your mic signal has been amplified to line level, it's ready for recording, which means you're going to need something to record it (like a portable digital recorder, or a computer with the appropriate software), and something to monitor it (like headphones or speakers).

Assuming, that is, that you don't want to further preprocess your signal. There are literally hundreds of little gadgets you can get to tweak your sound before it gets into your computer. Many of them are best-suited to live sound, DJ work, and music recording studios. There are, however, two that are commonly marketed to and/or mentioned by home producers. One should be avoided at all costs. The other is worth considering.

Compressors and Noise Gates

In simple terms, a dynamic range compressor manages the dynamic range of your signal by pulling down volume peaks and then boosting the rest of the signal. New producers (whether of music or of spoken-word) love compressors, because, on the face of it, they offer two very desirable benefits. First, they increase the loudness of the signal, which reduces the need for post-production mixing. Second, they are said to "prevent" clipping (in reality they minimize it), that unpleasant buzz/fuzz sound that comes from pegging above 0db on your recording equipment. Whether as outboard accessories or done in software using plug-ins or standalone tools like the freeware "Levelator," their appeal is hard to argue with.

Compressors do have their place in the pipeline, and we'll get to that in chapter 15. For spoken word applications, though, that place is not in outboard gear. Because it changes the volume and signal density on the fly, it raises the noise floor unpredictably (no compressor is smart enough to tell the difference between signal and noise), destroying your ability to do proper noise management. By compressing the dynamic range, it also flattens the harmonic curves of the human voice. When employed by an inexperienced user, the result is a signal where breaths, consonants, and mouth noises are amplified to distracting levels, creating a harsh, unpleasant sound. If you're doing this to your signal before you record it, you have no chance to back up and correct your engineering mistake, and you'll ruin your performance.

Noise gates try to correct the opposite problem—rather than trying to prevent clipping, they squelch noise below a certain threshold. If the signal levels drop below your gate level, the noise gate clamps down and mutes the channel completely. When the signal once again breaks above that threshold, the gate lifts, and the entire signal passes through.

Newbies mistakenly believe that this makes your signal cleaner. It doesn't. When that gate lifts, all the noise comes through with signal. This means that two unpleasant things happen when you use a noise gate: First, your baseline noise level is forever changing, which means your audience will notice if you set your threshold too high. Second, it will also cut off the decay, giving the ends of your words a disturbing clipped sound. Since the only time we hear clipped sounds in the real world are when someone's shouting or panicked or suddenly silenced, this clipping will, no kidding, give your audience an adrenaline spike. Making your audience anxious is not a best practice.

But it gets worse. Because cheap headphones and media players employ compression and consonant-boosting EQs, the unpleasant sound that gates create are amplified and made more obvious by cheap consumer equipment. Noise gates have no place in the signal chain of spoken word audio, whether as a software tool or in outboard gear.

So, if these tools are so awful, why do they exist? Well, something that's awful for the human voice is excellent—when used properly—for guitars and drums. The noise gate is designed to eliminate amp buzz bleed-over from guitars, and to reject stage noise on drum kits, so that the instrument only breaks through when it's being played, which frees the engineer up to do more artistic flourish work at the board.

Similarly, compressors are particularly nice for drums in club environments, as they help bring the characteristics of different drums together and give them more punch. But even when used for their intended purpose, they can still be used poorly, resulting in music that is uncomfortably loud or lacking in richness. If you've ever heard a song described as "overproduced," overuse of compression is usually one of the culprits.

Though compressors and noise gates are also sold separately, the most popular units combine both in one box. Both tools are available as software. In chapter 15 we'll talk about how to use compression properly for spoken-word in post-production. As far as using it in your pre-recording signal chain, save yourself some money and a whole lot of work, and just say no.

Outboard EQ

Here we move from the destructive to the divine. The single best piece of extra outboard equipment you can buy is an outboard 31-band equalizer (EQ). This will let you shape your sound before it goes into the recorder, which is useful for a few different things.

For one thing, it gives you an extra opportunity to squelch noise and take the "air" out of the mix—meaning that you can preferentially mute all the frequencies where the human voice doesn't occur, which can alleviate (or even eliminate) the need for noise cleanup in post.

For another, you can use it to shape your voice for different characters—pulling the bass out when performing female characters and boosting it for male characters, for example. When narrating, I run through a stereo 31-band stereo EQ. I have one channel set to leave the signal pretty much alone, and I use this channel for character voices. I have the other channel tuned for narration, bringing out the sweeter, more intimate characteristics of my voice and attenuating the harsher ones. Combining this with some mic technique, I can read both narration and character voices in one pass, then just pull my narration track from the left channel and my character voice track from the right channel.

Finally, you can use the outboard EQ in conjunction with your mic's response curve to enhance or flatten that curve. This way, if you can only afford a $99 Shure SM58, but your voice sounds better in a $300 Beyerdynamic M201, you can tune the signal on a $100 outboard EQ to closely approximate the sound you'd get with the Beyer.

These are wonderful pieces of equipment, and are the single best non-essential add-on you can get for your studio. For best results, place them between your board and your A/D (or, if your A/D is built into your board, use them on a send/return circuit, as detailed in your board's manual). But do bear in mind that they are non-essential. You can produce a stunning audiobook even if all you've got is a good dynamic mic and a cheap preamp hooked up to the computer you already own.

Recording Device

After the last several chapters, you'll be relieved to hear that recording is the easiest part of the process. You can use a portable recorder as mentioned in the previous chapter, you can use the computer you already have, or you can re-purpose an old laptop or netbook. If you've got a computer with a USB or Firewire port, you've got almost everything you need already. The rest is just best practices and software, which we'll cover in the next chapter.

Monitoring

The last pieces of hardware you're going to need are arguably the most important aside from the microphone: monitors.

Monitors are the speakers that you use to monitor the signal while recording and mixing, which typically means you'll need two sets: a set of headphones for recording, and a set of speakers for mixing. Not just any set of speakers will do—if you use the ones built-in to your laptop, you're liable to find yourself answering quality complaints with the immortal catchphrase familiar to all amateur software engineers:

"I don't know what your problem is. It worked fine on my system."

In other words, your mix will sound like crap, and you won't know why.

Laptop speakers are lowest-bidder type items, and have characteristic weaknesses. This means that, if you rely on them when you're tuning your EQ and doing your noise-cleanup work, or when you're mixing in music and Foley, you'll put a lot of work in for a product that doesn't sound good on a car stereo or on iPod earbuds.

Earbuds, speakers designed for gaming, or advertised "with bass boost" and other features "to make your audio pop," etc. all have the same problem: Whether due to defect or enhancements, they don't let you actually hear what you're doing.

Good monitors are accurate speakers (i.e. they have a flat response curve), and, like mics, they're worth spending money on. When you mix on flat speakers, your product will sound good almost everywhere. You can skimp on almost everything else to save money—skimping on your mics or your monitors, though, will really hurt you.

However, like mics, spending doesn't necessarily mean splurging. Good desktop studio monitors can cost upwards of $600 a piece (not a pair), but spending that much is strictly unnecessary. Studio monitors that are good for audiobooks can be had for ~$150/pair, but a good set of consumer bookshelf speakers can run as little as $60.

Desktop monitors won't help you when you're recording, though. Whether you're one who prefers to listen to themselves constantly, or just one who checks sound quality occasionally, you need a pair of good headphones.

Studio headphones range from $60 to $200, but the stuff between $60 and $100 is so good that you won't get a lot of incremental benefit out of spending more. Any of the phones from Sennheiser, Sony, Shure, or AKG will do handsomely. Avoid phones with active noise cancellation—they interfere with what you're mixing—and avoid "Audiophile" phones, as they can be tuned for listening pleasure rather than accuracy. Instead, prefer phones with "Studio" in the description, as these are the most accurate. They generally come with integral screw-in adapters that let you plug them into either 1/4" or mini-jack headphone ports, so a single set will do for both your mixing board and your laptop. Since studio phones come with 6' coiled leads, you'll need an extension cable if you're using a desktop computer stashed under your desk.

Headphones have one characteristic point of failure: the cable. Cables that are hard-wired in will work loose over time, and as those connections loosen, noise will creep into the system. The audio quality will decay, and you can wind up (after several years of hard use) with phones that are no longer accurate. Fortunately, a number of phones in this price range have detachable bayonet-lock style cables, which means that when the cable wears out, you can just replace the cable rather than replacing the entire package. It's the one "special feature" that's worth looking for on headphones.

The only other thing to worry about is ergonomics: if your head is larger or smaller than average, you'll want to make sure you get a pair that'll fit it comfortably. Most studio phones are adjustable to fit a wide range of head sizes, but if you're buying a set online, do check the spec list to make sure. Also, another ergonomic feature, make sure that you get ones with ear-surrounding foam. This keeps extraneous noise out and makes them comfortable to wear for long stretches of time. Cheaper models sometimes skimp on this essential feature.

If you're doing single-read audiobooks without a lot of music or Foley, there's no need to splurge for desktop monitors: your headphones alone will be perfectly adequate for editing and mixing. If you're doing audio dramas, full-production full-cast, or using extensive Foley or incidental music in a single-read book, you will need a set of desktop monitors for two reasons:

1) Ear and neck fatigue

Headphones are heavy, and they squirt sound right into your ears. During long work sessions, they'll wear you out and wreck your frequency discrimination.

2) Phase games

The success of a complex stereo mix depends on how the signals from the two speakers interact within the room. If you mix only on headphones, you can inadvertently set up a situation where you get unexpected harshness or muddiness in a real room.

Once you've got your headphones and monitors, it's time to hook your gear together. Your studio signal path should look like this:

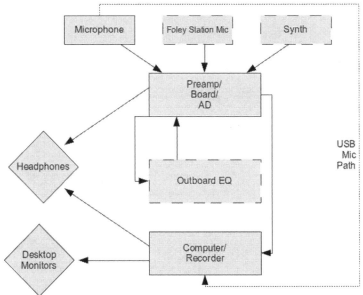

Figure 10.1: Outboard Signal Path. Dashed borders represent optional equipment. Dotted line is optional signal path for use only with USB microphones

Once you're all wired up, you're ready to start recording.

172

Making Tracks

Part V
Production

174

Making Tracks

Chapter 11

The Art of Laying It Down

S o, you've got a good book you want to record, you've bought your equipment, you've wired up your studio. Now, you've got to catch some sound and put it in some kind of order.

Sound recording and editing software falls into two general categories: The Sound Editor, and the Digital Audio Workstation (DAW). Either alone will suit, but they work best when they're used in concert with one another.

Sound Editors

Sound editors are designed for trimming and transforming sound effects, bumpers, and other short form work. The workflow is ideal for doing noise-cleanup work, making rough-edits to vocal tracks, and creating unique sound beds and effects. They are destructive programs, meaning that when you make a change to a sound in the program, it changes the sound as stored on the disc. If you overrun your undo buffer, you're out of luck.

This doesn't mean you can't do long-form work on them. Early in my independent film days, before I'd outfitted my own studio, I used sound sound editors to hand-mix the sound tracks (dialog, Foley, and music) for several short films and two feature-length productions. If you ever have occasion to do a complex mix with one of these, you'll find out very quickly why you shouldn't: Because every edit and FX decision you make is irrevocable, it's an utter nightmare for long-form work and mixing.

So if it was such a nightmare, why did I do it this way? Well, sound editors have an interface that feels natural and familiar to anyone who's used a computer extensively, and I've been using a computer since before I could read. The tool more suited to the job, a DAW, requires an understanding of procedural editing and routing, and those are things that aren't obvious if you haven't worked with live sound. At the time, as a rookie freelancer, I made the typical mistake of thinking I could make shorter work of the projects using the tool I knew than if I took time to learn the tool I didn't.

The result? I spent about 4x more time on the projects than I needed to. I got results that were comparable to what I'd later learn to do with a DAW, but I took the long way around.

Due to the simplicity of their interfaces, and the fact that they're so useful for quick rough-editing, I prefer using a sound editor to record my tracks and prep them for proper editing and mixing.

Here are the things you need in a good sound editor:

Recording and Playback Functions

For obvious reasons: Record to capture your sound (if you're using your computer as your recording device), and playback to check your work. Also called "Transport Controls."

Waveform Display

The waveform is the shape that the signal amplitude takes over time. We covered how this works in chapter 5. This display tells you, at a glance, whether your signal is clipping, or whether it's too weak. In editing, the waveform is all-important. In recording, it's damn nice to have.

Spectral Analysis

Spectrum analyzers come in two flavors: static, and real-time.

Although real-time analyzers are preferable, they are also a bit harder to come by. At the very least, you want a good static spectrum analyzer. By selecting and analyzing a bit of sound, you'll be able to see what frequencies are coming into your system, and what level they're at. That gives you the information you need to tune your EQ, to trace down noise sources in your outboard gear, and to do noise-cleanup in post. Here's a shot of one:

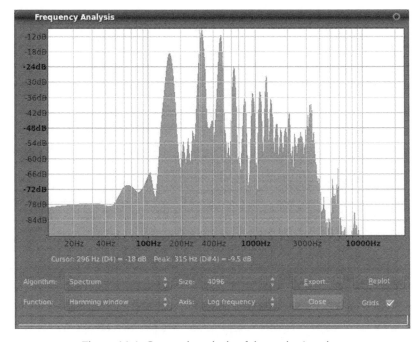

Figure 11.1: Spectral analysis of the author's voice

Along the Y-axis, we see the relative volume of the signal matched against 0dB. Along the X-axis, you see the frequencies laid out logarithmically (hence the "log frequency" text in the "axis" list box).

There are a lot of things we can read from this plot of my voice. First, since I'm a tenor, we know that all the signal below 120Hz is just noise. If you look to the left side of the graph, you'll see some pretty strong noise down in this range. We can thus use this for a rough reference to calculate the signal-to-noise ratio, which is ringing in at a healthy 50-60dB.

We can also see the profile of my voice; my fundamentals and harmonics on sharp display. The fundamental is that first big peak at around 180Hz, with harmonics popping out at 360Hz, 540Hz, 720Hz, etc. The relative strength of all of these frequencies is what determines the timbre of my voice. Way off to the right, you can see the fundamentals of my consonants at between 4.5 and 5.5kHz, with the consonant harmonics popping in at around 9kHz.

Mapping out the fundamentals and harmonics of your voice is called "typifying," and learning your typification curve is essential to successfully EQing your voice.

Note: Your typification curve will change depending on how tired you are, how recently you've eaten, and (if you're a woman), the timing of your menstrual cycle. Typify your voice over the course of a month, and then schedule your recording sessions so that you'll sound like the same person from session to session, and you'll keep your production quality consistent.

Real-Time Analyzers are also available as outboard gear, as stand-alone programs, and as features of some sound editors and DAWs. With RTAs, you can see the sound spectrum as it comes into your system. Though they aren't necessary when recording audiobooks, as you get more comfortable with audio you'll appreciate the shortcut they offer.

In sound editors, a good Spectrum Analyzer is essential. A good RTA is an optional extra, and should not come at the expense of a static analyzer.

Track Separation

Particularly important if you've got a stereo microphone or if you're applying different outboard EQ curves to each channel, the ability to easily split your stereo tracks to mono and work on them separately is essential. If it takes more than two or three mouse clicks to do this, you may want to re-think your choice of program.

Uncompressed Audio Export

By "uncompressed" I mean file compression, not dynamic range compression (which we discussed earlier in the book). File compression works by throwing away parts of the signal that are barely audible to humans, then using mathematical algorithms to reconstruct the missing pieces upon playback. Compressing a file once makes it portable with minimal noticeable quality loss. However, files that are re-compressed (for example, if you open it up to edit it, then save it again) get more information thrown away, and this degrades the quality of the signal.

Some consumer audio programs will only record or export to compressed formats like mp3, m4a, or wma. These programs are not suitable for recording products that you intend to deliver to customers. Make sure that *every* program you use will export to WAV, PCM, AU, AIFF, or a similar uncompressed format at the same sample rate you're using to record (44.1kHz or better, as discussed in the "Sampling" section of chapter 5).

Good Noise Reduction Tools

If you've managed your signal well, you may never need these, but it's nice to know they're there just in case. Noise reduction tools perform a variety of tricks (phase-reversed noise cancellation, EQ tweaks, etc.) to remove noise from a signal. You start with feeding the noise remover with a sample of the noise you want to get rid of (usually your studio's room tone), then tweak the parameters so that it removes only the noise you want to get rid of. They must be used with a very light touch to preserve your signal's quality, and they take a while to get the hang of, but they're good to have at hand if you need them. Consider these a "rescue tool of last resort."

System Plugin Compatibility

Each major operating system (Windows, Mac OS, Linux) has its own native plugins API(s). For Windows, these are VST plugins. For Mac, AU is the native plugin format. For Linux, LADSPA and LV2 are the names of the game. Most computers come with some native audio plugins pre-loaded with their operating system—at the very least, you want your sound editor to be able to use the hidden advantages your computer already possesses.

Note: Because Mac, Windows, and Linux all run on the same hardware, many programs on each platform can use plugins designed for other platforms. The more APIs your software is compatible with, the more options you'll have.

There are literally hundreds of good sound editors on the market at dozens of different price points. As with so many other things in the wonderful world of audio, price does not correlate with suitability. At every price point from free to $1000, there's at least one (and often more than one) program that will suit.

For my money the current best-of-the-basics that meets all of the above is a freely available open source program called Audacity. It's a sound editor available for all consumer platforms (except iOS and Android), and is very mature and well-tested. It's one of two main programs I use in my own pipeline, and it's the source of many screenshots in this book.

DAWs

Digital Audio Workstations are procedural (as opposed to destructive), real-time mixing, routing, and sequencing environments that are designed to mimic what racks full of equipment and patchbays, and they're every bit as capable as the hardware they replace. One of the practical upshots of this is that, while sound editors use their plugins and tools as "FX" (effects)—transforming the audio itself in a destructive way—DAWs use those same plugins and tools as "filters," meaning that they are applied to the signal in-line just as they would be if you were using outboard components.

This procedural aspect means that you can mix and match your EQs, reverbs, and other sweetening until it's just right, without ever having to worry that you're making irreversible decisions. Ditto for editing—your edit decisions are infinitely adjustable by dragging the ends of the tracks in and out. This makes dealing with your timing incredibly efficient. Once you're used to how they work, DAWs can reduce your production ratio by a factor of 2 or better. Much, much better.

Like sound editors, DAWs can be used for recording, and are often preferable in multitrack environments. However, due to their procedural nature they're less well-suited for noise-cleanup and other first draft work. The DAW works fastest when you feed it tracks that are ready for final assembly.

Most mixers with integrated A/Ds come bundled with feature-limited DAW software. This "feature limiting" typically is a limit on the number of tracks you can use, but if you're doing a single-read audiobook you'll only need six tracks or so to do even the most full-featured job.

However, if you don't have a pre-loaded or bundled piece of software (or the one you've got just doesn't suit your tastes), and you want to go shopping for one, prepare for a bit of sticker shock. Professional DAWs like ProTools and Cubase and Apple Logic run anywhere from $150 to $650 and up, with plugins running extra. However, there is a very good open-source DAW that is absolutely free to use. Ardour is available for all platforms, and also talks to LADSPA, LV2, and VST plugins.

Sound Input

Chances are, your computer has more than one sound device: the card it came with, and whatever device you're using for your A/D converter. In order to record sound, you need to select your input device—usually this happens within your recording software.

With the correct input selected, hit record, and start reading.

182

Making Tracks

Chapter 12

When You're Not Recording a Book

Foley, Feedback Shows, and Voice Mail

There is something almost alchemical about seeing a mass of flub-prone raw tracks transmogrify into a tight piece of work that can hold your listeners enraptured for hours on end, of being elbow-deep in the process every step of the way. Like a discordant symphony where the notes all swirl around and around, closing in on a central chord, before resolving on a massive crescendo, the entire process—grinding and exhausting though it often is—can feel like magic.

Is it any wonder that some folks find it addictive, and look for reasons to indulge their addiction in public places? If you find yourself searching for new projects, analyzing the reverb characteristics in your favorite restaurant, or spontaneously wanting to record conversations for posterity, you may be one of these unfortunate souls. If you are, and you have an audio business model that's conducive to indulging this obsession, here are a couple good excuses to get back into the studio and record things that aren't exactly audiobooks.

Foley

Foley, as mentioned earlier, is the art of creating sound effects. While you can gather Foley in the field using a portable recorder to capture the actual sounds that the actual events make, many (if not most) sounds can be approximated in the studio. In some cases, the fake version you record in the studio sounds more real than real. Verisimilitude is the key.

Figure 12.1: A Foley artist drops a bowling ball onto a concrete pad.
Note the rock and the frying pans near at hand.

To set up a Foley studio within your existing recording studio, you'll want a highly directional, very flat microphone (a hypercardiod or shotgun condenser or an accurate dynamic such as the Beyerdynamic M201), positioned optimally to pick up the sound you're recording, and a range of props: mason jars, wood blocks, litter boxes, bowling balls, bricks, leather gloves, chains, produce, pasta, phone books, beef roasts—the list is endless.

A wooden mallet smashed into a melon, for example, provides an excellent head smashing sound. Wrapping celery in a washcloth and snapping it gives you the sound of a neck breaking. Treading in a litterbox full of different consistencies of litter, sand, and gravel gets you different footstep effects. A frying hamburger can sound suspiciously like searing flesh. And that's nothing to what you can get out of effects when you add a touch of reverb or tweak their EQ.

To get into more depth than this requires a book of its own, and there are loads of resources online. Read up on them and experiment—it's loads of fun.

Snagging Pre-Made Foley

Of course, there are already a lot of stock sound effects in the world that can be had for free or cheap. An Internet search for "Stock Sound" will turn up oodles of retailers, many of whom sell entire sound collections themed along certain lines, to save you the endless hours of searching through samples.

There's also a place called The Free Sound project at freesound.org, where you can find tens of thousands of Creative Commons-licensed sounds uploaded by the people who recorded them, which are free to use according to the terms of whatever CC license the uploader stipulated. They're clearly labeled with their licensing terms, and they have a great search engine, so it's very easy to use.

When browsing stock sounds, don't just look for the obvious ones (recordings of actual events), think also of analogous ones and search for those. The sound of squealing rabbits is far more chilling than the sound of a screaming human child, but if you play it right, the rabbit sounds more genuine. In real life, a ray gun would probably sound something like a lightning bolt, but the quintessential blaster sound is made by striking a high-tension steel cable with a hammer. Going this less-obvious route can bring a great, and unique, texture to your sounds that will make your audience sit up and take notice.

Special Shows

Just as audiobook listeners have grown to appreciate (and even prefer) author-read books, there is also a healthy crossover population between audiobook listeners and podcast listeners—for the audience, after all, it's all coming over their iPod. If you include a contact email or voicemail soliciting listener feedback in your books or podcasts, you will get it, and it is a beautiful thing. The people who care enough to contact you directly are people who are more likely to move into your "true fan" column. These are the people you need to sustain you through a career, and their engagement creates a fun production opportunity for those who are so inclined: The Feedback Show.

A feedback show is, basically, a show where you answer audience questions on a regular basis. You can do this either individually, which is more intimate, or with a panel of other authors or friends. This latter is a higher-energy format, which listeners find addictive and inviting, and it will generate additional feedback in the form of thematic, craft, and business questions designed to generate interesting conversations among the panel members.

To prep for a feedback show, go through your recent fan mail and voice mail and pick out the items most likely to provoke an interesting or entertaining response (monologue if you're alone, discussion if you have cohorts with you), then winnow that stack down to a dozen or two messages.

While you're recording, it's a good idea to alternate between voicemail and email as much as possible, for aural variety. If you have a co-host or two, have them read the email. Start every segment with the fan's message, then, no matter how far afield the discussion ranges, bring it back around to the fan's message at the end.

Shows like this need some different engineering tricks than you'd use for recording an audiobook.

First, you'll want a voice mail number and a way to pipe it into the show. The number you can get for free from k7.net or from Google Voice. These services accept incoming calls and convert them to sound files, then drop them in an email box.

To pipe them into the show, use a 1/8" to 1/4" TRS cable to route the sound from your computer's speaker-out to a line level input on your mixing board or A/D, then queue your voice mails up in a media player program and control them from there (or, alternately, do the same thing, but from your iPod). Do a levels test before you actually record, to make sure it's coming in at the same level as your voices. As levels can vary between calls, you may need to ride the faders on your board.

Wired up this way, the signal will pass straight into your recording setup with your mic signal.

Second, if you're going to have co-hosts, you will need more microphones, more mic stands and cables, and (optionally) more headphones—and, if you get more headphones, you'll need a distribution amplifier (~$160). You're also not going to be able to get away with a simple USB A/D, you'll need an actual mixing board or a proper multitrack portable recorder.

The mics and cables are self-explanatory—everyone needs a mic, and every mic needs a cable. The board, similarly so—each mic needs a preamp, so a four-person show will need a board with four preamps. The headphones and distribution amp are to allow everyone to listen live to the voice mails without introducing feedback (the sonic whine type, not the fan mail type) issues. If you don't want to spring for that, though, you can make creative use of the "Solo" button on your mixing board. Solo the voice mail track while the voice mail is playing, then mute it when it's not, and hook your monitor speakers up to the headphone jack on your board, and everyone will be able to hear the track without screwing up your mix.

After you have an hour or two, call it a wrap, stop the recording. Add some intro and exit credits, give it a listen-through and cut out awkward silences and any comments/discussions that you don't actually want going out into the world, and then drop it to your podcast feed. The whole process takes about six hours, and you can do it as infrequently as every quarter. People will stay subscribed, and it gives you a point of regular contact where you can announce upcoming titles, special events, convention appearances, special editions, contests, etc. You won't be annoying your listeners with such things—the entire reason they've subscribed is to keep up with what you're doing. Between episodes, you can drop samples of new audiobooks as well, and their podcatcher will pick it up and load it to their media player just like it was any other episode.

Remember, though, that when you do this you do risk alienating people if you go off on a tear about party politics, religion, or other sensitive issues. If you have a polemical personality and can't moderate it in public, and your pet rants are of a sort that might alienate chunks of your readership, you might want to think twice about this one. Or, if you have the disposition, you could turn that personality quirk to your advantage by caricaturing yourself as a loveable curmudgeon—just be sure to always make your audience feel included, not attacked.

Shows like this are not for everyone. Each one takes a few hours to produce and, like radio, the success of a show is often personality driven. But if you have a friend or two who make good cohorts, and you have a fun time talking on-mic and staying in touch with fans, it's a good way to service and drive your hard-core fanbase.

189

When You're Not Recording a Book

Making Tracks

Part VI
Post-Production

Making Tracks

Chapter 13
Slice and Dice

Up to this point, when it comes to your production, I've concentrated mostly on what happens between the text and the hard disk—your performance and recording—because those are the fundamental elements of a good audiobook. Now that we're in post, it's time to take off your performer's hat and put on your producer's hat, and from the producer's point of view, there is one truth about what happens in post:

The performance is made (or lost) in the editing room.

This means that a bad performance can be raised, a good performance can be perfected, and an amazing performance can be utterly ruined. You see it happen all the time in movies—it also happens with audio. Without ever entering into sweetening or FX, the edit will completely transform the recording.

The Goals of Editing

There are three things you need to accomplish in your edit:

• *Clean-Up*

In the clean-up, you cut out everything that detracts from the performance: knocks on the door, bumps to the microphone, the sound of you taking a sip of water, page rustles, the stretches of silence from when you were reading ahead, performance-inappropriate breath noises—you get the idea.

You'll also cut out bloopers (though you may want to save the funny ones for use as bonus content, if your business model is friendly to that sort of thing). Be careful when you cut, though, and only eliminate truly blown takes. Takes that are partially good will come in very handy when editing for performance, which I'll cover next.

Because this is relatively brainless work, while the other two aspects of editing are intensely creative, many editors prefer to do this step on its own rather than combining it with other steps. That's why I talk about your "rough edit" as distinct from your "edit." The "rough edit" always refers to the clean-up.

• *Performance*

Editing for performance isn't just a process of eliminating bad takes, it can also be a process of creating good ones by piecing the bad ones together.

You will have bad performances: tongue twisters, flubs, places where the sentence just would not fit in your mouth, etc. When that happens, you will inevitably choose to record the sentence in chunks, parsed artificially so that you can perform it properly and move on. However, you will often find that when you get into the editing bay the pieces of the sentence don't quite match up—trying to put them together gives you an audible splice in the middle of the sentence where your tone, pace, or vocal characteristics changed (probably due to the rising levels of frustration as you recorded).

When this happens, you've got two options: you can re-record the sentence again (risking vocal mismatch with the older recording), or you can try to save the take by splicing it at a non-obvious point. For example, rather than putting the cut point at a comma, you might put it in the middle of the word, during a phoneme (like an "s" or a "th") that isn't affected by tonal delivery.

This trick isn't just useful for saving your butt when you've got problem takes, it's also useful for enhancing a performance that's technically good but that might be emotionally not-quite-right. By splicing together different pieces of different takes, you can bring out the delicacy and subtlety that might be present in your text but missing from your performance.

With this technique, and a number of others we'll explore in this chapter, editing ceases to be a critical task and becomes performance creation. When editing for performance your goal is to draw your listener's attention to the points in the story you want them to notice, and evoke in them the feelings you wish to evoke—but to do so in a way that is stylistically consistent throughout your book.

• *Timing*

Although the audience will experience this as a transparent aspect of your performance, this is something you need to edit for particularly. Just as when performing, the timing is all about the rhythm and pace of the words and the placement of silences. When editing for timing you may do things like inserting breaths where none existed before, extending (or shortening) dramatic pauses, quickening the pace of delivery in tense sections, etc.

Setting Up Your Projects

Before we get into the nitty-gritty, a quick word on projects. Audio editing is a resource-intensive process for your computer, so the longer your project file is, the more it can bog your system down. It can also bog you down. A twelve-hour audiobook is a huge undertaking, and editing requires precise moves, down to the millisecond. If you've got your whole book in a single file, you're going to be spending a lot of time trying to locate spots in the file—and, if your project file gets corrupted, you're going to lose the entire book.

For these reasons, as well as a few others that you'll discover as you work through your first few books, I've found that the optimal size for a project file is the length of a single CD (70 minutes) or less (I actually prefer to work in half-hour increments, since it makes it easier to create serialized episodes from the same project files). You may move to larger assembly files when it comes time to put the whole thing together, depending on the requirements of your marketplace, but when you're editing and mixing, stick to chunks of text between 5,000 and 10,000 words—you'll find the work goes much quicker and is much easier to keep a handle on.

The Basics of Editing

No matter what program you choose, editing uses four basic tools: Cut, Paste, Copy, Crossfade. In most programs, the first three work using the same tools you'd use in a word processor: Select a section, then hit CTRL-X (or COMMAND-X on Macs) to cut, CTRL-C (COMMAND-C) to copy, and CTRL-V (COMMAND-V) to paste. And, just like in word processing, editing with these three tools is a straight-ahead process of cutting out what you don't want, and relocating those things that you want to put someplace else.

The waveform above, for example, of a sentence that reads:

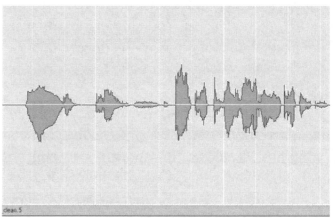

Figure 13.1: Waveform of a sentence

"Orange, pale, dark—like tarnish settling on copper" but is performed more like "Orange, pale. Dark, like tarnish settling on copper." Starting from the left, you see silence, then a few words (orange, pale), then a breath (which is the long small caterpillar-looking waveform), then the rest of the sentence, then a trailing breath at the far right. For the sake of argument, let's say that the breath in the middle of this sentence isn't situationally appropriate—it draws attention to the performer's breathing instead of serving a useful narrative purpose—and we want to get rid of it. We've got a couple options for how to deal with it.

If the pause is the right length, but the breath is the objectionable part, we want to replace the breath with an equal amount of silence (room tone). We'll pull this silence from the lead-in to the sentence by selecting a range of the right length (equal to the entire pause between words, not just the breath), copying it (CTRL/CMD-C), then selecting the entire pause—including the breath—and pasting (CTRL/CMD-V) the copied silence over it. Now listen to your work and make sure that the splice doesn't have any artifacts (check out the next section of this chapter for the kinds of artifacts that you can inadvertently introduce while editing).

If, on the other hand, the pause is too long and eliminating the breath will correct the timing issue, select the breath and cut it (CTRL/CMD-X).

Now, let's say we want to keep both the breath and the rest of the pause, but the breath itself is too loud. If you're using a sound editor, you would select the breath and reduce the volume. If you're using a DAW, you'll take care of this during automation (see Automation in chapter 14).

Finally, let's imagine that the breath itself is desirable, but it's too long. In this case, you'll want to cut a sliver from the middle of the breath and crossfade the two ends together. In a DAW, this is done by sliding (Click+Drag) the two clips until they overlap—the DAW will automatically crossfade them. If you're working in a sound editor, you'll move the second half of the sentence to a new track, drag it so the tracks overlap, and fade down the volume on the first track while fading up the volume on the second track (using either a "fade in" and "fade out" effect from the FX menu—usually labeled "Effects" or "Plugins"—or by using the envelopes, which we'll cover in a bit).

Mid-word Cuts

The clay of human language are phonemes—single sounds that, when strung together, form syllables and words. Diphthongs, vowel-consonant combinations, and single word sounds are all varieties of phonemes. In editing, your job is to take the clay you laid down on your hard drive (your raw recording), and make your sculpture. The audio is just a pile of phonemes. They're not special, they're not sacred, and the order in which you laid them down may have nothing to do with how they come out on the other side.

Remembering this will save your butt in a variety of situations. Consider, for example, a beautiful monologue delivered with pitch-perfect inflection, but in the middle of a long word, you ran short of breath and didn't aspirate an "sh" properly. Or, perhaps the electrical in your house popped briefly—not enough to screw up your equipment, but enough to trash an "o" sound. Or maybe you hit a blooper, backed up, and started again so you have a few words of overlap, but because of differences in delivery style, there is no obvious splice point between the words in take 1 and the words in take 2.

In all these situations, your solution is the same: a mid-word cut.

There are two ways to do this. The first, and easiest, is to make the cut at the syllable division. For example, if you have the sentence "The mismatched fabulists frolicked among the daisies," but you blew the second half of the sentence and only recorded a retake with a two word overlap at "fabulists frolicked," you can make syllable cuts anywhere you see the slashes: fab/u/lists fro/licked. Because of the way most English speakers slur their vowels, you'll probably have your best bet at u/lists.

However, this will only help in some circumstances. In others—such as patching dropped syllables—you'll have to delve into the more advanced technique. Basically, this one's a game of matching phonemes. Look for places in the middle of words (via copy, not cut) where the phonemes match, and steal phonemes from neighboring words to patch (via paste) the errors.

Unvoiced sibilants and fricatives (f, s, th, ch, h, x, z, sh) are the best for this, followed, in decreasing order of usefulness, by voiced nasals and gutturals (ng, n, g, k), voiced plosives (p, ed), long vowels and diphthongs (a, e, i, o, u, oi, oo), short vowelss (ah, eh, ih, aah, uh), and unvoiced plosives (t, d, b, p).

It's easy to get so enthralled with this technique that you lose sight of the difference between "fixable" and "better to fix than to re-record." If errors like this are occurring only once in every page or so, it's much quicker to fix than to re-take (and you avoid performance matching issues). However, if this is happening frequently, you'd be better served honing your delivery and re-recording.

Fades and Envelopes

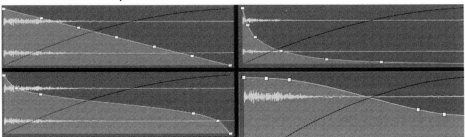

Figure 13.2: Top Row: A straight fade, an asymptotic fade. Bottom row: A variable slope fade, a partial fade

A fade is a volume reduction (fade down) or increase (fade up) over time. When the fade goes all the way to or from silence, it's called a fade out or a fade in (respectively).

In sound editors, a full fade is done by selecting the audio you want to fade and using a fade out/fade in from the FX menu. However, these FX generally only create a straight-sloped fade, which rarely sounds natural (above, top left). An asymptotic fade (where the curve swoops and tapers—above, top right), a variable slope fade (above, bottom left), or a partial fade (above, bottom right) will usually sound more natural. In order to create these more complex fades, you need to use the envelopes, or automation.

All modern editing programs can graphically represent your volume curve with an envelope. This is a multipoint bézier that describes the volume curve (the level at any given point in time). In sound editors, these curves are edited by clicking and dragging the points on the envelope, and new points are usually added by clicking on a stretch of blank line. You can use envelopes to adjust relative volume levels—dropping a louder performance to match a quieter

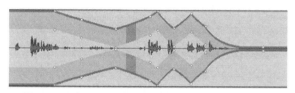

Figure 13.3: A volume envelope

one, or vice versa—and thus smooth out the transition between cuts. You can also use negative envelope spikes to fix pops that make it through your pop filter. This kind of relative volume adjustment within a track is the most basic form of mixing.

In DAWs, while you can tweak envelopes directly, you'll more frequently draw them through automation. DAWs also use envelopes to track automation curves for panning and for effect plugin parameters.

Editing Artifacts

An "artifact" is any unintended effect of signal processing. Editing can introduce a few that might be invisible to you, but will leap out at your listeners and brand your production as amateurish. These are:

• *Volume Mismatch*

A volume change that isn't motivated by a change in the story. Usually this happens because you moved closer to the mic or took a breath between takes—or forgot to breathe or stepped back from the mic—and when you started up again you were quieter or louder. In post, when cutting the intervening crap between the two takes, you're left with a performance whose volume jumps around in a way that sounds unnatural and doesn't match the story. This artifact is the reason you'll need to do a mix on your edited audio, even if you're not adding any music or Foley.

Note: Early on, you're going to notice this artifact a lot, particularly between sentences. It's normal for English speakers to start a sentence or thought quite loudly and then peter off toward the end as they run out of breath. After all, in the real world, once you have the attention of your audience, you can afford to relax a little.

This is why programs like Toastmasters are excellent for newbie audiobook readers: public speaking encompasses techniques that get rid of this—and other—vocal habits that will cost you a lot of post-production time.

• *Vocal Mismatch*

A tonal quality change that isn't motivated by the story. Can be caused by ragged breathing, choking on your water, shouting at your children to be quiet while you're recording a love scene, or because you tripped over some foreshadowing in your book that put you in an emotional space that's better suited for the climax of the book. Like with a volume mismatch, the rough-edit takes these behind-the-scenes cues away, and the audience is left hearing a change that doesn't make sense to them, which makes them hear the performance rather than the story.

If you have alternate takes, the best solution is to cut them together somewhere in the overlap, usually in the middle of a word rather than at a pause. Not always, but almost always, this will take care of the problem without re-recording.

However, if you don't have alternate takes or overlapping segments of sequential takes, you're going to have to go back into the recording booth to lay down a patch.

• *Half-breaths*

When you cut a breath out, or trim a silence, you always run the risk of cutting into the middle of a breath. Inhalations are worse for this than exhalations, since you typically can't see inhalations on the waveform. But you can hear them, and your audience definitely will hear them. Cutting into the middle of a breath won't only draw attention to your bad production technique, it will also induce anxiety in your listeners, which is an emotional experience you don't want associated with your production work (even if you do want it associated with your story because you are, for example, writing suspense or horror). Even with good breath control as a performer, you risk this kind of artifact any time you make a cut. The only way to avoid this one is to check your work after every cut, and be very, very anal about it.

• *Attack Snipping*

You'll remember from chapter 5 when we reviewed the different parts of the sound, how the "attack" is the initial audible portion of a sound or a phoneme. When editing, it's easy to slip with the mouse and cut the attack too close. This is much more noticeable with consonants (which have sharp attacks) than with vowels (which generally don't), but in either case it makes the effected word feel abrupt. You'll have heard this (and the next few) artifacts on poorly-cut radio ads, and now that you know what to listen for, you'll be able to see quickly how jarring it is. If, upon listening to your work, you discover that you've snipped an attack, you can either step back and redo it (assuming you're using a DAW or your undo buffer hasn't overrun), or you can copy the attack from the same phoneme in a different word and paste it in (this only works if you grab a chunk of audio that has the same lead-in sound, whether that sound is room tone or another phoneme).

• *Release/Decay Snipping*

The opposite of the above, this is where you artificially cut off the end of a phoneme at the end of a word, for the best possible reason: often, when you reach the end of a phrase or the end of a long word, you'll unconsciously let a breath go, or grunt through your nostrils, or swallow, and these sounds can make it into the recording, resulting in a sloppy, unpleasant sound. Trimming these sounds from the gaps between your words is desirable—trimming them back so far that you compromise the naturalness of the sound isn't.

Most commonly, people tend to chop trailing consonants (such as p, d, and t), because they haven't yet learned to spot the little spike that such consonants put in the waveform.

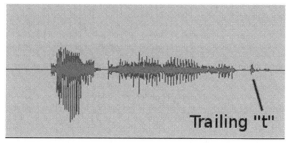

Figure 13.4: The sentence "Don't count on it." You can see the trailing "t" as a spike at the tail end.

When you cut these trailing consonants, you make your diction sound sloppy and sometimes can change the apparent accent of your narrator. Respect the consonants.

Less common, but no less problematic, is cutting short trailing nasals, glottals, and vowels. Phonemes like "ng" and "n" and "g" and "ch" and "ay" have resonance that carries on for a millisecond or three after the primary sound dissipates. When you chop these off, it sounds like the reader has swallowed their tongue—a sound your listener won't appreciate. However, sometimes when performing we hold on to these phonemes too long, and it ruins an otherwise excellent performance. To properly shorten one of these phonemes, fade it out rather than cutting it off hard (this also works with sibilants like "s" and "th").

• *Awkward Pauses*

When you get to shifting words around and adjusting timing, you will sometimes find yourself erring on the side of "too slow" or of long pauses sitting between words that don't need them. When you're editing, you'll often be dealing with audio chunks of a few seconds of a time, and this problem is hard to see in microcosm. Listening through your work once you think you've got it nailed will show you where these pauses are. When you find them, trim as necessary.

• *Hyperdrive*

The opposite of the above, this is where you've got a great performance, but the narrator never pauses to take a breath, either literally or figuratively. Back in the bad old days when books had to be distributed on tape or CD, books had to come in at a certain length, period. If you went ten minutes past a multiple of ninety minutes (for tape) or seventy minutes (for CD), you were saddled with extra production and shipping costs that could screw with your profit margin. This led to a convention (now largely abandoned) of trimming all the dead air out of a book. The word-rate came in at an average 150 words per minute (which is fast but nor unreasonably do), but it was a steady 150 words per minute. With no variation in rhythm, with no dramatic pauses, even the best performance gets static and exhausting.

When you're editing, it's easy to let this creep in. The hyperfocus you get in the edit bay leads you to naturally focus on the words rather than the story and performance. To keep this from happening, you'll need to do two things. First, every few paragraphs you need to zoom out and listen to your work. Then, for those times when you catch hyperdrive creeping in (as it inevitably will), keep a swath of clean room-tone handy, and copy/paste that into the too-short silences between words to loosen things up. Don't feel bad about it, and don't worry about the running time until you've finished editing the whole book. There are tricks to making things fit CD distribution without wrecking your performance. For now, just let your book breathe.

Wrap-Up

All of the techniques in this chapter, unless otherwise specified, will work in any sound editing program. In the next chapter, we'll deal with the extra tools that DAWs bring to bear, which can cut your editing and mixing time by a factor of two or more.

A Word About Room Tone

A consistent noise floor—or at least one with level changes undetectable to the human ear—is a must in an audiobook. At the head of every track, you should record 30-60 seconds of room tone, because you're going to need it. It will be the basis for your noise reduction efforts, it will be the place you check to measure for any EM interference, and it will be the material you patch in between words any time you cut a breath or insert a pause.

If you've decided to use a sound editing program to cut your project, you'll have to do as mentioned previously: copy and paste the room tone over the bits of audio you want to cut out.

If you're using a DAW, you can use this same approach—edit your audio and, as you go, fill the gaps with clips of room tone. However, if your signal is clean enough (i.e. your room tone needs to be below -80db and you need a 60db spread or better between signal and noise) you can save yourself a whole lot of work with the following technique:

1) Create a separate track for your room tone and move that 30-60 seconds from the head of the recording to that new track.

2) Set the volume of that track low enough that the signal is *barely* detectable on playback.

3) Loop the room tone clip so that it plays for the length of the project.

4) Edit the rest of your project as normal, but don't worry about inserting room tone in between the cuts. Just let the room tone on the new track fill in the gaps.

5) After you've cut the first minute or two of your project, listen to it with the most unsympathetic ear you can muster. If you hear the room tone levels shifting at the cut points, your s/n ratio isn't good enough on that recording to use this trick. However, if it is, you can carry on as normal and cut your editing time by 20-50% while you're at it.

Chapter 14
. . . .
DAWs
Slide-edits, Automation, and Mixing

DAWs and Sound Editors

Digital Audio Workstation programs (DAWs) have the workflow edge over sound editors in three important respects:

*1) DAWs are **procedural***

Instead of changing on the audio directly, DAWs record instructions that the computer uses to modify your signal as it plays from the hard disk. Like filters on a camera lens, it doesn't change the underlying signal, but it colors it before it reaches the listener. This means that any and all changes you make to it (EQ, FX filters, volume automation, panning automation) are infinitely tweakable right up to the moment of export.

*2) DAWs editing is **non-destructive***

A destructive operation is one in which the source material itself is altered. In a sound editor, when you cut or paste a segment of sound, the change you're making is permanent—the changes are written to the sound file on the disk. Hence, they're destructive. DAWs, on the other hand, write your edit decisions to a text file and present the results to you in the workspace. This means that you can later access anything you cut out, should you make a mistake or decide that you want to substitute an alternate take.

*3) DAWs are **automatable***

Every effect and parameter can be changed over time, in real-time, and those changes can be recorded and played back, and the recordings of those changes can be edited. This process is called "automation."

These add up to significant workflow speed-up compared with sound editors (once the workflow is mastered), and to a greater recoverability from errors due to bad calls in judgment, too-close editing, and other mistakes that editors are prone to. Because of the way assets are managed, DAWs are also not nearly as vulnerable to data corruption.

Although their learning curve is much steeper than a sound editor, these advantages are such that the time cost of mastering the DAW is easily recouped over the course of a single full-length audiobook. A professional-sounding single audiobook produced on a DAW can take half as much time as the same book produced on a sound editor (assuming identical-sounding finished products). More complex projects offer even greater time savings—full-cast and audio drama work can take 4-to-6 times as long on a sound editor as on a DAW.

The DAW Interface

The first time you open up a DAW, you might feel overwhelmed. While sound editors are evolved from older software paradigms, DAWs are evolved from older hardware paradigms. What you see in front of you on your monitor (or spread across multiple monitors, as a full-featured DAW can easily use four screens simultaneously with no duplication of information) is a software implementation of an old-fashioned recording studio.

For the purposes of this little tour, I'm using Ardour, a professional open-source DAW that is freely available for Windows, Mac and Linux operating systems. All DAW programs operate essentially the same way, with minor differences. For other freely-available programs, sorted by platform, see the list in Appendix B.

The first sight you'll be greeted with when you open your DAW is a main window like this one:

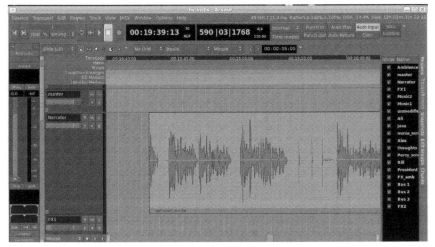

Figure 14.1: Ardour Main window

Fortunately, it has a few elements in common with a more basic sound editor program. Along the top, you have your transport controls (play, stop, record—plus loop and skip) and just to the left of that you'll see a jog/shuttle slider, which speeds up or slows down playback for audible scrubbing—this is like listening to an audio tape with a variable-speed, reversible motor—while to the right you see a timecode display, which tells you where you are in your project.

Below these (and many other controls which I won't cover in this book), you have a canvas, which can be populated with tracks, and the basic edit controls work much the same way as in a sound editor. However, this is where the similarities end. Whereas in a sound editor your sound files create and define your tracks, in a DAW the tracks are workspaces where you can lay down audio, and then slide it around to your heart's content. Audio clips can be trimmed from either end by clicking and dragging the edge of the clip. Overlapping two clips will create an automatic cross-fade between them. You can use as many tracks as you want, as well as buses and MIDI tracks, mixing them using automatable volume faders.

Off to the left of the track, you see the track name and controls.

The name is for labeling so you can keep track of what's on it, and is entirely for your convenience. The button with the red dot in the middle is the "record arm" button. When this is depressed, incoming audio will be written to this track when the transport is set to record. When not depressed, audio will not be written even if you press the main record button. The "m" button mutes the track, the "s" button solos the track (i.e. mutes everything else that isn't also solo'd), and the "a" button allows you to display the track's automation curves. The long bar is actually a horizontal volume fader, which is one of your volume control surfaces (see "Control Surfaces" below). The other buttons are used for interacting with various outboard equipment, and aren't something you'll ever need to touch unless you really get into this stuff, in which case you'll need to thoroughly read the manual for your software.

Further left still, you see something that looks suspiciously like a channel strip on a mixing board, and it behaves the same way. Signal moves from top to bottom, starting with a field for pre-fader plugins, inserts, and sends, then below that you see a fader with a track-specific VU meter, then a field for post fader plugins etc. Below that you have pan pots, which control the balance (one for each channel of the track). Those tracks can be routed into the master bus (which is your output), or through sub-mixes for a variety of reasons that will usually only come in handy if you're doing full-production work for audio dramas or full-cast (see chapter 14 on *side-chain processing* and chapter 16 on *environmental audio* for further details).

Along the right side, you have a tabbed field that gives you access to the bookkeeping aspects of your project: saved alternate versions, asset list, track and bus display control, edit groups, an index list of chunks that appear on your canvas, etc.

And this is only the beginning.

Mixing and Routing

DAWs are all about mixing and routing. In addition to the main window, DAWs have a number of child windows. The first of these looks suspiciously like a mixing board:

Figure 14.2: Mixing window

This is the Mixer window, and it shows a channel strip for every track and bus in your project. This is the window you'll be interacting with if you do simultaneous multichannel mixing, and it's also what you'll deal with when you do your output. The VU meter on the master bus is the one to watch to here: this is where all the signal sums, and clipping here will translate to clipping in your product. When dealing with spoken word, this is the only place where it's appropriate to use a compressor/limiter, and you'll use it as a safety measure rather than as a volume maximizer (see "Compressors" in the next chapter).

Unlike a mixing board, the signal flow here isn't fixed, but is controlled by the routing window.

The nest of spaghetti in Figure 14.3 shows signal flow moving from left to right. On the left is a list of all the outputs available, and on the right is a list of all the inputs available. Every track and bus has one output and one input per channel. Each send has one output per channel. However, unlike a real mixing board (where your physical cables limit you), you can hook up any number of inputs to any number of outputs.

These are the main windows common to most DAWs. Further

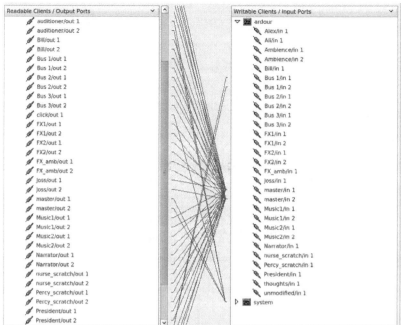

Figure 14.3: The routing window—for Ardour, this is actually handled by an outboard program

windows to control specific functions feature in different programs, and most plugins will spawn their own control windows as well.

Sends, Buses, and Inserts

In chapter 9 when we talked about mixing boards, I briefly touched on sends, inserts, and buses. The same principles for signal flow in board layout are at work inside the DAW, so now might be a good moment to go back and read the section on mixing boards. Go ahead, I'll be here when you get back...

...all up to speed again? Good.

So, in a DAW, routing within the system works by shuttling signal from tracks to buses, either directly or through pre- and post-fader sends.

A send is a signal tap on a track that *sends* the signal to another place for processing—this place is called a *bus*.

A bus, like a track, is a signal repository. Unlike a track, it doesn't originate or contain a signal, it merely serves as a waypoint for signals routed through it.

The difference between a pre-fader send and a post-fader send is that the post-fader send's baseline signal is controlled by the fader instead of by the signal coming straight off the track.

When signals are combined on a bus, the process is called *summing*. Controlling the relative volumes of the different signals is called *mixing*.

When you use a send to split a daughter signal to a separate bus before it's mixed back in with the mother signal on the master bus, this is called *side-chain processing*. That process looks like this:

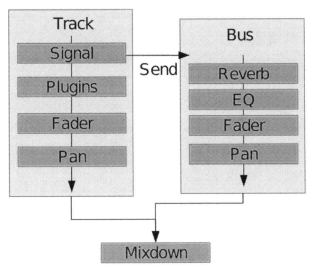

Figure 14.4: Diagram of side-chain processing

Side-chain is one of two kinds of signal processing you can do. The other is in-line processing.

For in-line processing, you use plugins as *inserts* on a bus/track to affect the sound on that bus/track. Like sends, inserts can be pre- or post-fader, though for the kinds of projects we're concerned with here you'll rarely use a post-fader insert. If you look just at the left hand side of the diagram above, and ignore the bus at right, you can see what in-line processing looks like.

Side-chain processing isn't the only use you might chose to make of buses. You can also use them for sub-mixes. For example, you may wish to mix your music together before mixing it against your vocal performance. Such a setup would look like this:

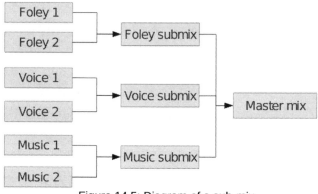

Figure 14.5: Diagram of a sub-mix

Plugins

Plugins are auxiliary signal processing programs that are called by the DAW to accomplish specific tasks. Basically, if it can be done to an electronic signal, you can do it with a plugin. In the next chapter (chapter 15) we'll cover the three plugins most frequently employed by audiobook producers: EQs, Reverbs, and Compressor/Limiters.

Important: A good DAW will let you save your plugin settings as pre-sets, which saves an immense amount of time when you move from project to project, or even from track-to-track in the same project. This is a must-have feature.

The Basics of Automation

The speed of the editing controls and the flexibility of routing control are two of the things that make DAWs fast and useful. The third, and perhaps the most important, is automation.

In a live-sound environment, parameters like volume and panning are controlled in real-time by the sound engineer to produce a mix that continually adapts to a changing musical landscape. But just as each musical performance is subtly different, each time an engineer performs a mix there are subtle differences. Automation is the ability to record the moves from a mixing session to be repeated on demand. It allows an engineer to capture a good baseline mix, and then tweak it afterward to make it shine.

Like music, audiobooks require mixing to equalize volume levels and bring out the dynamics of the performance. Performing that mix in a sound editor requires manually drawing the envelopes. While this is practical for a 30 second radio spot, doing it for a 12 hour audiobook is arduous and eats a god-awful amount of time. Automation is the answer.

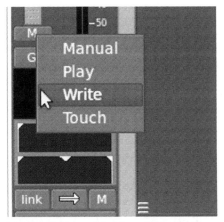

Figure 14.6: Picture of Ardour fader automation control button, with menu deployed. You can see the pan pot control button below—look for the "M"

In your DAW, you'll see little buttons (like the "M" buttons in the picture above) sprinkled throughout. These are automation control buttons, and, in addition to appearing next to your faders and pan pots, they will appear next to parameters in some plugin control windows. Wherever they appear, the principle of operation is the same. Since you'll be dealing mostly with fader automation (i.e. volume control), for the sake of simplicity this is what I'll focus on.

Each of these buttons has four settings:

1) Manual (M)

This is the default setting. When set to "manual" the fader will stay wherever you leave it, just like happens on a regular mixing board.

2) Record (R)

When "record" is activated, and you press "play" on the transport control, the fader will record all the moves that you make while your audiobook plays.

3) Touch (T)

This setting is for tweaking. It will play back previously-recorded automation, and it will also automatically record any changes you wish to make while you're playing back your performance. This way, you can listen to a mix you've just done and selectively retouch portions where you made the wrong move. Touch will overwrite whenever your finger is on the control surface (see next section), and will play back whenever it's not. It's a good idea only to use this setting when you're revising, as bumping the control surface while "touch" is activated will change your automation curve.

4) Play (P)

This setting locks your controls to the automation curve. All automation controls (where automation is present) should be set to "play" before final export.

There are two things you want to accomplish through mixing your vocals:

First, you want to even out the volume by subtly reducing the dynamic range of the performance. You can anticipate the moves you'll need to make by watching the shape of the waveform just in front of the cursor—bumping the volume up subtly when things are quiet, dipping it subtly when they near saturation, and dipping it sharply and quickly if you hit a sudden spike (perhaps a plosive that got through your pop filter).

Second, mixing allows you to enhance the performance. When you performed the book, you modulated your tone and pacing. During intimate or suspenseful stretches, you might have whispered, or gotten close to the mic and spoken in low tones to get intimacy. During moments of disconnection and coldness, you might have backed up and spoken loudly to create emotional distance. When performing, volume and intimacy are inversely proportional. But when mixing, the further forward you pull a sound, the more immediate it is. Therefore, you will find it expedient to mix whispers louder than they might otherwise be, and to mix matter-of-fact speaking slightly quieter than it might otherwise be. This kind of mixing adds that last level of shine to your performance, and keeps you in your listener's head.

> ## When Automation Isn't Enough
>
> Due to the quickness of human speech modulation, there will be some occasions when you'll need an automation curve to be much sharper than you can get by adjusting it in real-time. When you find yourself in this situation, fear not. Just as in a sound editor, you can edit the envelopes that you've generated through your automation. Display the automation (in Ardour, you do this by pressing the "a" button in the track header), then move the points on the curve with your mouse.

Fortunately, these two goals don't usually stand in opposition to one another. When they do, bias yourself in favor of the second goal. And always always *always* bear in mind that the mix should be transparent to the listener. Subtlety is the watchword for all the volume changes you'll make when mixing your vocals.

This section on automation has concentrated on volume control, but to truly unlock the power of a DAW, bear this in mind: Almost all parameters for all plugins, and all mixing parameters, can be automated in exactly this same way. The only limits are those of your aural imagination.

Control Surfaces

You access and change your automatable parameters through your control surfaces. These appear in software as faders, sliders, and rotary pots, and you can control them with your mouse.

But the mouse isn't your only option. You can also bind the controls to an external surface that mimics the workings of a mixing board—faders, pan pots, buttons, and all. This gives you a much finer level of control and a much quicker mixing experience than you get working with your mouse. These devices work via the MIDI control language, so in theory you could use any MIDI control device (including keyboards and DJ equipment) for this. However, there are some that are purpose-built for mixing. Most of them are very expensive, but there are a couple good options available for the home studio on a budget (there are many more than I can list here):

1) The Behringer BCF2000

This is an outboard hardware device that runs over USB. It has 8 motorized faders, 10 pots, and a couple dozen assignable buttons. It works splendidly with just about any DAW on any operating system, and currently retails for about $300. If you're going to be doing full-cast or audio drama work, I seriously recommend this piece of hardware.

2) TouchDAW

This is an app for touchscreen phones and tablets running Android (phones, Kindle Fire, Google Tablets, etc.). It turns said touchscreen device into a DAW control surface, using your USB port. This nifty little software program costs about $5, so if you already own an Android phone or tablet, this is a seriously cheap and useful way to go. Ideal for use on single-read audiobooks if you're running it from a phone, and suitable for more complex productions if you're running it on a tablet. The TouchDAW website has host programs/drivers that allow a TouchDAW device to connect to Windows, Mac, and Linux machines.

3) V-Control Pro

Similar to TouchDAW, for iPad. Connects to Windows and Mac.

4) DAW Remote

Another touchscreen DAW controller. Runs on the iPhone. Connects only to Mac.

Only a few years ago, external control surfaces cost upwards of $1000, so most of us had to make do with mice. Now, that's not the case. Since you can get them for the price of a smartphone and a cup of coffee (~$250-500—or less—including the cost of the smartphone), there's no reason to abstain, particularly if you already own a smartphone or a tablet. Using external control surfaces will seriously speed up your work. I cannot recommend them highly enough.

Chapter 15
Making It Sweet

Whether you're just mixing your voice in isolation, or you're mixing it against environmental audio, music, Foley, and/or other voices, there's more to a gorgeous sounding audiobook than just the volume. In addition to the mix, you may to want to sweeten your voice, and perhaps add some aural character differentiation. For thoughts, you might want to add reverb. If you've got aliens with speaking parts, you might also want to selectively add a touch of reverb or vocal distortion. From the simple to the complex, this is how you sweeten your vocals.

EQ

Equalization is the selective amplification (boost) and attenuation (cut) of specific frequencies, and is the most important form of processing you can do. In EQ'ing a human voice, you will change its character, emotional presence, and urgency. You can mute harsh nasals, remove sloppy sibilants, rescue a muddy recording, and create different profiles for different character voicings.

More radically, you can make your voice sound alien, extra pronounced,

Here are some of the basic types of EQ filters you can build:

1) High-pass filter (also called a low-cut filter)

When you mute all frequencies below a certain cut-off point, and leave all frequencies above that point open (or boost them), you've created a *high-pass filter,* so-called because you're allowing the higher frequencies to pass through.

2) Low-pass filter (also called a high-cut filter)

A low-pass filter is the inverse of a high-pass filter: dump the high frequencies and leave or boost the low frequencies

3) Comb filter

In comb filtering, you leave the fundamentals and the harmonics alone, but dump everything in between. So-called because the resulting EQ controls looks like a comb, with some teeth way up, and gaps between them plunging to zero. This is a trick you can use for noise management, but it's also useful for creating alien and mechanical voices, particularly if you create a comb filter based on the fundamentals and harmonics of some sound *other* than the voice you're applying the filter to.

4) Vocal enhancement filter

This is your typical sweetening move, this is an EQ curve created to bring out the warmth and intimacy (or other particular characteristics in a given person's voice. As you mature as a producer, you'll find that you develop an archive of such filters for different characters you play, and for other actors you may hire in from time to time.

5) Wall-of-sound filter

Where some parts of the spectrum are notched out to make way for music or foley. See "Wall of Sound" below.

In order to build these filters for a given purpose, it helps to know the frequency characteristics of the human voice. Here's a breakdown of the various bands in the human vocal range, and what they add to its flavor and texture:

1) 40-120Hz

Low-end resonance. There's no actual information here, but a small touch of these frequencies evokes power and authority in singers. In your listener's speakers (excepting subwoofers), anything below 100hz will just come out as noise, and most consumer earbuds can't reproduce these frequencies anyway. The presence curve in the SM58 and similar dynamic vocal mics adds resonance at 120Hz when you speak directly into them at ultra-close range. Cutting all vocal frequencies below 120Hz is always advisable in spoken-word productions.

2) 160-250Hz

Vocal fundamentals—the primary frequencies produced by your voice—live here. If you're a basso, your fundamentals are at the very bottom of this range. If you're a soprano, they're at the very top. You can find your fundamental frequency by looking at a spectrum analyzer. The harmonics from this frequency proceed up the spectrum as multiples of the fundamental.

3) 315-500Hz

This is where the harmonics of your fundamental are most important. This is where the timbre and character of your voice emerge.

4) 630Hz-1kHz

This is your conversational range. Low-end nasals and vowel clarity exist here. If you cut the lower frequencies and slightly boost this range, you'll get a telephone-like quality to the voice.

5) 1.25k-4k

The most complex range, 1.25k marks the low end of the vocal clarity range. These are where the fundamentals of the sounds made in your head (as opposed to your chest and throat) come into play: consonants, swallowed nasals, and such. Boosting too heavily between 2k and 4k will blur consonants like "v" "m" and "b," making them indistinguishable. Selectively cutting and boosting through this range can separate them, making them more distinct than they sound coming out of your mouth. If you're mixing against music, this is one of your best Wall of Sound opportunities (see below)—slight boosting at 3k for the vocals and a slight dip at 3k on the instruments will make the consonant fundamentals cut through. Be careful, though, of being too enthusiastic here. More than a slight boost throughout this range will fatigue your listener's ears.

6) 5k-8k

Slight boosting here can accentuate the sharpness of your voice. Slight cutting will make it muddy (useful for doing voices of very old characters or ones with poor diction). The fundamentals of consonants like "t," "f," and "s" live here. 8k is the top end of the vocal clarity range.

7) 10k-16k

The harmonics for your vocals live here. The human ear is very sensitive to this range, and too much boost will create unpleasant sibilance. On the other hand, if you have a harsh "s," subtly notching this band down creates a nice de-essing filter. Anything over 16k should be cut completely, as it just comes through as hiss.

EQs come in varieties, defined by their bands. A 3-band EQ, also called a DJ EQ, is what you'll have on your mixing board. It breaks the spectrum into lows, mids, and highs. A 10- or 15-band parametric EQ is usually sufficient for most voices (parametric refers to how the system interpolates between the control points). At the top end, the 31-band parametric EQ gives you the greatest possible control.

As you create the various EQ curves you need for your voice, be sure to save your pre-sets.

The Wall of Sound

The Wall of Sound is the name of a technique pioneered by Phil Spector to produce music using multiple, distinct layers of reverb that saturate the entire audio spectrum. When applied to general mixing though, it refers to a subset of the technique: Creating distinctive places in the audio spectrum for each and every element.

This is done with your EQ on a per-channel basis. First, you apply an EQ to each track. Next, in those EQs, you dump the parts of the signal that aren't important. For the human voice, everything below 120Hz can go (if you're an alto or a soprano you can dump quite a bit more). For sound effects of all sorts, the frequencies depend on the particular sounds you're using (you can figure these out using the spectrum analyzer). For some sounds, you can cut the fundamentals and boost the harmonics—for others, you'll want to do it the other way around. For many, you'll hit upon a combination of the two that will give you what you want. Ditto for music, and for voices mixed against music and Foley.

Since even the simplest audiobook is likely to contain music in its opening and closing sequences, here's the breakdown of the audio spectrum of music:

1) 31-63Hz

Drum, double-bass, tuba, and pipe organ fundamentals live here. This is where the music gets its sense of power. If overemphasized, these frequencies will create a muddy sound.

2) 80-125Hz

Tympani fundamentals live here—too much boost creates a "boom" that will bleed up the spectrum. Guitar amplifier hum has its second and strongest harmonic at 120Hz, so if that's causing you problems, this is where you cut it.

3) 160-250Hz

Drums and electric bass, and the third harmonic of amplifier hum live in this range.

4) 315-500Hz

Strings such as cellos, violas, and the lower end of the guitar range have their fundamentals in this range, as do tom-toms, bongos, snare drums, and some other percussions.

5) 630Hz-1kHz

Higher strings, such as violins and the higher notes on a guitar, have their fundamentals in this range, as do pianos, keyboards, many woodwinds, wood-blocks, etc. Boosting this range will give your instruments a horn-like blare.

6) 1.25k-4k

High harmonics for strings, this is where their clarity comes through. Guitar fret noise, the sound of the drumstick or the hand smacking the skins of a drum, and other performance artifacts also live in this range. Beware of ear fatigue when boosting too much in this range.

7) 5k-8k

This is the harmonics range that gives your sound its clarity and definition. Cutting at 5k will attenuate the presence of the music, making it sound more distant. The scratchy qualities of string instruments come out here, so if you're wanting to create "Psycho-strings" you'll boost subtly in this range. The fundamentals of cymbals typically live here.

8) 10k-16k

Cymbal sizzle and overall music "brightness" live here.

The goal of the Wall of Sound EQ technique is to produce a signal spectrum where a certain element is dominant at every frequency, rather than having any two elements competing for supremacy at a particular point in the spectrum.

The more elements (voices, sounds, music) you have in your production, the more essential this technique becomes. We've all heard "muddy" sound, where a piece of music or conversation requires conscious effort to decode. It's the kind of thing you hear in a crowded room when trying to focus on a conversation. Muddy sound creates listener fatigue, irritation, and will eventually make your audience turn off your production—and because of age-related degeneration in hearing, the older your listener is, the sooner they'll hit their limit.

On the other hand, a crisp, clear sound is a joy to listen to. It's a physical and psychological relief from the noisy world we live in. It makes your production inviting, safe, relaxing. If you're doing full-production sound for audio drama or full-cast, this technique gives you wider latitude to weave your illusion and seduce your audience.

Restoring Harmonics

One of the downsides of digitization is that it can destroy harmonics that bear a certain mathematical relationship to sample rates (see *Sampling* in chapter 5). If your voice has exactly the wrong resonance, you can have the best equipment in the world, and deliver the best performance in the world, and still come out with a recording that sounds mechanical and lifeless. This will happen to perhaps one person in ten thousand, but if you're the lucky one you can spend a lot of time trying to figure out what went wrong, with no success.

Fortunately, these harmonics can be restored mathematically, by building harmonics that are nearest-neighbor to the lost data and letting the listener's ear fill in the gaps, and many DAWs include a plugin for this effect, called "Tube Warmth." Every tube warmth plugin functions differently, but the controls are usually quite simple. If you find yourself in need of this effect, play around with the settings until you get the desired result—then go away for a while and come back and listen, to make sure you haven't overdone it.

Ring Modulation

Ring Modulation is one of a number of "alien" sounding FX you can apply to a voice, but I single it out here because it has one of the iconic sounds that people associate with alien voices in science fiction radio and television. In *Star Wars*, a ring modulator combined with a phaser gives Darth Vader's voice its mechanical quality, while on *Doctor Who*, the Cybermen and the Dalek voices both come from the use of a ring modulator in combination with sweep, EQ, and reverb FX.

Tube Amp

Not the same as Tube Warmth. This plugin amplifies the signal in the way that gives electric guitars that trademark fuzz tone, the Tube Amp is useful for re-creating the effect of talking over a telephone (when used in concert with a high-pass EQ) or a distorted CB radio (when used in concert with a ring modulator). Any track where you apply a Tube Amp will need to be mixed differently, since the point of these things is to spike the volume into clipping territory. Placing the Tube Amp and its related FX as pre-fader inserts will allow you to then control the output volume with the fader, while still holding on to the artifacts this FX chain produces.

Reverb

Reverberation is the sound that persists in a space after the initial sound has ceased. When you stand in a church or a warehouse, the reverb is all the sound that bounces back at you. The delay between the initial sound and the echoes, the time the echoes takes to decay, and the phase games played by the reverberating sound waves all work together to create the aural sense of space. Stand in a live room and sing, and you can hear the shape and composition of a room because your brain knows how to interpret reverb, even if your conscious mind does not.

In audio engineering, artificial reverb is used to give sounds that sense of space and texture. In a single-read audiobook, you'll use it exclusively for things like thoughts, dream sequences, and the like. In a full-cast audiobook or drama, you may opt to do environmental soundscaping, in which case you'll use the reverb to put your characters into an aural room appropriate to the scenes in your story.

In the old days, reverb was accomplished by using physical spaces or devices. These days, everything happens in the computer using mathematical convolution, but the basic species of reverb are still named after the physical process they're meant to imitate. They are:

1) Plate reverb

Plates were old-style reverb machines that ran sound through plate metal and mixed the metal's resonance back with the original signal. This style of reverb produces a haunting, bright sound. It's what you think of when you imagine a "thought echo."

2) Spring reverb

As with the plate, but using a spring instead of a plate. These produce a darker sound than plate reverbs, and are more commonly used with instruments than with voices. When applied to vocals, they convey a sense of menace, and thus work well in FX chains for voices of demonic or alien characters.

3) Chamber reverb

In the analog days, a reverb chamber was a room (often a locker room, a restroom, or a basement) where engineers would set up speakers at one end and microphones at the other, to capture the resonance of the space. With chamber reverb plugins, you'll get a number of presets designed to simulate environments like cathedrals, gymnasiums, concert halls, forest glens, etc., and you use these as the base sound profile for your reverb room.

Each of these basic types of reverbs have a number of controls in common that you can use to tune them:

1) Wet/Dry mix

With all FX plugins, your "dry" signal is the one you've not yet run through the processor, and the "wet" signal is the result of the processing. In reverb, the wet/dry mix is the volume relationship between the sound of your reverberation and the sound of your primary signal. New engineers have a tendency to overdo reverb (i.e. set the wet signal level too high)—in most instances, a very light touch is all you'll need.

The wet/dry ratio is very useful when soundscaping for audio dramas. For example, if your characters are all in a cathedral, and the action has one of them is walking toward the POV character from far away, you can simulate this by automating the wet setting in your reverb.

To set this up, use a chamber reverb with a cathedral preset as the basis of a side-chain effect. Place the reverb on a bus (call the bus "Cathedral"). When the talking character is walking toward the POV character (and thus the listener), automate the wet level to decrease over the course of the monologue. At the same time, on the initial signal track, automate the volume so that it increases at the same rate. The result is a completely convincing illusion of someone walking toward the listener through a cathedral.

2) Delay/Pre-Delay/First Reflection

All these terms mean the same thing. It's the time, in milliseconds, between the attack of the dry signal and the sound of the first wet reflections. The longer this is, the bigger the reverb space will seem to be.

3) Decay

This is the amount of time the reverb will take to tail off into nothingness.

With these three parameters (and other controls that vary by the particular reverb plugin you're using), you create the shape of your room. However, reverb can often produce very harsh, unpleasant artifacts, just as it can in real life—imagine standing in an empty garage with two friends and trying to hold a three-way conversation with all those high harsh frequencies bouncing back at you. To correct this problem, add an EQ as the last element in the side-chain, and use it to tune the reverb as needed.

Using a simple plate reverb to produce your thought echo is dead easy. Mastering chamber reverb for environmental effect takes a lot of practice to train your ears. I recommend starting simple in your early productions, and building from there.

Compressors

Finally, we come to the most abused type of signal treatment: dynamic range compression. I've already rehearsed at length the reasons why you don't want to use this willy nilly, as it can destroy your signal—now I'm going to let you in on the two techniques that are useful in spoken word work.

First, though, let's look at the basic controls on a compressor:

1) Threshold Level (in dB)

Measured either by peak amplitude or by peak loudness (RMS) depending on the plugin, this is the point at which the compressor will kick in.

2) Attack

In milliseconds, the amount of time it will take the compressor to clamp down on the signal once it's triggered. Some compressors, such as those with lookahead limiters, allow you to set this parameter to zero.

3) Release

The amount of time the compressor will take to release its hold on the signal. For both the attack and the release, the amount of time specified defines a slope. Thus, the compressor will start to release as soon as it's fully engaged, and it will release progressively. For vocals, you typically will want to set the attack as short as possible, and set the release at between one and two seconds. This keeps the release from being obvious to the listener.

4) Pulldown Ratio

Everything that strays above the threshold will be attenuated according to this ratio, resulting in a curve that looks like this:

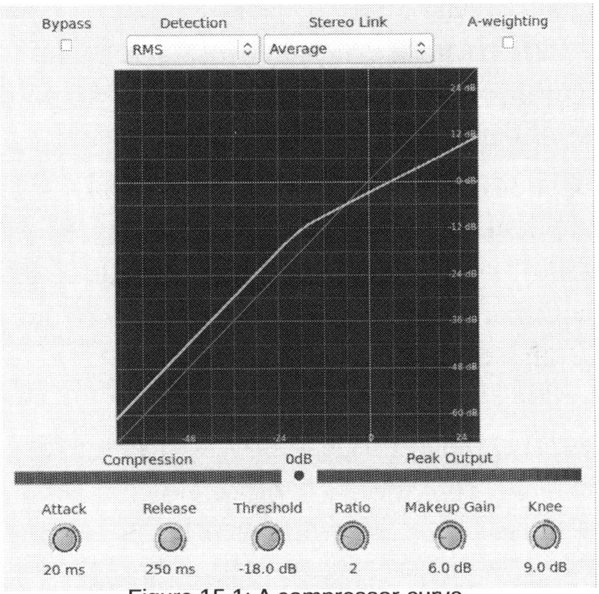

On this graph, an uncompressed signal would look like a straight diagonal—the gray diagonal line provides the baseline reference. You can see the pulldown by the amount of flattening where the curve changes as it hits the threshold. That change is called the knee.

Figure 15.1: A compressor curve

1) Knee

This controls how sharp the knee of the curve is. The larger this number is, the gentler the transition from compressed to uncompressed parts of the signal.

2) Make-up gain

When the compressor kicks in, the overall volume goes down. Make-up gain tells the compressor how much to amplify the compressed signal to keep it in parity with the rest of the track, where the compressor isn't engaged. In the screenshot above, you can see the makeup gain in the distance the green line (or, if you're reading this in black-and-white, the thicker bendy line) rides above the thin straight gray diagonal before the knee.

Some compressors also have other goodies, such as band separation, which allows you to separately compress lows, mids, and highs. However, for audiobook purposes, a very simple compressor is all that's necessary.

The first way you might want to use a compressor is for a "soft squash." If you're an animated narrator (or have hired one), the dynamics of the performance can range so broadly that hand-mixing everything can become tiring. A very light-touch compressor, can come to your aid in this case.

To create a soft squash, place a pre-fader compressor on your narrator's track. Set the threshold ridiculously low, at around -36db, with a shallow ratio of 1.2:1 to 1.5:1, and a decay time of five or six seconds. If you've set it properly, this compressor should engage the moment you start speaking and stay engaged all the way until the end of your project. The resulting subtle reduction in dynamic range will make your mixing job easier without destroying the dynamics of the performance or introducing any unpleasant or noticeable artifacts.

The other proper use you can make of a compressor is as a ""safety compressor", to protect your final mix from clipping. Think of it as a safety net of last resort, catching any stray volume spikes that managed to slip through your net as you mixed.

To create a safety compressor, place the compressor on the master bus as a pre-fader insert. Set the threshold fairly high, at around -1dB, so that it'll only kick in when your signal is actually going to clip. Use a shallow ratio, no bigger than 2:1, and just the barest touch of make-up gain. If your compressor has a limiter, set the limiter at 0dB, so that it will hard-clamp should the compressor miss anything. If not, add a declipper in the chain after your compressor to accomplish the same thing. Done it this way, assuming you've done a good job mixing your vocal track, your compressor should kick in only rarely (if ever), saving you from embarrassing artifacts without screwing up your mix.

Chapter 16

The Sound of Dreams
Taking Your Production to the Next Level

The Way It Used to Work

The world of audio theater began with a single delivery channel, and traditional stage theater companies performed their stage plays clustered around one or two microphones. It was The Golden Age of Radio. Families gathered near the radio every night to hear the adventures of The Shadow or Philip Marlowe, or tales of creeping terror in Lights Out, or the strange worlds of X Minus One, or comedies starring Lucille Ball, or even the first soap operas.

With one speaker, and one channel, good actors and writers and live-Foley artists had to transport their audiences to previously-unimagined places, all using equipment not much more sophisticated than a campfire and a practiced voice.

The Way It Works Now

In the intervening decades, we've gone from one channel to 7.1 surround, from live-performance to non-linear editing, and from AM radios to home theaters and personal media players, but the success of any audio production still depends on the connection between the writer, the performer, and the listener. Even if you only ever use free and open source software, cheap or hand-me-down audio equipment, and your best friend's old laptop, you have more tools at your disposal for making spectacular soundscapes than the guys who did the soundtrack for Star Wars.

As you get into production, you'll find a kazillion shiny tools, FX, and tricks that you're going to be tempted to experiment with. By all means, experiment with them! But be careful when deploying them in an actual production.

Just as in the old days, the job of us tech folks is to help the listener slip into a dream by enveloping them in your story's environment. Our productions should facilitate and enhance, not browbeat and bully.

Believe it or not, that means that the most important technical element isn't how good your production sounds. It's how consistent it sounds. A consistently plain production without any embellishments will play better than a production that is sporadically embellished. Your sound design is creating an illusion, and the integrity of that illusion gives the listener permission to let go and let you guide his consciousness.

Expectations

The key to creating a good illusion is managing your audience's expectations, and your book's first chapter is where you set those expectations. The elements you have to play with are: Your noise floor, your decisions about environmental audio, about sound effects, about how to handle thoughts vs. dialog, about soundscaping, stereo positioning, and incidental music.

Once set, you must stick with these conventions for the length of the production. By all means, step your production level up between books as you get better at what you do, but for heaven's sake, don't start with mediocre audio and work up to spectacular over the course of one book. You'll jar your listeners, and you might lose them. Treat each production as a single spell you're casting over your audience. Make movies for their minds.

In this chapter we'll go over all the technical enhancements you can add to any audiobook or audio drama to make for a lush production. These are modular techniques: employing one does not mean you must employ any of the others. However, when you employ them in combination, there are some tricks for how to make them work together in a way that gives you maximum dramatic punch and keeps your illusion intact. In the following chapters, I'll cover all the additional production and production management techniques you need to produce a full-cast audiobook or audio drama (over and above a traditional audiobook).

Here they are, from the most basic to the most complex:

Noise Reduction

Sometimes, even when you've managed your noise through the whole chain—from your room, to the power, to the EM—you can wind up with a signal that's just not quite clean enough for audiobook work. Maybe you've got a recording setup where you can't quite get the microphone far enough away from your computer, or your preamp is just a shade too noisy. In this situation, there are a number of techniques you can employ to squelch the noise just that extra little bit you need to push your production to professional standards. In this section, I'll cover three of the most accessible methods for digital noise reduction—each is best suited to a subtly different kind of noise.

The first is an application of something we talked about in the EQ section: Comb filtering. This method works best on a source of constant pitched noise, such as you'll get from a fan whose speed doesn't vary. Run a spectrum analyzer on the room tone and find your fan noise—it'll show up as a large peak (the fundamental) with a series of smaller peaks propagating toward the higher frequencies (the harmonics). Use your EQ to attenuate the fundamentals and the harmonics, but leave all the other frequencies alone. If you're very lucky, the fundamentals and harmonics of the noise will not intersect with the fundamentals and harmonics of your voice. Count your blessings, apply the EQ, and check the result to make sure your voice still sounds fabulous. If you're unlucky, and this method destroys your voice, find some way to eliminate the noise—either by tracking down the source and killing it, or by moving or reconfiguring your studio.

The second and third method both used the built-in noise removal tool in Audacity, which is essentially a sophisticated multi-band noise gate. Many other programs have similar tools or plug-ins, but the principles in the following mini-tutorial are applicable across most of them. The trick with these tools is to use a very light touch.

To start with, select a section of room tone, about a second long. Open the Noise Removal tool. You'll be presented with the following dialog:

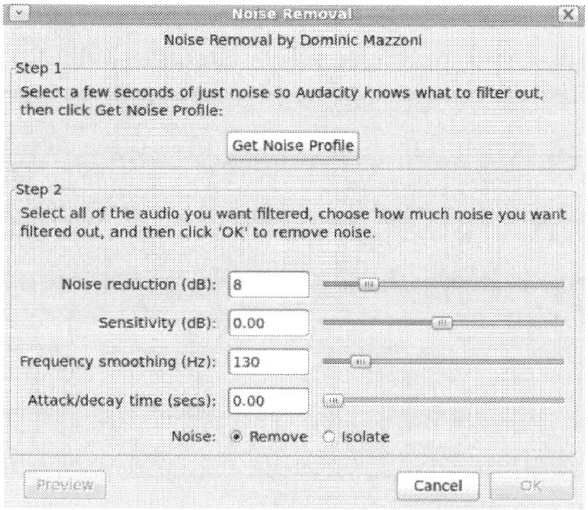

Figure 16.1: Audacity noise removal tool

Hit the "Get Noise Profile" button. The window will disappear, but the tool will do a spectral analysis of the bit you selected.

Now, select the entire track and re-open the Noise Removal tool. This time, look at the section that says "Step 2." This selection has four controls that allow you to tweak for the noise you've got. "Noise Reduction" is the amount of volume reduction applied to anything caught in the gates. "Sensitivity" controls how much tolerance the tool has for deviation from the noise sample—a lower number means more tolerance, and thus makes the plugin more active. The "Smoothness" control controls the breadth of frequencies of the different gate bands—the bigger this number, the broader the bands, and often, the muddier the result will be. Attack/Decay sets how closely the gate portions of the tool will cut to your noise floor.

The numbers above will create a middle-of-the-road noise filter that will marginally reduce the noise in your track without impinging audibly on your voice, in most cases. You may need to tweak them, but be very careful to use a light touch—it's very easy to overprocess and destroy your audio with artifacts.

Once you have your sliders set, make sure the "Noise" selector at the bottom is set to "Remove" and hit "Okay." Depending on the length of your track, the computer may need to think for a while. When it's done, listen to the result, paying special attention to any tinny artifacts—even slight ones will cause problems, because they are exactly the same kind of artifacts introduced by mp3 compression, so exporting to mp3 for sale on download sites will exaggerate them and make your audio sound ugly.

The second way you can use this tool is for noise isolation. This gives you more control, and is useful for different sorts of noise, so it's worth a try if doing things the first way doesn't give you the result you want. For this method, you'll first need to duplicate your track, then operate on only one of them. Do everything the same way you would if you were using the tool for noise removal, but instead of checking the "Remove" field, check the "Isolate" field. Once you click "Ok," you'll be left with a track filled with room tone, slightly disrupted by the spaces where your dialogue used to be.

Now, phase reverse the noise track (in Audacity, you do this with the "Invert" tool). You'll remember from our chapter on acoustics that a phase-reversed signal cancels out its opposite when the two are added together. You can thus control the intensity of the noise reduction by adjusting the volume on the noise track up and down until you find the exact right setting—you'll be able to hear the result as you play the track back. Once you get your desired result, go to the "Tracks" menu and select "Mix and Render." This will mix your two tracks down to a single track.

Using the Noise Removal tool only works well when you have constant noise. Noise that varies in level or pitch can't be effectively digitally cleaned—the amount of processing you'll have to apply will introduce unpleasant artifacts. In such instances, you're better off re-recording.

If the techniques above don't work to your satisfaction, and you have no way to re-record a cleaner source track, you'll need to investigate more advanced techniques such as Notch Filtering. A notch filter takes a single frequency as a center frequency (use your spectrum analyzer to find the troublesome peak), a "width" for how far on either side of your center frequency the filter will apply, and then kills everything in the band you've defined. Notch filtering (usually using half a dozen or more notch filters applied in succession) is the only way to eliminate EM noise from a recorded track.

However, sometimes there is intermittent noise that you can't help—for example, an aircraft flying overhead, or a dog barking. When you're recording, and these things happen, stop performing until the noise passes, then cut the waiting time out as you edit. If you talk over these events, you'll lose the audio anyway, it's better not to try. Audiobooks are not conversation; you can't trick your listener's brain into ignoring anomalous background noises by speaking louder or with better emphasis.

Stereo Positioning

Once you move beyond cleanup, stereo positioning is the most basic form of audio enhancement you can do. By positioning your different voices around the "room," you create a sense of place, as well as easy separation between the characters in the scene. This is a trick that's useful in single-reader audiobooks with rapid-fire tagless dialogue, particularly if your reader isn't an accomplished voice actor.

This technique works by changing the weight of the signal in the left and right channels. A dead center signal pushes 50% of its signal to the left speaker and 50% to the right speaker. An audiobook mixed dead center is "monaural stereo" or "stereo-mono," meaning that you have two channels containing identical signals. The moment you break out of a 50/50 distribution, you're dealing with a true stereo signal.

To learn how to position people around the room, close your eyes and listen next time you're in a small group. Have people reposition themselves, and then resume the conversation. Without opening your eyes, you'll be able to point directly at each friend and name them, because your brain uses a trick called "signal subtraction" to place near-field sound sources in your mental map of the room. Basically, if you're getting 10% more volume in your left ear than your right ear, then your brain will map the sound to 10% (about 18 degrees) left from straight ahead.

When positioning your characters in a "room" with your pan pots, you're using this same trick. The easiest way to do it is to pick where in the room each character is, then pan the track to the correct L/R position, then close your eyes and listen in order to check your work.

The simplest way to organize your room is to stick your narrator at or near dead-center (positioning your narrator 1-2% off center can enhance the feeling of intimacy if you're using multiple voices, but you never want to deviate more than that), then position your characters elsewhere around the room. Be sure to be consistent about where you put your characters in a scene (easiest to do if you put each character's lines on a different track and just set the pan pot for that track, even if you're only using a single reader).

The next layer of complexity involves the automation and/or envelope features (see chapter 14) on your pan pot. Using this, you can move your characters around the room, or simulate characters pacing or approaching and retreating from one

Caveat

Some of your audience will be listening to their audiobooks at work, and they'll do it on with only one earbud, letting the other dangle so they can hear their bosses and coworkers. If you do extreme panning (beyond about 25%L-75% right or the reverse), they're not going to be able to make out what's going on in the other earphone. Best practice is to mix all your dialog and important sound effects in this middle 2/3 of your l/r sound space, leaving the edges for purely decorative touches that won't diminish comprehension if missed by the listener.

another in scenes of high tension. This is a very effective dramatic technique, but it does take a bit of work to make it gorgeous. This process is called automated stereo positioning.

This technique works very well in conjunction with soundscaping (see description later in this chapter), and if you're using stereo positioning on your voices, you'll want to make sure the soundscape follows the same conventions you establish for your voices.

Volume Games

Just as you can play with your characters' left/right placement in the room, so you can play with their apparent distance from your listener. There are two aspects to this game, and we already covered one of them in the section on reverb in chapter 15. This one has to do with the volume at which you mix the character.

The principle is really simple: the farther away someone is, the quieter their voice sounds. Don't have your actor try to simulate this by speaking lower or louder when recording—the characteristics of the human voice change at different volumes and with different kinds of projection, and their distance from the microphone will also affect the way they sound (less so with condenser mics than with dynamic mics, but condenser mics have presence curves too)—just do it in post with your envelope and automation controls.

Just as with panning, you can automate the volume curve in your DAW to create the illusion that your character is walking around the room (in this case, toward or away from your POV character).

And, just as with panning, you have to use this trick in moderation, as audience members who listen in loud environments (such as on a commuter train, or in a car, or in a factory) will begin to miss words and plot points if they're spoken at a volume that doesn't cut through the background noise of their real-world environment.

Soundtrack Music

Soundtrack music encompasses title music, scene transition

bumpers, and chapter break ditties that re-create for the listener the structure they would have experienced as a reader leafing through the paper version of your book.

The current convention is to employ an opening title theme that runs under the front matter and production credits at the beginning of the book, then to employ a two or three second clip from that theme (or a separately recorded short extract) to signify perspective and/or time shifts within a scene, a slightly longer clip to signify a hard scene change, and a slightly longer still and/or thematically distinct piece for chapter breaks. Each of these should be distinct from one another, so that your audience is firmly oriented every time they hear the cue. If you want to get fancy, you can have a couple different scene change markers made up so that you can use each as a leitmotif for a character or a location. However fancy you chose to get, stay consistent—and make sure that the convention you're using is simple enough that it will be immediately intelligible to your listeners.

Thoughts vs. Dialog

When you write a book, there are three common conventions for handling the thoughts of characters. The first is to handle it in narration, for example:

"George thought that Allen was a bit of a jerk."

The second is to treat it like dialog:

"'He's a bit of a jerk,' George thought."

And the third is to treat it like a direct injection into the narrative flow:

"*What a jerk.* George sipped his tea and smiled."

In an audiobook, it's a good practice to set your thoughts apart audibly while preserving the original style of the text. The most common convention is to handle the first example as normal narration, to handle the second as a closer, softer delivery by the reader, as if he were talking to himself, and to handle the third by applying a very slight, ethereal reverb to the line.

This is not the only possible convention. Whether you follow the traditional convention or create your own, be sure to keep the same convention throughout any given book. I have a "thought" preset that I created for my reverb, so I never have to think about it.

Incidental Music

When you use music to heighten the tension, mark events, or evoke emotion in a scene, that's called incidental music, and it's one of the big things that screams "production values." When you start using it, you're moving from "movies for your mind" as a metaphor to actually making movies without pictures.

Incidental music can be custom-composed, it can be specially licensed, or it can be cobbled together out of public domain and stock sources. This can easily become the most expensive part of your production—but if you're careful, you can do it for free or nearly free.

"Source Music" is a special form of incidental music, as it's music that actually originates within the story. If your character is at a ball, the orchestra in the background is source music. If she's singing, or playing the radio, or playing an instrument, that's source music.

I mention this because if you use incidental music in your production, your audience will expect that any source music in the story—particularly songs that are important at dramatic moments, or that serve as plot point—will be present in the audiobook as incidental music. This isn't a problem if the songs in your stories are obscure, are in the public domain, or are being re-sung/re-performed by characters in the story—all of those are cheap. But this can be an enormous money sink when you've got a story that revolves around something by the Beatles or U2 or is soundtracked (in the text) with all the Top 40 hits from your childhood. The rights to music like that are not cheap.

So, when deciding on incidental music, be sure to calculate budget. I got my business-start in the world of independent film, so I was acutely aware of these issues when I started producing audiobooks, and it actually affects the way I treat music in my books. If a book is one I may want to turn into a sumptuous full-cast audiobook production (instead of a traditional audiobook, for example), I write around the expensive music. I may refer to it, or pay homage to it, but if I use it to soundtrack a scene I never specify whether it's the original recording or a cover. This gives me greater flexibility when I put on my producer's hat. Conversely, if I have a book that demands that kind of expensive music, I'll produce it as a single-reader version rather than as full-cast.

See chapter 17 for resources on licensing and dealing with the legalities around music.

Soundscaping

Soundscaping is to audio as landscaping is to land—it defines the texture and feel of your aural environment.

The first soundscaping level is your baseline background noise for the scene. For example, if you have a scene taking place on a loading dock, your soundscape will consist of the bed of forklifts, factory fans, workmen shouting in the background, palates being dropped, etc., all at a low enough level that it doesn't swamp your narration or dialog. You can get soundscapes like this prefabricated from stock houses and from The Free Sound Project, or you can build them yourself with recordings of particular locations, objects, and machines, augmented with synthesized noise beds, carefully mixed and EQ'd, and otherwise sweetened.

If your ambiance is a real-world environment, sometimes a good recording of that actual environment will work best. For alien environments, repurposing and tweaking other sound effects (such as fans, car window motors, wind, etc.) is usually your best bet. Using real sounds adds to the sense of reality—Ben Burtt, sound designer for Lucasfilm, was in large part responsible for the authentic feel of the Star Wars universe. None of the effects he used in the film—not the lightsabers, not the engine hums, not the blaster fire—were synthesized. All were re-purposed and remixed real-world sound events that he'd recorded on a portable tape recorder.

That said, sometimes careful use of a synthesizer can help you create good baseline room textures. Synthesizers and electronic instruments are not the same thing. Electronic instruments are a subspecies of synthesizer that are tuned with specific, pre-designed voices that are either entirely artificial, or are based on recordings of real-world instruments, or a mix of the two. The kind of synthesizer you'll use for ambient sound is a software program (or hardware device) that lets you adjust a number of electrical parameters that generate and shape waveforms from electrical signals.

Using a synthesizer is a technical art beyond the scope of this book, but many good resources are available—or you can just load one on your computer and play with it. You'll get the hang of it very quickly, and free synthesizers are available for every platform.

Synthesized or real, the background sound effects create your aural texture.

The second level of soundscaping is made up of your "hero" sounds (in all media production, "hero" elements are ones that happen in the foreground where the audience can carefully scrutinize them). These are sounds motivated by the action of the story. A door opening/closing, footsteps, gunshots, the sound of a character sipping tea. If a sound effect emerges from the action, it's a hero sound effect.

When you make the decision to employ sound effects, there's a basic counterintuitive rule about audio productions that will help you preserve the consistency of your illusion:

Audio illusion works from the top down, rather than the bottom up.

This is exactly the opposite from how things work in movies. This is because in movies, you can see the environment you're in, and if you don't also hear the environment, the feeling of unreality sets in.

With audio, you have no other cues, so your mind will fill in whatever isn't present, so long as the illusion is worked consistently. Therefore, if you have the ambient sound in place, your audience will expect the hero sounds to be similarly rich. However, if you use hero sounds only to heighten drama (in a predictable way), your audience will fill in the background themselves. So, the modular relationship of the different levels of soundscaping starts with the hero effects, then works downward.

Your hero effects should be mixed at the same general level as

> ### Important
> Bear in mind that a lot of your audience will be listening in the car. Avoid, as much as possible, sound effects like police sirens or sounds that a car might make when it's breaking down, as they can make nervous drivers panic, swerve, get into accidents, or pull over to the side of the road to figure out why their car is trying to explode. If you must use such effects, mix them softly and give them an EQ pass to emphasize the fact that they cannot possibly be coming from anywhere besides the car stereo.

your audio if they are plot points, and slightly below your audio if they are textural. You must be careful in selecting your sound effects, as some stock effects have environmental sound embedded in them—if that sound does not match what you're doing in your lower-level soundscaping, they will break your illusion. Isolated sound effects without environmental reverb are always preferable source material. All of the techniques in this book for dealing with editing and sweetening dialogue are also applicable to hero sound effects.

Your background effects, on the other hand, should be mixed low enough that they don't distract from the dialog or narration, and they should be loopable—meaning they shouldn't have regularly occurring, distinctive and anomalous sounds or volume spikes, and their edges should match up in such a way that a simple cross-fade between clips will make your ambiance sound seamless. In other words: they should not draw attention to themselves.

An example of an anomalous region: In a soundbed for a crowded bar, a single voice shouts out or laughs distinctively in a way that breaks above the din. If your audience hears such a sound once, they won't notice it unless you draw further attention to it. If they hear it twice within a minute or two, they'll suddenly spot the artificiality, and your illusion will falter.

Whether dealing with of hero effects, background effects, or ambiance, when mixing your sounds with dialogue, be sure to use

Wall of Sound style EQ to make room in the spectrum for everything.

Environmental Audio

Another way to enhance and deepen the illusion is to put your characters into a "room" by running their voices through a reverb+EQ combination configured to closely mimic the acoustic properties of the environments you've placed your characters in.

This is one of the biggest game-changers in spoken-word entertainment. Audio dramas and particularly the BBC have long done this to an extent, but it was Dirk Maggs who first took this technique to its limit and used it to unite ALL the proceeding techniques into a level of production that's now the gold standard in audio drama. To hear how this sounds, pick up any of the Hitchhiker's Guide to the Galaxy productions from 2004-2006 (the Tertiatry, Quandary, and Quintessential phases) and listen to them. To get an idea of how this differs from the way things used to be done, listen to them next to the original BBC productions of the Primary and Secondary phases. Each of these is available through BBC Audio at most audiobook outlets online.

The time investment in using this technique, once you've mastered it, is trivial. The time investment required to master this technique is enormous. Because of the work of Dirk Maggs and others, audience expectations for books and dramas using this production technique are very high.

Evolving Your Style Over a Series

I started this chapter talking about consistency within the production being the key to your illusion. If you're starting out with this, and you have lofty production ambitions, you can find yourself seemingly trapped in a Hobson's choice, where you either have to master a long list of admittedly complex techniques before you can put out a product, or you have to resign yourself to putting out crap.

This is a false choice, and if you fall for it you're going to cost yourself a lot of money in terms of lost earnings. Properties that aren't on the market can't generate income. They also can't generate word-of-mouth, which drives future income.

The solution to this Gordian knot is to prioritize your projects according to the level of production you've decided they need. Start with a short story collection that will sound fabulous as a single-read. Follow that with a novel with opposite-gender points of view, and have the other actor read all the parts and narration that are appropriate to their sex while you read those appropriate to yours. Do a few of them like that, and with each book, add a new tool—minimal sound effects here, minimal incidental music there, etc. After you've got a few books under your belt, following this progression, you'll have trained yourself into all the techniques you need.

Gregg Taylor's journey epitomizes this evolution. *His Decoder Ring Theatre* audio drama/podcast began life using a single, very cheap, condenser mic. While he did use sound effects and music, the early episodes are thinly produced, clumsy affairs with a lot of engineering mistakes. However, the writing started out at the level of "very good" and has progressed to jaw-dropping. Over the show's ten year (so far) run, he's trained himself to be a top-notch producer, with each episode getting slightly more sophisticated than the one before it.

But even in the early episodes, where you can hear the dimensions of Gregg's apartment living room, where you can hear the electronics in the USB microphone, where you can hear the bad post-production and crummy mp3 encoding software, the quality within each episode was consistent. That consistency meant that even an insufferable audio snob like me could tune out the technical imperfections and hear the story—and the story was always excellent. If you write an excellent story, and your production is consistent, your audience will stay with you while your craft as a producer and performer improve. Just as with writing, so with production: the story is everything. All you have to do as a producer is *not screw it up*.

246

Making Tracks

Chapter 17

Putting it All Together
Program Structure, Title Sequences, and Music

Once you've got the book recorded, and edited, it's time to assemble the whole thing. Generally speaking, the program of your audiobook should be laid out like so:

1. Production Company tag

If you don't already have a production company name, this is the time. It could just be your publishing imprint: "MyPub Audio Presents..."

2. Book Title

3.Author

If you're reading the book yourself, this usually goes "Written and read by..." or "Written and performed by..."

4. Author contact information

Optional, but putting your website address here and at the end can drive traffic to your other properties.

5. Performance credit(s)

If you're not reading the book yourself, the reader should get credit here. If it's a full-cast production, you can put this off to the end credits for everyone but your narrator.

6. Copyright Date and any additional information regarding first publication, etc.

7. Music Composer Credits

Only appropriate if you've got custom-composed music.

8. Adult Content warning on books where it is appropriate

Optional, but growing in popularity, for the benefit of audience members who might listen with children in the car.

9. Front Matter

Epigraph, Dedication, Foreword, etc. Some producers will also record the back cover copy and place it alongside the front matter.

10. The Story

1. Bumpers to delineate scene changes, POV shifts, or chapter changes. These can be Foley, music cues, or extended silences.
2. CD-specific bumpers. For the beginning of the disc, these should go:

    1. Book Title

    2. Author Name

    3. [Disc number] of [Number of Discs] *or* Chapter [x], Continued

Basically, something to let your listener know where they are.

11. Back Matter

Author's Note, Author's Bio, etc.

12. Closing Credits

Credits for licensed music and Foley (where credit is required by licensing terms), additional performers, the producer/director/anyone else who helped out with the production. If you're a one-horse show, and reading the book yourself, just credit your production company ("MyPub Audio," as above) and pimp its website. Include author contact info (voice mail number, email address, and/or website) to help drive traffic to your other works and recruit the more enthusiastic fans.

13. Disclaimer

"This is a work of fiction, any resemblance..." etc.

14. Preview of another book

You've got a captive audience, you might as well try to hook them on another book that you're producing. If it's not currently available, be sure to list a release date at the end of the preview.

Title Sequence

Your opening title sequence (consisting of items 1-8 on the above list) sets the tone for your story. If you're using theme music, you'll want it to run throughout the opening sequence, properly EQ'd so it doesn't muddy your voice.

The same holds true for the end title sequence (items 11-12 on the above list). Send them off with a sense of closure and style, just as you would if you were producing a movie or a TV series.

Music

So now you've got your book recorded and edited, and your title sequence vocals laid out, but you need some music for the title and credit sequences, for the between-chapter bumpers, and maybe to add a bit of groove to the action.

The legal situation around music is complicated. Not only do composers and songwriters have copyright to their music and lyrics, the arrangers and performers have rights to their interpretations and executions of the music, and the recording engineers have the rights to the recordings themselves. As you can imagine, it can get really sticky really fast.

The situation is so messy, in fact, that two organizations exist for the purpose of collecting and dispersing licensing revenue for the commercial use of copyrighted music: The American Society of Composers, Artists, and Publishers (ASCAP), and Broadcast Music Incorporated (BMI). In order to get the right to include a copyrighted recording of a popular song in your audiobook, you must go either to the band itself, or buy a license through ASCAP or BMI (depending on who their publisher is and/or which organization they're a member of). Prices vary from the very reasonable to the unbelievably expensive.

If you're using a public domain recording of a public domain performance of a copyrighted song, you still will need to buy a license—just as you do if you include popular song lyrics in your book. For text reprints, you get a reprint license. For audiobooks, you need what's called a "mechanicals" license. Fortunately, these are much less expensive than licensing the original popular recording—this is why it's always cheaper to have a cover band's rendition of your favorite Led Zeppelin song than it is to license a Zeppelin recording.

Fortunately, those aren't your only options. In addition to licensing popular recordings, and licensing mechanical rights that let you record your own version for your book, there are some other less troublesome and/or less potentially expensive options open. From most expensive to least expensive, they are:

1) Work with a composer

Granted, the cost will depend on the composer you use, but if you have a generous contract (where you only get the rights to use the music in the audiobook) and you work with a fresh-faced composer (undergrad and graduate level music composition students are wonderful), you can work a deal that's inexpensive for you and very valuable to them. Mutual advantage—and good contracts—are key to making these relationships work.

2) Do it Yourself

If you've got musical training and an electronic keyboard, you can compose your own music—or record your own performances and arrangements of public domain music. You don't have any legal or royalty expenses to worry about here. It will only cost you the time you spend performing, the time you spend learning MIDI sequencing (which is how computerized music is put together), and the money you spend on the keyboard (anywhere from $100-1000).

3) Licensed Stock

Many companies exist to supply stock music, which is music you can use for a one-time or renewable (every 1,000-10,000 units sold) licensing fee without paying additional royalties. You buy it, you buy the right to use it in your productions. Digital Juice is one such (very popular) company, and they also deal in Foley, but they're far from the only game in town. Magnatune is an iTunes-like store that sells stock licenses for all the tracks it carries, and on very reasonable terms. Searching for "stock music" on Google will bring up many others covering all genres of music, performed by no-name performers but often with great virtuosity. Be careful to read the licensing agreement when you buy stock music, as occasionally a shady company will specify "non-commercial use only" or specify that they are "not responsible for errors and omissions"—which means that if they forgot to clear the rights to their music, you can't sue them, but the copyright holder(s) can still sue you.

4) Free Stock

Like licensed stock, but without the payment part. These are usually one-horse shops—a composer or a band turning out music and releasing it under liberal Terms of Service licenses (or Creative Commons licenses) as a loss-leader, to build a name, or for the sheer love of it.

As with all things, be sure that you read the license so you understand what usage limitations you must abide by to stay legal.

A few good sites that put out good-quality stock:

http://www.purple-planet.com

http://www.soundjay.com

http://www.royalty-free-music.com

and many, many more...

5) Public Domain

Then, of course, there's the public domain. As the name implies, anything that's in the public domain is free to use, modify, adapt, chop up, etc. It's not under copyright, nobody owns it, anyone can use it. Anything produced in the United States before 1926 is in the public domain. After that, things become spotty and dicey, and you can't use the production date as a guide.

Probably the most ready source of public-domain music is the Internet Archive at http://www.archive.org, and its search engine allows you to search by license type. However, it's a user-driven site and accepts no responsibility for files which are mislabeled (and there are many that are labeled public domain which are manifestly not). The Public Domain is a complicated field, but you can get a comprehensive, easily-digestible orientation in the graphic novel *Bound by Law? Tales from the Public Domain* published by Duke University Press in 2008. A freely-available digital version can be found at https://law.duke.edu/cspd/comics/.

Chapter 18

The Last Mile
Track Separation, Export, Quality Control, Delivery Formats, and Tagging

Once you've got your edit and your mix done, and your safeties all in place, it's time to export the file and package it for release. At this stage, you have one major creative decision left to make:

How are you going to divide up the book?

Track Separation

Now that you've got a nice long audiobook all put together, you need to figure out how to divide it up. For online distribution, this is simple: the major audiobook marketplaces want books uploaded at one chapter per file, plus front and back matter, plus a commercial sample. You'll be delivering in high bitrate mp3 (128kbps or better).

For CD distribution, you're dealing with hard constraints in terms of the length of each disc, along with the option of track division points, which offer a navigation interface that doesn't exist in the mp3 format.

Some recommendations:

Audio CDs run 70 minutes each, so your files should be divided in such a way that each CD is as close as possible to 70 minutes long without going over. More CDs in your book means greater duplication and distribution expense. Tracks within those

CDs should be 4-10 minutes long, to provide for ease of navigation for audience members who listen in their cars.

To create track separation without significant duplication of your work, you want to approach the problem on two levels. First, in the way you set up your DAW files, and second, in the way you index within those files.

Your DAW project files should be organized so that each contains one to three chapters (5-10k words), and have a maximum running time of 70 minutes. This will make each of your projects about the same length as a CD, and will also keep them short enough that they're easy to navigate when you're working on them. Insert range markers to serve as track dividers on the cue sheet for your CD master files (the process for this varies widely by program, so you'll need to consult your DAW's manual. This can't be done in most sound editors).

Now, export the project to your CD-quality master: A 16 bit stereo WAV or AIFF file with a sample rate of 44100Hz. See your DAW's manual on how to do this for your program.

If you're working in a sound editor, you're not going to have the advantage of range markers, and you'll have to slice your project up and export each CD track-length section manually.

Fitting To Length for CDs

Which brings us to the sticky problem of fitting your stories to length for CD distribution. If you intend to distribute on audio CD, your final running time (including any front and back matter, bumpers, title sequences, previews of other audiobooks, etc.) must be as close as possible to a multiple of 70 minutes without going over. If you're over by even a second, you've just bought yourself the expense of duplicating and distributing another CD—it's not a huge cost, but it does add up. And, if you're only over-budget by a few minutes, you also put your audience in the annoying position of having to change CDs in the middle of your climax or falling action.

There are a few ways you can deal with this. The most radical is to run part or all of your project through a time-stretch plugin. If used with great restraint (less than 2% time compression), the artifacts it produces are inaudible even to the most discriminating audiophile. On a 12 hour audiobook, a 2% time compression applied uniformly over the whole thing will net you a ~14.4 minute reduction in length.

Need a greater length reduction? If you're willing to accept a slight up-shift in the pitch of your voice, you can play a fun game with sample rates. If you recorded at 44.1kHz, you can play that file back at 48kHz. It'll speed your reading up by 8%, which is just big enough that it can edge you over into hyperdrive territory, and it will pitch your voice up by 8% as well (about the equivalent of two whole notes on the piano), but if you're in dire straits, it's something to keep in mind. To do this, open your 44.1kHz file in Audacity, then set the track rate to 48kHz in the track controls while leaving the project rate (bottom toolbar) the same. When you export it it will retain the pitch and time shift.

But, depending on how your book is apportioned over those CDs, even a 30 minute shift might not make a difference. For example, if you're cutting your CDs at natural story breakpoints instead of at the 70 minute mark, you'll wind up with a variety of disc-running times (usually anywhere between 60 and 70 minutes). If you're doing this and wind up with a short (less than 20 minutes) overage, time shift isn't going to help you. You're going to need to reapportion your book across the CDs.

20 minutes is the magic number. If you have more than 20 minutes of overage, you're into "it's too big to worry about" territory. At that point, unless your book is very long indeed, you're not going to compress it without going back in and manually trimming the silences and screwing up the timing in the rest of the book. At this point, rather than compressing, you're better off expanding. You've already bought that extra CD, you might as well use it—and there are a couple excellent uses you can put it to, such as:

1) Author Afterword

An extended author's note, an interview about topics covered in the book, or another similar personal message to your fans can go well here.

2) Previews

A 20-40 minute preview of your next audiobook is the best advertising you can ever buy. Even if you produce it specifically for this slot, it's worth doing. By the end of this preview your audience will be hooked, and they'll immediately head out to Audible or iTunes or Audiobooks.com and get their next fix. When previewing a book that is not yet on the market, include a release date.

Quality Control Check

Once you've got your file exported, you need to do a four-level QC check.

Level One: The Audacity Test

Open the exported master in Audacity and visually inspect the waveform. Look for any dropouts, spikes, clipping, or other problematic areas. Then, listen randomly through it—a second or two every few minutes—and make sure the loudness and clarity and vocal quality remain consistent. If you discover any problems, note them on a scratch pad, go back into your DAW, and fix them. If you don't discover any problems, it's time to move on to QC level two.

Level Two: The Toyota Test

Load your master onto your iPod or burn it to a CD and take it for a drive in an economy sedan. Take it on the freeway and listen to it at 70mph. Can you hear all the vocals clearly, or is the road noise drowning them out? If you have a rich production, can you hear the music and Foley well enough? Can you still hear the narrator clearly, despite the road noise and the music and the Foley? Can you hear all the voices that clearly?

If it passes with flying colors, it's time to take it to level three.

Level Three: The Proof-Listen

With everything on track sonically, it's time to give the book a proof-listen. Do not try to mainline it. Listen to a couple hours of it a day, and listen closely while reading along with your text. Listen for flubs, stumbles, missed lines, mispronunciations, and malapropisms that slipped by you the first sixteen thousand times you heard them (during the performance and edit). Make notes on each of these on a scratch pad: the nature of the error, the time at which it happened to the nearest second, and the text of the line as it should have been. If you've got a rich production, make the same notes on Foley and music cues that are mis-timed or mixed too hot.

Take these notes, go back into the DAW (or the booth, if necessary), and fix 'em. Re-export everything, and move on to level four.

Level Four: The Test Audience

Now, hand off the whole production—from title sequence to the end of the post-book sample—to someone who's willing to sacrifice 12+ hours of their life on the altar of your business (you're more likely to find success if the victim in question likes your writing). Have them take notes on any problems.

A 12 hour audiobook retails for $25-35 when not discounted, meaning that it will cost your audience between ~$2 and $3 an hour. On an hour-by-hour basis, audiobooks aren't the most expensive form of popular entertainment, but they are among the most expensive units of entertainment your audience will ever buy (right up there with full seasons of television on Blu-Ray).

The cruel reality is that, while there is no such thing as a perfect book, there is such a thing as a perfect audiobook. A perfect audiobook is one that renders clear and understandable and enjoyable the words on the page, as written. Anything over that threshold is gravy. Anything under that threshold is unprofessional. Enrich your performances and your productions as much or as little as you want, but never skimp on that level of perfection—and never let your enhancements get in the way of that perfection. Your listeners are used to perfection, and they will not be inclined to forgive you for not delivering. Considering the price they paid for it, you can't really blame them.

Delivery Formats

Your audiobook will go to market in a variety of formats.

1) For CDs, you'll need a raw 16/44.1 stereo WAV or AIFF files divided, each 70 minutes long or less, and accompanied by a cue sheet specifying track divisions. If you're burning the CDs yourself, you'll need a CD burning program that understands cue sheets (most of them do).

2) For online distribution, either to a distributor or to a specific storefront, your client will specify the file type and metadata needed.

3) For podcast, you'll want 96kbps 16/44.1 joint-stereo encoded MP3 files. Most audio programs can export mp3—to be able to specify bit rate, sample rate, and stereo encoding method, you may have to click on the "Options..." or "Advanced" button in your export dialog.

Tagging

MP3 and similar deliverable file formats allow you to attach metadata to the file, including cover art that will display on the media player's screen, author info, publishing company info, track number, a link back to your website, and just about anything else you care to include. This is called "Tagging," and the format that most media players recognize is the ID3 tag.

To do your tagging, you'll need an ID3 editor. You can find these for all platforms, at price points ranging from free to $30. Since the current best-of-breed for any given operating system is constantly changing, I'm not going to make any recommendations here. Instead, search the Internet for "MP3 tagging [your operating system name here]" and you'll come up with an embarrassment of riches.

The Road Goes Ever On

Now, at long last, you're ready to release. There's nothing more to do besides packaging and shipping, whether you're uploading or sticking something in the mail. The book is done, the labor's over, you can retire to your sun porch and sip a tropical drink and wait for the new stream of nickels to start paying off.

But as you sit there, you may find it difficult to ignore the sound of new stories in your head. The keyboard calls you, it needs feeding. There are more books to write. And that microphone seems awfully lonely. Perhaps it's time you fed it a bit more sound. And somewhere out there in the wider world, in a few hours, someone is going to reach the end of your audiobook and wonder...

Where's the next one?

260

Making Tracks

Appendices and Notes

262

Making Tracks

Appendix A
Breakout Using CeltX

Regardless of what format your audio productions take, doing a script breakout can save you a goodly amount of production time. Breakouts make it easier to keep track of your progress, to make notations for post production, to pre-direct yourself (saving re-takes), and to read in different characters with different voices separately, enabling you (or your actors) to more easily maintain character consistency.

You can do this in a word processor, but dedicated scriptwriting tools will speed up the process enormously. Here's a quick-and-dirty tutorial on doing it with CeltX, a freely-available open source tool that you can download at http://www.celtx.com

Step 1: Export Your Novel

CeltX will import a novel in HTML format, but not in .doc or other popular native word processing formats. Open your story or book in your word processor, export it as HTML, and move to step 2.

Step 2: Start a New Project

Open CeltX, start a new project using the "audio play" project template.

Step 3: Add Your Novel

In the "Project Library" sub-window, click on the plus sign. From the dialog that pops up, select "Novel." Click on the resulting empty novel, then in the "Novel" pull-down menu, select "Import." A file selection dialog will appear. Select the HTML version of your novel and click "OK."

Step 4: Set Your Scene

CeltX is basically a rewrite of the Firefox web browser, so the interface works in much the same way—you can open multiple scripts and novels and control windows in neighboring tabs. Open your blank script in one tab and your novel in the other.

Select the script window. On the top line, you'll see a blank scene heading line saying "Scene 1:" with nothing after it. Give your scene a title, like "Front Matter," since the first thing you'll be recording is the title sequence and/or front matter of your book. When you make the change, you'll notice that the "Scenes" panel at bottom left will change to reflect the your alteration. This little window is the key to quickly navigating your script—it will auto-generate a table of contents based on the Scene Headings that you use.

Hit the ENTER key, and you'll go down one line to a line that's formatted as a "Production Note"—you can tell by the styles list box at the top of the script tab. These styles are the key to your breakout. Change this list box to "Character" and then type "Narrator" in as your opening character voice. Hit ENTER again, and you'll drop to a new line auto-formatted for dialog. Now it's time to start moving things across from the novel.

Step 5: Move Your First Chunk of Text Across

In the novel tab, select your first block of text—the front matter (title page, dedication, etc.) by highlighting it, just as you would in a word processor. Copy (CTRL/CMD-C) the text, then click over to the script tab and paste it. You'll be left with a fairly unformatted block of text that you now need to break out.

Step 6: Break Out The Text

On the first line of your pasted text, re-select "Dialog" in the styles list. Your text will auto-indent itself to the next paragraph break. At the end of that paragraph, if you hit ENTER again, you'll be auto-shuttled to a new "Character" line. If no character has changed, hit CTRL/CMD-ENTER and you'll be given a line-break but you'll stay in the "Dialog" style, then just hit DELETE to bring the next paragraph into the Narrator's dialog.

Keeping the copy in "Dialog" has some serious advantages later on, as we'll see in a few steps.

The styles list box doesn't just let you select scene headings, production notes (which you can use for inserting direction), dialog, and character. You can insert music cues, Foley cues, and a number of other things that basically amount to pre-planning your performance and post-production, which can save you quite a lot of time later on.

If you find yourself in the wrong style with a chunk of text, the obvious way to change styles is to use the list box. The quicker way is to use TAB, which will change the style on a rotating basis. If you work in a mouse-centric way, breakouts take forever. Use the keyboard shortcuts (like TAB, CTRL/CMD-ENTER, DELETE, ENTER, etc.) and, once you get used to it, you'll make very short work of a book. After a little practice, you'll find yourself able to break out a whole novel in about eight hours.

Repeat this copy/paste/breakout process throughout the novel, labeling each of your characters as appropriate to your story, giving cameo characters names like "man 1," etc., and using new scene headings for every chapter. The result will be an indexed script that you can pull sub-scripts from, at will, which you can then load onto your e-reader (or print out) for reading in your studio.

Step 7: Check For Formatting Loss

All the switching between styles you'll do in this breakout process will sometimes result in formatting loss, particularly bolds and italics. I've found it useful, after breaking out every chapter, to quickly scan the novel tab through for bolding and italics and make sure they've carried across to the script tab. I always find some things that got lost in translation. These are easily fixed in the script tabs using the word processor-style controls along the top of the tab.

Once you've got your script formatted, it'll look something like the example in Figure A-1.

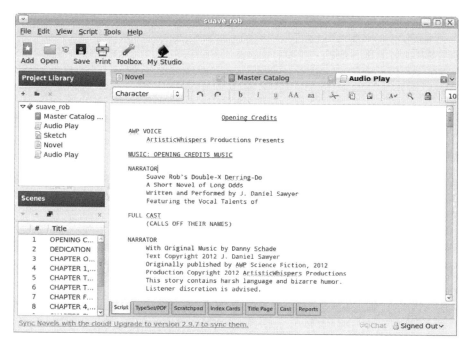

Figure A.1: A Formatted script in CeltX

Step 8: Making Your Script Do Tricks

Once you've got the script broken out, you can use your scriptwriting software to do all sorts of things.

For example, if you click on the "reports" tab at bottom, you can directly pull all the lines for a given character (which will include any production notes you included under the character name for a given line). You can use this to count lines/words for the characters (important in calculating payment rates for full-cast and audio drama work), to export scripts for given characters, etc.

If you open the Mater Catalog tab (double-click on "Master Catalog" in the project library pane), you'll get a complete list of characters in the book, with a list of scenes those characters are in and fields for annotation. You can use this to keep track of cast, make notes to yourself about what voices or accents you're employing for each character, etc. In short, you've got the ability to do complete production management.

Step 9: Exporting Your Breakouts

You can export using one of four methods. First, you can simply print the script or any reports you generate from the script. Second, you can select and copy the text directly across to a word processor. Third, you can export as HTML by selecting the "Script->Export" drop-down menu at the top of the screen. Fourth, you can click on the "TypeSet/PDF" sub-tab in the bottom of the script tab, then hit the button that says "Save PDF." Of the four, the third is most versatile, as HTML can be edited by any word processor, printed, or converted to an ebook and loaded onto an e-reader.

Appendix B
List of Free Editing Programs by Type

Many of you will use the software that came bundled with your A/D converter or mixing board. However, if the software you got is time-limited, or crippled, or doesn't suit you ergonomically, take a look at these free programs before you decide to drop several hundred dollars on a commercial package. Free/Open Source software developers have put professional-level programs within reach of everyone. Here's an as-current-as-possible list of the best-of-breed free sound editors and DAWs, grouped by type.

Sound Editors
- Audacity (Sound Editor) (Windows, Mac, Linux)
  - Rezound (Sound Editor) (Linux)
- Sweep (Sound Editor) (Windows, Linux)

DAWs
- Ardour (DAW) (Mac, Linux)
- Qtractor (DAW) (Linux)
- Traverso (DAW) (Windows, Mac, Linux)

Appendix C
Additional Resources

We covered a lot of ground in this book, and some of it was necessarily cursory. Here are some essential resources for deeper study that you may find very useful:

Scriptwriting

• *The Complete Book of Scriptwriting* by J. Michael Straczynski

One of the few resources to cover script annotations in depth, including for audio drama, I can't recommend this book enough. Important for anyone doing audio dramas, and very useful background information for anyone doing script breakouts—includes a lot of information on how to embed direction instructions in the script.

Legal

From Duke University Press
Bound by Law? Tales from the Public Domain
https://law.duke.edu/cspd/comics/

From Nolo Press:
• *The Public Domain*
• *Getting Permission*
• *The Copyright HandBook* (absolutely essential—every writer and producer should have this book and memorize it. This is the definitive guide to the core legal climate in which you operate your business)
• FAQ on hiring independent contractors and freelancers can be found online at: *http://www.nolo.com/legal-encyclopedia/contractors-freelancers*

Voice Acting

The Complete Voice and Speech Workout: 74 Exercises for Classroom and Studio Use by Janet Rodgers

The Art of Voice Acting, Fourth Edition: The Craft and Business of Performing Voiceover by James R. Alburger

Sound

Foley artist Scott Paulson has a number of excellent videos on YouTube where he demonstrates Foley technique. Start with this one: https://www.youtube.com/watch?v=szyht9jc8PE

Academy Award-winning sound designer Ben Burtt recorded a commentary track on the DVD of *Star Wars Episode I: The Phantom Menace,* which is essential listening for anyone attempting to learn soundscaping. In it he goes into detail about where he acquired the sounds for the Star Wars universe, how he altered them and layered them, and how he brought them together into a coherent whole to create one of the most stunning audio universes ever realized.

Although I mentioned it in the text, I must mention it again. The film *Radioland Murders,* a farcical murder mystery set in the midst of a radio drama studio, has a lot of wonderful on-camera Foley work (you can see the artist creating the sounds you're hearing). It will give you a lot of ideas, and it's wonderful fun to boot.

Finally, check out a book called *The Foley Grail* by Vanessa Theme Ament for in-depth, up-to-date techniques for creating your own sound effects.

Acknowledgments

In addition to the dedicatees of this volume—who between the three of them taught me the art of audio and lent me gear to bootstrap my studio (Mary Mason and Lynx Crowe of Missing Lynx Productions) and pushed me to re-purpose those skills from producing corporate audio and video into producing my own audiobooks (Scott Sigler)—there are a few other people deserving a hat tip or two.

First and foremost, serious thanks are due to Kristine Kathryn Rusch and Dean Wesley Smith who asked the questions that started this project rolling. Serious mensches, both of them—if you are ever lucky enough to work with such scrupulous and inquisitive folk, take advantage of it.

Second, my business partner Kitty NicIaian, who tolerated (with great enthusiasm) this side-venture from the normal course of business.

To Joanna Penn and ML Buchman, who both prodded me about a new edition of this book, and without whom I'd never have looked back and decided it was worth doing.

To the excellent authors in the once-thriving Podiobooks community—Nathan Lowell, Philippa Ballantine, Tee Morris, Seth Harwood, Abbie Hilton, Chris Lester, Christiana Ellis, and so many others too numerous to mention—with whom I've traded tips and voice work over the last few years.

And finally, to the folks like Steven H. Wilson and Gregg Taylor (who did it on their own), and the folks at Seeing Ear Theater, Above The Title Productions, and Full Cast Audio (and the hundreds of others who didn't start in the DIY space) who, working on their own and without coordination, have revived my favorite narrative form and given it an abiding vitality in the pantheon of the narrative arts: The Radio Drama.

Photo Credits

Chapter 5

Figure 5.1: A standard 440Hz reference waveform. Time, in seconds, is marked on the horizontal axis along the top of the picture. © 2012 ArtisticWhispers Productions.

Figure 5.2: A vocal waveform, clipped. © 2012 ArtisticWhispers Productions.

Figure 5.3: Two in-phase 440Hz waveforms. © 2012 ArtisticWhispers Productions.

Figure 5.4: In-phase waveforms mixed together. © 2012 ArtisticWhispers Productions.

Figure 5.5: Phase-reversed 440Hz waveforms. © 2012 ArtisticWhispers Productions.

Figure 5.6: Mixing down opposite-phase signals. © 2012 ArtisticWhispers Productions.

Figure 5.7: A piano solo waveform. © 2012 ArtisticWhispers Productions.

Chapter 6

Figure 6.1 Picture of a recording shroud. © 2012 ArtisticWhispers Productions.

Chapter 7

Figure 7.1 From left to right: A desktop stand, approx 5 in. tall;, a stick stand, extends to 6 ft.; a boom stand, 4ft. tall with 3ft. adjustable arm. © 2012 ArtisticWhispers Productions.

Figure 7.2: An AT4040 XLR Condenser mic in a shock mount. © 2011 Wikicommons user Kreuzschabel. License: Creative Commons Attribution Share-Alike 3.0.

Figure 7.3: A side-address mic with pop screen. Photo: Microphone électrostatique, by Eric Chassaing. License: Public Domain.

Figure 7.4: An omni-directional polar pattern. © 2007 Wikicommons user Galek76. License: Creative Commons Attribution Share-Alike 3.0.

Figure 7.5: A shotgun polar pattern © 2007 Wikicommons user Galek76. License: Creative Commons Attribution Share-Alike 3.0.

Figure 7.6: The Cardioid Family, from left to right: subcardioid, cardioid, supercardioid, hypercardioid © 2007 Wikicommons user Galek76. License: Creative Commons Attribution Share-Alike 3.0. Collage by ArtisticWhispers Productions.

Figure 7.7: The dual-capsule figure-eight polar pattern. © 2007 Wikicommons user Galek76. License: Creative Commons Attribution Share-Alike 3.0.

Figure 7.8: Response curve diagram for a Shure SM58, from Shure Inc.website.

Figure 7.9: A Front-Address microphone. © 2012 ArtisticWhispers Productions.

Figure 7.10: A side-address microphone with pop screen. See Figure 7.3

Chapter 8

Figure 8.1: XLR connectors. © 2012 ArtisticWhispers Productions.

Figure 8.2: 1/4" Connectors: TRS (top) and TS (bottom). © 2012 ArtisticWhispers Productions.

Figure 8.3: RCA cables. © 2012 ArtisticWhispers Productions.

Figure 8.4: Lightpipe/TOSLink cable end. 2006 Photo by English Wikipedia user Cyvh. License: Public Domain.

Figure 8.5: Connectors from left to right: Firewire (6-pin), USB mini and USB standard, standard MIDI (top) and MIDI-Joystick (bottom)

Figure 8.6: Insert a picture of the industry standard power cable. © 2012 ArtisticWhispers Productions.

Figure 8.7: Insert a Picture of a Velcro tie. © 2012 ArtisticWhispers Productions.

Chapter 9

Figure 9.1: Blue Yeti, a popular high-quality USB microphone. Photo by Evan Amos. License: Public Domain.

Figure 9.2: A mixing board, annotated with board geography. © 2012 ArtisticWhispers Productions.

Figure 9.3: A board channel. © 2012 ArtisticWhispers Productions.

Chapter 10

Figure 10.1: Outboard Signal Path. Dashed borders represent optional equipment. Dotted line is optional signal path for use only with USB microphones. © 2012 ArtisticWhispers Productions.

Chapter 11

Figure 11.1: Spectral analysis of the author's voice. © 2012 ArtisticWhispers Productions.

Chapter 12

Figure 12.1: A Foley artist drops a bowling ball onto a concrete pad. Photo: Foley Room at the Sound Design Campus. © 2011 Vancouver Film School, Used under Creative Commons Attribution 2.0 license

Chapter 13

Figure 13.1: Waveform of a sentence. © 2012 ArtisticWhispers Productions.

Figure 13.2: Top Row: A straight fade, an asymptotic fade. Bottom row: A variable slope fade, a partial fade. © 2012 ArtisticWhispers Productions.

Figure 13.3: A volume envelope. © 2012 ArtisticWhispers Productions.

Figure 13.4: The sentence "Don't count on it." You can see the trailing "t" as a spike at the tail end. © 2012 ArtisticWhispers Productions.

Chapter 14

Figure 14.1: Ardour Main window. © 2012 ArtisticWhispers Productions.

Figure 14.2: Mixing window. © 2012 ArtisticWhispers Productions.

Figure 14.3: The routing window—for Ardour, this is actually handled by an outboard program. © 2012 ArtisticWhispers Productions.

Figure 14.4: Diagram of side-chain processing. © 2012 ArtisticWhispers Productions.

Figure 14.5: Diagram of a sub-mix. © 2012 ArtisticWhispers Productions.

Figure 14.6: Picture of Ardour fader automation control button, with menu deployed. © 2012 ArtisticWhispers Productions.

Chapter 15

Figure 15.1: A compressor curve. © 2012 ArtisticWhispers Productions.

Chapter 16

Figure 16.1: Audacity noise removal tool. © 2012 ArtisticWhispers Productions.

Appendix A

Figure A.1: A Formatted script in CeltX. © 2012 ArtisticWhispers Productions.

Also By

The Clarke Lantham Mysteries
And Then She Was Gone
A Ghostly Christmas Present
Smoke Rings
Silent Victor
He Ain't Heavy
In The Cloud
Blood and Weeds
The Bodies In The Basement
The Sky Miners (forthcoming)

The Kabrakan Ascendency: A Mannix Families Saga
The Briggs Defection *(coming July 2017)*
The Orinthal Deception *(coming August 2017)*
The Hartman Gambit *(coming September 2017)*
The Singh Hegemony *(coming October 2017)*
The Reeves Directive *(coming November 2017)*
The Mannix Initiative *(coming December 2018)*

Suave Rob's Awesome Adventures!
Suave Rob's Double-X Derring-Do
Suave Rob's Rough-n-Ready Rugrat Rapture
Suave Rob's Amazing Ass-Saving Association *(April 2017)*

Standalone Works
Down From Ten
Ideas, Inc.
The Resurrection Junket
Hadrian's Flight
The Auto Motive *(May 2017)*

The Every Day Novelist *(Nonfiction)*
Business 101
In Thirty Days *(April 2017)*

Writers Guides *(Nonfiction)*
Science Fiction Weaponry: A Guide for Writers *(with Mary Mason)*
Throwing Lead: A Writer's Guide to Firearms (and the People Who Use Them) *(with Mary Mason)*
Making Tracks: A Writer's Guide to Audiobooks (and How to Produce Them)

Short Story Collections
Sculpting God: Bedtime Stories for Adults
Frock Coat Dreams: Romances, Nightmares, and Fancies from the Steampunk Fringe
Tales of the Lombard Alchemist *(coming June 2017)*

The Lombard Alchemist Tales *(shorts)*
At The Edge of Nowhere
Chicken Noodle Gravity
Sunday Morning Giraffe
The Serpent and the Satchel

Short Stories
Angels Unawares
Buried Alive In The Blues
The Coffee Service
Cold Duty
Lilith
The Man In The Rain
Self-Sustaining
Train Time
We Create Worlds
On Matters Most Austere

About the Author

A longtime award-nominated audio/video producer and tech journalist-turned novelist, J. Daniel Sawyer's abusive behavior toward the English language finally landed him in trouble with the release of his hard-boiled Clarke Lantham Mysteries. When not speculating about crime and punishment, or laying out twisted visions in his sci-fi thriller series The Antithesis Progression or his cabin fever comedy Down From Ten, he bends his mind toward corrupting his fellow authors with educational books like Throwing Lead: A Writer's Guide to Firearms (and the People Who Use Them) and Making Tracks: A Writer's Guide to Audiobooks (and How To Produce Them).

On the rare occasion that he escapes his cavernous studio to see the light of day, he slips away into the wilds of the San Francisco back country where he devotes his energies to running afoul of local traffic ordinances in his never-ending pursuit of the ultimate driving road.

Should you be so inclined, you can communicate with this shady character, as well as find stories, podcasts, articles, and other literary abominations at http://www.jdsawyer.net

Made in the USA
San Bernardino, CA
24 April 2017